Cognitive Psychology & Cognitive Neuroscience

Authors and Image Credits
listed on page 178

Originally published on Wikibooks.org
Wikibooks is a project of the Wikimedia Foundation
THIS PUBLICATION IS NOT OFFICIALY
SPONSORED BY WIKIBOOKS OR WIKIPEDIA

Published by
Seven Treasures Publications

Published by
Seven Treasures Publications
SevenTreasuresPublications@gmail.com
Fax 413-653-8797

Printed in the United States of America

ISBN 978-0-9800707-8-1

COGNITIVE PSYCHOLOGY AND COGNITIVE NEUROSCIENCE

by Wikibooks contributors

Developed on **Wikibooks**,
the open-content textbooks collection

Main authors: Aschoeke (C)   Tbittlin (C)   LanguageGame (C)   Itiaden (C)   Pbenner (C) · Mheimann (C) Jkeyser (C)   Ddeunert (C)   Marplogm (C) · Pehrenbr (C)   Ifranzme (C)   FlyingGerman (C)   Sspoede (C) · Asarwary (C)   Lbartels (C)   Smieskes (C)   Apape (C) · Ekrueger (C)

The current version of this Wikibook may be found at:
http://en.wikibooks.org/wiki/Cognitive_Psychology_and_Cognitive_Neuroscience

Contents

1 COGNITIVE PSYCHOLOGY AND THE BRAIN

live version • discussion • edit lesson • comment • report an error

Introduction

Imagine a young man, Knut, sitting at his desk, with his tired eyes staring at a monitor, surfing around, trying to find some worthy articles for his psychology homework. A cigarette rests between the middle and index fingers of his left hand. Without looking, he stretches out his free hand and grabs a cup of coffee located on the right of his keyboard. While sipping some of the cheap discounter blend, he suddenly asks himself: "What is happening here?"

Around the beginning of the 20th century, psychologists would have said, "Take a look into yourself, Knut, analyse what you're thinking and doing," as analytical introspection was the method of that time.

A few years later, J.B. Watson published his book *Psychology from the Standpoint of a Behaviorist*, from which began the era of behaviourism. Behaviourists claimed that it was impossible to study the inner life of people scientifically. Their approach to psychology, which they assumed to be more scientific, focussed only on the study and experimental analysis of behaviour. The right answer to Knut's question would have been: "You are sitting in front of your computer, reading and drinking coffee, because of your environment and how it influences you." Behaviorism was the primary means for American psychology for about the next 50 years. One of the primary critiques and downfalls of behaviorism was Noam Chomsky's 1959 critique of B.F. Skinner's "Verbal behaviour". Skinner, an influential behaviourist, attempted to explain language on the basis of behaviour alone. Chomsky showed that this was impossible, and by doing so, influenced enough psychologists to end the dominance of behaviorism in American psychology.

As more researchers were once again concerned with processes inside the head, cognitive psychology arose on the landscape of science. Their central claim was that cognition was information processing of the brain. Cognitive psychology did not dispose the methods of behaviourism, but rather widened their horizon by adding levels between input and output.

Modern technology and new methods enabled researchers to combine examinations of public actions (latencies in reaction time, number of recalls) with physiological measurements (EEG and event-related potentials, fMRI). Such methods, in addition to others, are used by cognitive science to collect evidence for certain features of mental activity. From this, references and correlations between action and cognition could be made.

These correlations were inspiration and thenceforwards the main challenge for cognitive psychologists. To answer Knut's question the cognitive psychologist would probably first examining Knut's brain in that specific situation. So let's try this!

Knut has a problem, he really needs to do his homework. To solve this problem, he has to perform loads of cognition. The light is gleaming into his eyes, transducing it from his retina into nerve signals by sensory cells. The information is passed on through the optic nerve, crosses the brain at the lateral geniculate nucleus to arrive at the central visual cortex. On its journey, the signals get computed over complex nets of neurons; the contrast of the picture gets enhanced; irrelevant information gets filtered out; patterns are recognized; stains and lines on the screen become words; words get meaning, the meaning is put into context, analyzed on its relevance for Knut's problem, maybe stored in some part of memory. At the same time an appetite for coffee is creeping from Knut's hypothalamus, a region in the brain responsible for controlling the needs of an organism. The appetite, encoded in patterns of neural information, makes its way to the motor cortex where it is passed on to the muscles into Knut's arm.

A lot more could be said about this, and Knut's question remains unanswered, but this should be enough to point out the complexity of cognition and the brain's importance. In this chapter, we are going to dig deeper into the question of what cognitive psychology is and how it became this way, and then draw connections to the brain and explain some of its most important parts.

Defining Cognitive Psychology

Cognitive Psychology is a psychological science which is interested in various mind and brain related subfields such as cognition, the mental processes that underlie behavior, reasoning and decision making.

In the early stages of Cognitive Psychology, the high-tech measuring instruments used today were unavailable. The idea of scientifically scrutinizing what was going on in a human mind was first established during the late 19th century.

Psychology Laboratories were based on measuring observable features such as *reaction time*. Nonetheless, there was a technique developed called *analytic* introspection. The latter is a method that focusses on the subject's inner processes. Here, the subject has to give precise reports about his or her mental activity.

During the first half of the 20th century and naturally parallel to behaviorism, the behavioristic approach became the main issue in psychology. The main emphasis was the examination of outer expression of inner processes, rather than the mind itself.

Even though behaviorism had established itself as the mainstream, curiosity about the mind was not diminished. In the 1950s, this inquisitiveness was released in a new science named Cognitive Science. Cognitive Psychology became one of its subfields. The interdisciplinary approach of Cognitive Science enabled the use of modern technology and new methods to combine examinations of *public actions* (latencies in reaction time, number of recalls) with physiological measurements (EEG and event-related potentials, fMRI).

Hereby, references and correlations between action and cognition could be made. Cognitive Psychology is using these methods and additional ones such as *Single and Double* Dissociation and *brain lesioning* to collect evidence for certain features of mental activity. Because of those correlations that were found, the examination of the human brain and its functions has become one of the main challenges to Cognitive Psychology.

The role of the brain

Examination of brain damage has a long tradition. The Ancient Romans observed that gladiators with head injuries often lost their mental skills, whereas injuries to other parts of the body did not have such an effect. It was inferred that there was a possible link between the mind and brain. Today, the assumption that the mind is somehow implemented in the brain is taken for granted, and even the common-sense understanding presupposes a relation between mental and neuronal processes. Subsequently, research on the brain became more and more important, and the psychological methods being used shifted to systematic scientific examination of the brain. The crucial question then became: How is this relation realized, and what properties of the brain are capable of causing mental and cognitive events?

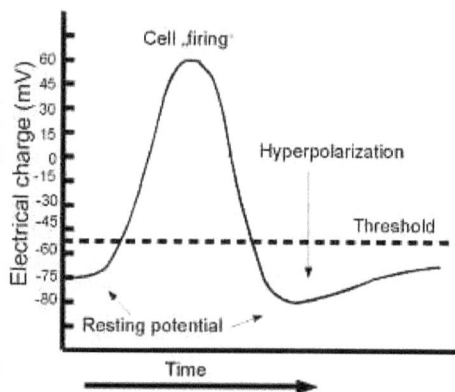

Figure 1.1 - The resting potential is initially around -70 mV relative to the outside of the cell. Once the threshold (-55 mV) is passed, the cell depolarizes and the polarity reverses up to +40 mV. Subsequently the cell hyperpolarizes and the voltage becomes more negative than the resting potential for a short period.

As it is not possible, in this introductory passage, to cover the entire configuration of the brain in an appropriate manner, we will just give a brief summary of the concepts behind neural signal transduction, and smoothly switch over to the anatomy of the brain. This in turn will then serve as background information in the attempt to link cognitive functions to brain structure.

In principle, there are two classes of cells in the human brain: **neurons** and glia. Both are approximately equal in distribution, though neurons seem to play the main role in information processing. The actual signal transduction takes place in different ways. On the one hand, there is mean electrical conduction, and on the other hand, there are complicated biochemical cascades which transmit the data. Both variants can be subsumed to the concept of action potentials (Figure 1.1), which generally carry out the signal transduction from one nerve cell to another.

For better conduction, the axons of the neurons are insulated by a so-called myelin sheath. The myelin in the human brain is produced by a certain class of glial cell, the oligodendrocytes. This is important because the decomposition of the myelin sheath is involved in diseases, such as as multiple sklerosis.

Once the information perceived by the sensory organs is transformed into a sequence of **action potentials** the data is, in a way, neutral, since it has no specific qualitive properties which indicate from which sense the signal was original initiated. But how is the information encoded? In other words, how can the variety of our conscious experience be caused by simple inhibition and excitation of nerve cells embedded in an admittedly complex system? Because of the lack of better metaphors, the answer is often given by comparing the brain to a modern digital computer. Parsing the world into objects, making inferences, having associative memory and the like can be analyzed by developing computational models. The underlying paradigm is that the information is represented by the rate of action potential spikes. How this is exactly realized is the aim of research of biophysics, a subdiscipline of neurobiology.

In cognitive psychology, however, the methods used differ. This is because the main interest is not devoted to the organization of single neuron circuits, but rather to the larger, functional units in the network.

References

- M. S. Gazzaniga, R. B. Ivry, and G. R. Mangun, Cognitive Neuroscience, Norton & Company, 1998, ISBN 0393972194
- E. Br. Goldstein, Cognitive Psychology, Wadsworth, 2004, ISBN 0534577261
- M. W Eysenck, M. T. Keane, Cognitive Psychology, Psychology Press, 2005, ISBN 1841693596
- M. T. Banich, The Neural Bases of Mental Function, Houghton Mifflin, 1997, ISBN 0-395-66699-6
- E. R. Kandel, J. H. Schwartz, T. M. Jessell, Principles of neural science, 2000, ISBN 0-07-112000-9

Links

- PDF file of the "ethics code" of the American Psychological Association
- Cognitive Psychology miniscript by Fabian M. Suchanek
- Famous papers in the history of cognition

live version • discussion • edit lesson • comment • report an error

2 PROBLEM SOLVING FROM AN EVOLUTIONARY PERSPECTIVE

live version • discussion • edit lesson • comment • report an error

Introduction

Gestalt psychologists approach towards problem solving was a perceptual one. That is, for them, the questions about problem solving were:

- how is a problem *represented* in a persons mind, and
- how does solving this problem involve a reorganisation or *restructuring* of this representation?

Restructuring is basically the process of arriving at a new understanding of a problem situation - changing from one representation of a problem to a (very) different one. The following story illustrates this:

Two boys of different age are playing badminton. The older one is a more skilled player, and therefore it is predictable for the outcome of usual matches who will be the winner. After some time and several defeats the younger boy finally loses interest in playing, and the older boy faces a problem.

The usual suggestions, according to M. Wertheimer (1945/82), at this point of the story range from 'offering candy' and 'playing another game' to ' not playing to full ability' and 'shaming the younger boy into playing'. And this is what the older boy comes up with:

He proposes that they should try to keep the bird in play as long as possible - and thus changing from a game of competition to one of cooperation. They'd start with easy shots and make them harder as their success increases, counting the number of consecutive hits. The proposal is happily accepted and the game is on again.

Insight

There are two very different ways of approaching a goal-oriented situation. In one an organism readily reproduces the response to the given problem from past experience. This is called *reproductive thinking*.

The second way requires something new and different to achieve the goal, prior learning is of little help here. Such *productive thinking* is (sometimes) argued to involve insight. Gestalt psychologists even state that insight problems are a separate category of problems in their own right.

Tasks that might involve insight usually have certain features - they require something new and nonobvious to be done and in most cases they are difficult enough to prevent that the initial solution attempt is successful. When solving this kind of problems one experiences a so called "AHA-experience" - the solution pops up all of the sudden. At one time they do not have the answer to a problem and in the next second it's solved.

Fixation

Sometimes, previous experience or familiarity can even make problem solving more difficult. In effect habitual directions can get in the way of finding new directions. This is called *fixation*.

Mental Fixedness

One approach to studying fixation was study wrong-answer verbal insight problems. To this, people tend to give rather an incorrect answer when failing to solve, than to give no answer at all. A typical example is, when people are told that, on a lake, the area covered by water lilies doubles every 24 hours and that it takes 60 days to cover the whole lake, and are asked: 'How many days does it take to cover half the lake?' the typical respond is '30 days' (whereas 59 days is correct).

These wrong solutions are due to an inaccurate interpretation, hence representation, of the problem. This can happen because of 'sloppiness' (a quick shallow reading of the problem and/or weak monitoring their efforts made to come to a solution). In this case error feedback should help people to reconsider the problem features, note the inadequacy of their first answer, and find the correct solution. If, however, people are truly fixated on their incorrect representation, being told the answer is wrong doesn't help. In a study made by P.I. Dallop and R.L. Dominowski in 1992 these two possibilities were contrasted. In approximately one-third of the time error feedback led to right answers, so only approximately one-third of the wrong answers were due to inadequate monitoring.

Functional Fixedness

Functional fixedness concerns the solution of object-use problems. The basic idea is that, when the usual way of using an object is emphasized, it will be far more difficult for a person to use that object in a novel manner.

Problem Solving - Modern Approaches

Problem Solving as a Search Problem

The idea of regarding to problem solving as search problems was invented by Alan Newell and Herbert Simon while trying to design computer programs which could solve certain problems. This led them to develop a program called General Problem Solver which was able to solve any well-defined problem that can be formalized like chess or the towers of hanoi, but was not able to solve any real world problem.

Any given problem consists of two special states namely an initial and a desired final or goal state. To represent all possible situations between the initial and the goal state, intermediate states were introduced. Additionally there exist a set of operators to move from one state to another. A solution is a sequence of actions describing how to reach the goal state. The simplest method to solve a problem, defined in these terms, is to search for a solution by just trying one possibility after another (also called trial and error).

As already mentioned, this method of problem solving is not capable of solving real world problems since it is usually not possible to formalize these problems in such a way that a search algorithm is able to search for a solution.

Means-End Analysis

Another way is to try to divide a problem into smaller ones by creating sub goals. This method is called means-end analysis and can be best demonstrated with the towers of hanoi problem. The initial state is a stack of discs of different sizes on a peg. There are three pegs (A, B and C) and the discs are on the left one. A disc has to be always placed on a bigger one or on an empty peg. The goal is to move the stack of disks to the right peg, but only one disc can be moved at once. The following recursive algorithm solves this problem by using the means-end analysis:

1. move n-1 discs from A to C
2. move disc #n from A to B
3. move n-1 discs from C to B

(n is the total number of discs)

With each recursive loop the problem is reduced by one.

This is an important everyday problem solving strategy - like, say, writing this chapter of the book. We describe one aspect after another to give you, the reader, an overview of the subject that is as comprehensible as possible.

Analogies

Analogies describe similar structures and interconnect them to clarify and explain certain relations. In a recent study, for example, a song that got stuck in your head is compared to an itching of the brain that can only be scratched by repeating the song over and over again.

Restructuring by Using Analogies

One special kind of restructuring, the way already mentioned during the discussion of the Gestalt approach, is *analogical problem solving*. Here, to find a solution to one problem - the so called *target problem*, an analogous solution to another problem - the *source problem*, is presented.

An example for this kind of strategy is the **radiation problem** posed by K. Duncker in 1945:

As a doctor you have to treat a patient with a malignant, inoperable tumor, buried deep inside the body. There exists a special kind of ray, which is perfectly harmless at a low intensity, but at the sufficient high intensity is able to destroy the tumor - as well as the healthy tissue on his way to it. What can be done to avoid the latter?

When this question was asked to participants in an experiment, most of them couldn't come up with the appropriate answer to the problem. Then they were told a story that went something like this:

A General wanted to capture his enemy's fortress. He gathered a large army to launch a full-scale direct attack, but then learned, that all the roads leading directly towards the fortress were blocked by mines. These roadblocks were designed in such a way, that it was possible for small groups of the fortress-owner's men to pass them safely, but every large group of men would initially set them off. Now the General figured out the following plan: He divided his troops into several smaller groups and made each of them march down a different road, timed in such a way, that the entire army would reunite exactly when reaching the fortress and could hit with full strength.

Here, the story about the General is the source problem, and the radiation problem is the target problem. The fortress is analogous to the tumor and the big army corresponds to the highly intensive ray. Consequently a small group of soldiers represents a ray at low intensity. The solution to the problem is to split the ray up, as the general did with his army, and send the now harmless rays towards the tumor from different angles in such a way that they all meet when reaching it. No healthy tissue is damaged but the tumor itself gets destroyed by the ray at its full intensity.

M. Gick and K. Holyoak presented Duncker's radiation problem to a group of participants in 1980 and 1983. Only 10 percent of them were able to solve the problem right away, 30 percent could solve it when they read the story of the general before. After given an additional hint - to use the story as help - 75 percent of them solved the problem.

With this results, Gick and Holyoak concluded, that analogical problem solving depends on three steps:

1. *Noticing* that an analogical connection exists between the source and the target problem.
2. *Mapping* corresponding parts of the two problems onto each other (fortress → tumor, army → ray, etc.)
3. *Applying* the mapping to generate a parallel solution to the target problem (using little groups of soldiers approaching from different directions → sending several weaker rays from different directions)

Next, Gick and Holyoak started looking for factors that could be helpful for the noticing and the mapping parts, for example:

Discovering the basic linking concept behind the source and the target problem.

Schema

This basic linking concept (see above) was called *problem schema*.

To activate a schema, *schema induction* is necessary.

One successful way to achieve schema induction by Gick and Holyoak: Before letting the participants solve the radiation problem the instructor gave them two stories to read, the one with the General and one with a similar outline. Now the participants were asked to write a brief summary about the similarities of these stories.

When the underlining similarities where indirectly emphasized in this way, 52 percent of the participants were able to solve the radiation problem without any hints given.

How do Experts Solve Problems?

With the term *expert* we describe someone who devotes large amounts of his or her time and energy to one specific field of interest in which he, subsequently, reaches a certain level of mastery. It should not be of a surprise that experts tend to be better in solving problems in their field than novices (people who are beginners or not as well trained in a field as experts) are. They are faster in coming up with a solution and have a higher success rate of right solutions. But what is the difference between the ways experts and nonexperts solve problems? Research on the nature of expertise has come up with the following conclusions:

- Experts **know** more about their field,
- their knowledge is **organized** differently, and
- they spend more time with **analyzing** the problem.

When it comes to problems that are situated outside the experts' field, their performance often doesn't differ from that of novices.

Knowledge:

An experiment by Chase and Simon (1973a, b) dealt with the question how well experts and novices are able to reproduce positions of chess pieces on chessboards, shown to them briefly. The results showed, that experts were far better in reproducing actual game positions, but that their performance was comparable with that of a novice when the chess pieces were arranged randomly on the board. Chase and Simon concluded, that the superiority on actual game positions was due to the ability to recognize them from the more or less 50,000 patterns stored in an expert's memory. In comparison, for a good player there may be 1,000 patterns and for a novice only few to none at all.

Organization:

In 1982, M. Chi and her co-workers took a collection of 24 physics problems and presented them to a group of physics professors, as well as to a group of students with only one semester of physics. The task was to group the problems based on their similarities.

As it turned out, the students tended to group the problems based on their *surface structure* (similarities of objects used in the problem), whereas the professors used their *deep structure* (the general physical principles) as criteria.

Analysis:

Experts often spend more time trying to understand the problem before actually trying to solve it. This way of approaching a problem may often result in what appears to be a slow start, but in the long run this strategy is much more effective.

Divergent Thinking

The term *divergent thinking* describes a way of thinking that doesn't lead to one goal, but is open - ended. Problems that are solved this way can have a large number of potential 'solutions' of which none is exactly 'right' or 'wrong', though some might be more suitable than others. It can be contrasted by *convergent thinking* - thinking that seeks to find the correct answer to a specific problem.

Divergent thinking is often associated with creativity, and it undoubtedly leads to many creative ideas. Nevertheless, researches showed that in the processes that result in original and practical inventions, things like searching for solutions, being aware of structures, and looking for analogies are also heavily involved.

The Evolutionary Perspective

In 1831 Charles Darwin began to develop the evolutionary theory which was meant to explain why there are so many different kinds of species. This theory also is important for psychology because it explains how species were designed through evolution and what their goals are. By knowing the goals of species it is possible to explain and predict behaviour.

Natural Selection

The mechanism of natural selection is the basic and most important one of which were introduced by the theory of evolution. It is this process that makes organisms with superior traits more likely to survive and reproduce. Without natural selection the growth of populations is exponential. For example an organism that reproduces once a day will create a population of about 2^{29} organisms within a month. In natural populations this is not the case and most populations are relatively stable, since most organisms do not have as many offspring as they might have. This is caused by the environment. Hence, if an individual is better at finding food or avoiding predators it is more likely that it will survive. This ability which enables the individual to survive will be passed on to the next generation. On the other hand if an individual fails to survive its disadvantages will not be passed on to the next generation. Over many generations this natural selection will lead to individuals that are better adapted to their environment. This process may also be called "reproduction of the fittest". Natural selection can only work if there are random changes in the genetic process, also called mutations. Only if these mutations are significant, natural selection can choose which version better solves the problem of "staying in the game of evolution".

As traits can only spread through reproduction, natural selection is a very slow process. The time until an individual is able to reproduce is called the generation time (approx. 20 years for humans). Evolution is such a slow process since natural selection can only choose from existing alternatives. That is, until a new trait becomes common it has to develop and spread in the whole population which of course takes much time.

Adaptation As a Result of Natural Selection

Variations in individuals are constantly tested whether they help to survive in the environment or not. This variation can be of any kind, for example an enhancement of the body or a new behaviour that enables the individual to solve certain problems which are necessary to survive or aids reproduction. These variations are called adaptations because they adapt the individual to its environment. Adaptations are structurally complex and support reproduction.

Psychological Adaptation

Evolutionary psychologists think of the mind as a modular system. This perspective on modularity was mainly developed by Leda Cosmides and John Tooby. It is based on the assumption that the mind has evolved by natural selection and therefore should solve the same problems as other organs namely survival and reproduction. Each module of our mind is responsible for one task (e.g. face recognition) and can be adapted by natural selection. So behaviour is not adapted directly but rather indirectly by modifying the underlying neuronal networks to produce adaptive behaviour.

Adaptations May Be Out-of-Date

A disadvantage of the slow evolutionary process is that when the environment changes quickly, adaptive functions and behaviour may be out-of-date. The result is that organisms are better adapted to the past and this is an important point if we think about human social behaviour and the development of cultures (see chapter Evolutionary Perspective on Social Cognitions for details).

Sexual Selection

Besides the theory of natural selection there is another one called the theory of sexual selection. It states that there is also a kind of selection between individuals of the same sex which leads to a development and spread of traits in males or females.

> Sexual selection depends on the success of certain individuals over others of the same sex, in relation to the propagation of the species; while natural selection depends on the success of both sexes, at all ages, in relation to the general conditions of life. —*Charles Darwin, 1871*

A famous example for sexual selection is the peacock. The evolution of its tail cannot be explained by natural selection only because it is neither very helpful to find food nor does it help to avoid predators, even the opposite is the case. But it makes the peacock more attractive to the opposite sex and therefore conducts to reproduction due to the fact that this oversized tail can only be worn by a male that is strong enough to wear a disadvantage.

Altruism

Natural selection favours the strong and selfish who acts in his own interest. But there are other traits like altruism which are very common in human behaviour and it seems that they cannot be explained by natural selection only. With regard to a whole group traits can be

Darwin argued that the female peahen chose to mate with the male peacock who had the most beautiful plumage in her mind (intersexual selection).

characterized as

- increasing the fitness of the individual (self) or
- increasing the fitness of the group.

Altruism obviously increases the fitness of the group, but decreases the fitness of individuals what at first glance conflicts with the theory of evolution and natural selection. But there are three attempts to explain why individuals decrease their fitness for the fitness of a group, namely

1. group selection,
2. kin selection and
3. reciprocal behaviour

which will be explained in more detail in chapter Evolutionary Perspective on Social Cognitions. We will focus here on reciprocal behaviour with regard to problem solving.

Reciprocal Behaviour

Why should an individual behave altruistic if it cannot be sure whether its recipient will also behave altruistic or not? Reciprocity is one explanation for these phenomena. That is, an altruistic individual will only offer an altruistic act to an individual which is known to be altruistic and will withhold altruistic behaviour to individuals which only act selfish. This exception prevents altruists from extinction and allows them to spread in population, but it presupposes that both individuals interact more than once and that they are able to recognize each other.

We can distinguish two types of reciprocal behaviour: direct and indirect reciprocity. The direct one is an exchange of altruistic behaviour between the same two individuals ("I scratch your back and you'll scratch mine") whereas the indirect one is between different individuals ("I scratch your back and someone will scratch mine"). The latter is even more complicated to explain, but it is a fundamental trait in our contemporary society. The basic idea to explain these phenomena is the development of reputation in society. That is, altruists decide whether or not to interact with someone according to the reputation of an individual.

(Iterative) Prisoner's Dilemma

The problem of cooperation is also topic in game theory a branch of applied mathematics where players try to maximize their winnings. There are many convergences between the theory of reciprocity and game theory, one famous example is the prisoner's dilemma. Two people A and B have been captured by the police, they committed a crime but the police is not able to proof that they are guilty, but they have enough evidence to arrest them for six months. Before A and B have been captured by the police they both agreed to keep silent. At the police department they were questioned in separate rooms and both have the choice to cooperate with his partner or with the police. If one betrays the other he will get free and his partner will have to serve for ten years. If they both betray each other they will both have to serve for two years. But if both keep silent, they only have to serve for six months.

Prisoner B		

		Stays Silent	Betrays
Prisoner A	**Stays Silent**	Both serve six months	Prisoner A serves ten years Prisoner B goes free
	Betrays	Prisoner A goes free Prisoner B serves ten years	Both serve two years

The dilemma is that both accused people do not know how the other has decided or will decide. Regardless how the other will decide, confessing the crime will improve the outcome. If A betrays B, A will get free or he will stay in prison for two years. If he does not betray B, A will stay in prison for six months or ten years depending on however B decides. So obviously the best choice is to betray the other. There is an interesting extension of the dilemma called iterative prisoner's dilemma. The game is played again and again so it is possible to punish selfish behaviour in order to support altruism. One good strategy for the iterative prisoner's dilemma is tit-for-tat. At the first round this strategy suggests to cooperate with the partner. All other rounds one will do whatever the partner did in the round before. If someone betrays his partner, he will get punished next round. On the other hand, if someone always acts altruistic he will get paid back. This strategy is nothing but reciprocity.

Consciousness

When bringing Problem Solving and evolution together, explaining consciousness is an important point to understand how we have come this far. The answer shall be given in three steps: (1) The advantages that consciousness gave us during the evolutionary process. (2) The observations, through which neuropsychology has approached consciousness. Observations of various kinds of impairment like blindsight, commissurotomy, hemineglect, anosognosia, and also another approach called "binding problem" which tries to explain how distributed activities of neurons make up conscious perception by means of EEG monitoring. (3) Finally, what is probably the most controversial step, dealing with some suggestions of how consciousness is involved in Problem Solving, namely (psycho-)functionalism, metacognition and situation models.

Evolution of Consciousness

When trying to explain consciousness from an evolutionary perspective, there are two possible options of approach. Either you specify the function of consciousness and thus give reasons for an evolutionary progress or you explain how our abilities we gained through evolution made it inevitable to make us conscious. Furthermore, it has to be considered at what time consciousness may have appeared, that is where we can find consciousness in animals. While the first two theories presented here will give reasons for why the function of consciousness has some benefits, the third theory is more about the development of the brain that was not caused by any benefits of cognition but nevertheless enabled the emergence of consciousness.

(*direct source* [1])

As a pioneer in this field, William James (1890)[2] argued that evolution pushes the behaviour of an organism into a direction that is of interest for it. The brain was seen as an instrument to make predictions and therefore also having the ability to choose among many possibilities. So consciousness is involved in reinforcing the favourable possibilities while repressing the unfavourable. James assumes that the evolution of consciousness happened at the same time at which the cerebrum had evolved. It allowed to selectively guide the nervous system in an environment that became more and more complex throughout evolution (1890/1891, p. 147)[2].

James distinguishes three classes of animal consciousness. The first class contains bilateral invertebrates (earthworms, leeches, spiders, and insects) that show a centralisation of the nervous system. The main criterion for this class is the differentiation between having a sensation and not having that particular sensation. Although this can only be considered as a primitive mental state, the detection of stimuli is thought to be a condition for consciousness. An example of scientific investigation was done by Keunzi and Carew (1991)[3] showing that the marine snail Aplysia californica reacted differently to light from various directions and could also be trained to behave in a certain way through conditioning.

The second class contains animals that do not only remember previous experiences but are also capable of equate them with present experiences. They are able to copy a model or in other words imitate a behaviour which is regarded as the beginning of conceptual thought. Here the animal class of cephalopods should be mentioned. Octopus vulgaris which belongs to this class was examined by Fiorito and Scotto (1992)[4]. They separated the octopuses into the "demonstrator" and "observer" group. The "demonstrator" group was trained with conditioning techniques to attack either a white or a red ball when offered both. Then an octopus of the "observer" group watched an octopus from the "demonstrator" group attacking a ball with the specific colour. The "observers" imitated the attacking behaviour rapidly, however they sometimes chose the ball with the respective other colour. Because of this choice, it is assumed that a primitive form of consciousness is involved.

The third class entails humans as well as great-apes (gorillas, orang-utans, chimpanzees) and cetaceans (whales, dolphins). In comparison to other animals they all possess a larger surface area of the cerebrum, the neocortex. The main feature of this class is the capability of self-consciousness which is according to James a more complex form. Gallup (1970)[5] introduced an experiment to find out whether animals or infants are able to distinguish "me" from "not me". Red dye is put on the forehead that can not be recognized except with the aid of a mirror. However, it is in question whether this method can be seen as a test for self-consciousness in the sense that there is an awareness of one's own thoughts.

These three classes were shortly presented because later, in the third part of the subtopic of consciousness, we will introduce a general definition for consciousness which will give us a different but quite similar classification and a suggestion of how to overcome this last problem.

(Blackmore, S. J., 2004 [6])

Another theory that contributes to the idea of consciousness having a function is held by Nicholas Humphrey. The main thesis is that consciousness has a social function. While animals like chimpanzees live in a social environment, humans are highly specialized to social skills. Humphrey believes that skills like understanding, predicting and manipulating the behaviour of others became necessary for our ancestors because, in a group, they were facing situations like deciding whether a group member is a friend or an enemy or when they should form alliances etc. He calls our ancestors having evolved this way "natural scientists".

How consciousness could have had influenced this can be shown by considering the following scenario. Imagine an early hominid Suzy seeing Mick with a large piece of food, with him sits her friend Sally. Suzy thinks about distracting Mick so that Sally could grab the food. But first she needs to ask herself various questions like "Is Sally going to share the food with her". In other words, she needs to put herself into the position of another person. Thus our ancestors developed a self-reflexive insight or an "inner eye" that gives us a perception like other sense organs, however, not of the outer world but of one's own brain activities (1986[7]; 2002[8]). According to this theory consciousness can be attributed to social creatures like great-apes, elephants, wolves and dolphins. But it would also claim that most creatures are not conscious.

The third theory which gains support from Robert Ornstein (1991)[9] is mainly about the necessity to withstand heat mainly for purposes of our head which means that the growth of the brain about 2 million years ago was caused neither by social nor cultural but physiological adaptation. The reason for this assumption is that the increasing size of the brain happened in advance of human characteristics.

First, the importance of cooling the head shall be emphasized. Human beings are sensitive to high temperatures because a rise of 1 or 2°C above normal can disturb brain functions and a rise of 4°C can cause a heat stroke. In addition, human beings lack a cooling system like dogs for example, they have a special blood circuitry which cools the blood when they start panting. One way to achieve cooling is an upright posture. It is assumed that bipedalism was influenced by a climate change that due to its dry conditions thinned the forests. Thus, hunting became a more reliable source for food than plants. But it also caused the temperature to rise in our body. An upright posture had the effect that at noon the sun hit a much smaller surface and more of our body mass is above the hot ground that had a vegetation of 50 cm (adopted from Peter Wheeler). After this evolutionary step it took about one million years until the brain started to grow. Anthropologist Dean Falk assumes that during this time our ancestors developed the net of emissary veins that lead in and out of the brain. In normal circulation these veins carry heated blood from the brain out to the surface of the skull in order to cool it down. If the brain temperature rises due to exercise like conditions, the blood flow in these veins reverses.

The second method our ancestors developed to withstand heat is increasing the cortical size (Konrad Fialkowski, 1986)[10]. On the one hand this enhances the cooling effect of the emissary veins mentioned before. On the other hand the abundance of neurons made it possible that other areas of the brain could take over tasks when there was a loss of neurons. An indication for such a development is that a small piece of the cortex looks like any other piece and except for the size it is even similar to that of other species. Also the density of the neurons is almost the same as for example in chimpanzees. This development could explain how the human brain gained a parallel organization which is preliminary for complex thought. The oversupply of supporting cells (glia) might have allowed more interconnections between neurons due to the space they fill up.

Compared to the previous theories consciousness has no function but is a result of the evolution of the brain. It is important to see that evolution as such is independent of intellect. We will come back to this later in part three because this hint is essential for the definition of consciousness and will be discussed in the short remarks on functionalism.

Neuropsychology and Consciousness

In philosophy there are many notions of consciousness. The topics of the second part are most likely ascribed to phenomenal consciousness which is about our subjective experiences. However, philosophers like John Searle and Thomas Nagel list three features of consciousness that seem to be essential: subjectivity, unity and intentionality. First we will deal with unity also referred to as the "binding problem".

The model of Wolf Singer[11] tries to explain the binding problem with a concept other than the classical one. The classical concept says that cognitive operation is the generation of explicit neuronal representations. These representations are realized by individual neurons that are tuned to particular constellations of input activity. Specificity is gained through selective convergence of input connections in hierarchically structured feed-forward architectures. But according to Singer this view has several disadvantages. It requires a high number of neurons and seems to be inappropriate for the encoding of syntactical structure and hierarchical relations of elements composed in a perceived object (Roelfsema, P.R., Engel, A.K., Koenig, P. & W. Singer, 1996)[12].

So the concept suggested by Singer is a distributed dynamical process which relies on self-organization. It is assumed that neurons are associated with so called functionally coherent assemblies that represent objects. The advantage is that one neuron can participate in different assemblies. Each neuron is tuned only to a subset of elementary features (colour, movement, orientation). This concept may be strong enough to explain phenomenal consciousness due to the combinatorial complexity and flexibility. In contrast single neurons show little difference in sleeping or anesthetized animals.

Now two important questions arise. What is the mechanism of selection that dynamically separates one assembly into two and how is an assembly labelled in order to be recognized by subsequent processes. To give an answer to the first question there are three possibilities. First, the inhibition of non-grouped responses, second, the selected response can be amplified and third, the selected cells fire in synchrony. However, it is unlikely that the modulation of discharge rates (action potential) is involved for the following reasons. An explanation of this type leads to ambiguities when considering the second question of how neurons are labelled. In addition, the processing time would be too high because for evaluation the action potentials first need to be integrated. Also different assemblies can not co-exist in time if they share the same neurons. Otherwise they would not be indistinguishable. This would only allow a sequential processing.

The main hypothesis is that selection and labelling is achieved through the synchronization which comes in with several advantages. It is independent of the firing rate of single neurons and can be used in parallel. Assemblies can follow one another much faster (Singer, 1999/2000)[13] and output activity has a high precision because of minimal latency jitter (Abeles, M. 1982[14]; Softky, W. 1994[15]; Koenig, P., A.K. Engel & W. Singer, 1996[16]). The processing speed increases because synchronized EPSPs trigger action potentials with a minimal delay.

With this hypothesis some preliminaries for selection have to be considered. Neurons must be sensible to detect coincident synaptic input. Further, they have to be able to coordinate rapidly in a context dependent way. One example of neurons working with high precision is the auditory nucleus where delays in the sub millisecond range are evaluated. Another example is the oscillatory responses of retinal ganglion cells which are transmitted to cortical neurons (Castelo-Branco, M., S. Neuenschwander & W. Singer, 1998)[17]. When awake these oscillatory patterns are in the gamma frequency range of 30-60 Hz (also see Crick, F. & Koch, C., 1990)[18]. In many experiments rapid synchronization has been observed in the visual cortex of cats. Fluctuations of the local field potential shifted the response latency accordingly to the polarization of the potential. In other words, these sub threshold oscillations can cause a delay in the response and thus are responsible for synchronization tasks.

Coming back to the binding problem, we can examine it with the study of attention. Attention can facilitate synchronization. In one experiment cats were trained to react to visual stimuli with a motor response. When they focused their attention, cortical areas that are involved in the execution of the task synchronized their activity. Immediately after the stimulus was shown, synchronization further increased. Thus, attention has the functional role of expectancy. It acts like a dynamic filter which in advance selects neurons that participate in the execution and therefore accomplishes binding.

Now we will have a look an various brain damages which reveal additional insights in the subject of consciousness.

Blindsight[6]

Lawrence Weiskrantz (1986[19]; 1997[20]) had been studying a patient called D.B. who lost vision in a large part of his left visual field due to the removal of a tumor that was in an area of his visual cortex. In an experiment a circle containing stripes was shown to him in the blind field. He said that he could not see anything within this area, for he was blind there. However, when he was asked to guess whether the orientation of the stripes is either vertical or horizontal, he answers correctly in 90-95 % of the time. (compare with hemineglect below)

Commissurotomy (split-brain)[6]

In the 1960s operations severing the corpus callosum had been carried out. This should prevent epileptic seizures spreading from one hemisphere to the other as the corpus callosum is the primary root where both hemispheres can interact. When the patients recovered they performed equally well on problem solving tasks and language as before. When considering the visual pathway, a cut through the corpus callosum prevents information from going from one side to the other (see picture). This affects paths that start from the nasal side. So one hemisphere will only receive information from the contralateral side of the visual field (here: left hemisphere only blue path, right hemisphere only red path).

Patient P.S. was shown a snow scene on the left side (right hemisphere) and a chicken claw on the right side (left hemisphere). Because the right hemisphere controls the left side of the body, he pointed to a shovel with the left hand and to a chicken with the right hand. When he was asked why, he said, "The chicken claw goes with the chicken, and you need a shovel to clean out the chicken shed" (after Gazzaniga & LeDoux, 1992). Other experiments show that this confabulation is common. No patient would admit that they have a split brain but invent a story that seems plausible to their reaction.

Hemineglect[21]

Patients that suffer from hemineglect ignore or pay no attention to the side of space contralateral to the lesion. For example when asked to copy a picture of a clock, they may only be able to draw the right half which in this case would be caused by a lesion in the right hemisphere. Hemineglect occurs within different frames which means that the symptom occurs with regard to the horizontal plan (left-right) or the vertical plane (top-bottom) or to non spacial frameworks which can be object based (e.g. words).

Each hemisphere seems to have an attentional bias on the contralateral side. This can be seen when you compare a chimeric picture containing a face that has a smile on the left side with the same picture mirrored. If you are right-handed which means that your emotional interpretation is better in the right hemisphere, you will perceive the first picture as being happier (Levy, J., Heller, W., Banich, M.T. & Burton, L.A., 1983)[22]. Another property is that lesion in the right hemisphere are more severe causing patients to slow on response time. In an experiment (Weintraub, S. & Mesulam, M. 1987)[23] where patience with left- and right-hemisphere damage and intact persons (control group) should mark items on a display, patients performed worse on the neglected hemispace respectively. However, patients with a right hemisphere lesion performed even worse than those with left hemisphere lesion. There are two possibilities to explain this. First, the attention bias is greater in the right hemisphere and second, the attention drops towards the ipsilateral side of each hemisphere while the right hemisphere does so with a higher gradient.

What is interesting is that patients still seem to process information of the neglected field. When patients were shown two pictures, the first presented 400 ms earlier in the neglected field, they responded faster if those pictures were related although they were not aware of the first one (Berti, A. & Rizzolatti, G., 1992)[24].

Anosognosia[6]

The unawareness of once disabilities is called anosognosia (Damasio, A., 1999[25]; Weiskrantz, L., 1997[20]). It occurs with the damage to particular parts of the right parietal lobe. For example patients who are unable to stand up still insist that they would be able to and at the same time make excuses that they cannot get out of bed. There are extreme cases like a blind patient told that he enjoyed watching TV (Sacks, O., 1992)[26].

Problem Solving and Consciousness

An explanation why consciousness plays an important role in the process of problem solving in itself leads to a problem because without a clear concept of consciousness one can always verify or deny its purpose. Therefore we will state a definition not claiming that it is correct but can be a ground of our discussion. It seems that such a definition presupposes that there is an objective description of a subjective experience. However, our approach assumes that consciousness is not the same as subjective experience and thereby explain consciousness without explaining why perception has a qualitative character. Nevertheless, we will also explain how sensations are related to consciousness.

To start up from the bottom, we will just ask whether a stone is conscious. Simply 'no' because stones are not alive. So what does life mean? Def.: Life is the part of the phenotype which is solely determined by the genotype excluding environmental influences on both phenotype and genotype (Mendel's law, mutation, genetic engineering). We can consciously change both and therefore we have to exclude them from definition. Otherwise we could not differentiate between life and consciousness. It does not mean that life cannot undergo an evolutionary process.

On the next level we have modalities which are experienced in a subjective way. The difference between creatures that are merely alive and creatures that can also perceive is that the former can only adapt through evolution whereas the latter can adapt during lifetime. An example for the first group is a virus while Aplysia californica would belong to the second group. The main idea is the ability to establish a representation of the environment. Through evolution these representations can gain an interpretative value for example the face of a tiger is interpreted as being dangerous (this idea goes back to Gerald Edelman). So we may conclude that sensations are representations plus their interpretation. How these interpretations are accomplished is still unknown.

Finally, we will just define consciousness in a way we can deal with it. Def.: Consciousness is the ability to establish structured sensations. The first notable property would therefore be that consciousness itself cannot be perceived. If you imagine that it is a structure, you might say it is perceivable but this for itself is not consciousness because it is just a semantic content as described below. So how do we understand this structure. It can be thought of as an axiomatic system where we can give content a meaning, that is we know what the world has to be like to fulfill a sentence of this system (see Ludwig Wittgenstein). From this we conclude that our sensations compose a semantic content

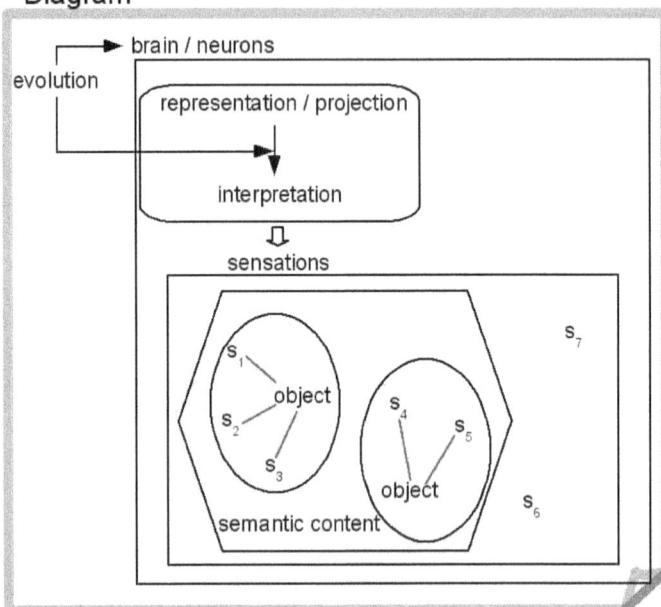

Diagram

binding that reflects conscious state
(static view: syntax, dynamic view: inference)

Consciousness diagram (GFDL - Marc Heimann)

(binding). Unfortunately we would have to guess that this is learned during childhood. One example is visual object recognition. We will show later that consciousness should not be defined over objects but, as we already did, over sensations. Then we may conclude that we have the possibility to transcend various systems because semantic and syntax are both realized on the sensational level. This allows us to perform metacognitive tasks because we can switch syntax to the roll of semantic enabling us to solve problems in a way that differs from evolution for it is done on a symbolic level. One example of how this definition can be applied is linguistic. Linguistic shows that there are various levels of processing like morphology, syntax, semantic, pragmatic. These levels altogether compose a system that contributes all its aspects for evaluating the meaning of a sentence.

Review

Defining consciousness as an ability to structure sensations, confabulation in this sense can be seen as its performance. People try to give something a meaning and it is important to see that they can do so despite the lack of information. Confabulation is a constructive process which can be performed without semantic content. Blindsight and hemineglect show that patients can perceive sensations (orientation, color, emotional expression). But they are unable to recognize objects which means that semantic content may not affect consciousness. Due to this double dissociation we can conclude that consciousness is independent of semantic content. Now we can say that problem solving may happen unconsciously for example when riding a bike. This can be accomplished due to plasticity (Kandel, E. R., Schwartz, J. H., Jessell, T. M., 2000)[27]. However, we suggest that consciousness must be involved when we face new problems. We will show examples where consciousness is useful and one example where it is inevitable.

Functionalism:

We will consider two questions. The first is how cognition can have a function that is relevant for the evolutionary process. The evolutionary process has to be viewed very precisely. It does not act upon individuals but upon generations of individuals. Next, the genetic information of an individual is randomly chosen from its parents which means that there is no preference of any feature in the genetic code (Ornstein, R., 1991)[9]. If you imagine the evolutionary process as a tree, cognition virtually increases the branching factor because individuals having a lifetime adaption may better cope with environmental obstacles. Thus, cognition does not influence evolution but having cognition does. This leads us to the next question asking how functionalism would allow subjective experience when it actually states that on certain inputs there will be definite outputs. Indeed the answer is already given with the distinction of evolutionary adaption and lifetime adaption. The abilities of cognition with regard to the evolutionary process have nothing to do with the abilities of an individual to perceive.

References

1. ↑ Nielsen, M. (?) William James and the evolution of consciousness. La Trobe University. Retrieved May 20, 2006 from http://cogprints.org/
2. ↑ [2.0] [2.1] James, W. (1890/1981). The principles of psychology. Cambridge: Harvard University Press.
3. ↑ Keunzi, F. M., & Carew, T .J. (1991). Aplysia californica. Behavioral and Neural Biology, 55 (3), 338-355.
4. ↑ Fiorito, G., & Scotto, P. (1992). Observational learning in Octopus vulgaris. Science, 256, 545-547.
5. ↑ Gallup, G. G., Jr. (1970). Chimpanzees: Self-recognition. Science, 167, 341-343.
6. ↑ [6.0] [6.1] [6.2] [6.3] Blackmore, S. J. (2004). Consciousness : An Introduction. New York: Oxford University Press.
7. ↑ Humphrey, N. (1986). The Inner Eye. London: Faber & Faber
8. ↑ Humphrey, N. (2002). The Mind made Flesh: Frontiers of Psychology and Evolution. Oxford: Oxford University Press.
9. ↑ [9.0] [9.1] Ornstein, R. (1991). Evolution of Consciousness: The Origins of the Way We Think. New York: Simon & Schuster Paperbacks.
10. ↑ Fialkowski, K. (1986) A mechanism for the origin of the human brain: A hypothesis. Current Anthropology, 28, 540-43
11. ↑ Singer, W. (?) Consciousness and the Binding Problem. Max Planck Institute for Brain Research. Retrieved May 20, 2006 from http://www.mpih-frankfurt.mpg.de/
12. ↑ Roelfsema, P.R., Engel, A.K., Koenig, P. & W. Singer. 1996. The role of neuronal synchronization in response selection: a biologically plausible theory of structured representation in the visual cortex. J. Cogn. Neurosci. 8, 603-625.
13. ↑ Singer, W. 1999/2000. Response synchronization: A universal coding strategy for the definition of relations. In The New Cognitive Neurosciences, Second Edition. M.S. Gazzaniga, Ed.: 325-338. MIT-Press. Cambridge, MA.
14. ↑ Abeles, M. 1982. Role of the cortical neuron: integrator or coincidence detector? Isr. J. Med. Sci. 18, 83-92.
15. ↑ Softky, W. 1994. Sub-millisecond coincidence detection in active dendritic trees. Neuroscience 58, 13-41.
16. ↑ Koenig, P., A.K. Engel & W. Singer. 1996. Integrator or coincidence detector? The role of

the cortical neuron revisited. Trends Neurosci. 19, 130-137.

17. ↑ Castelo-Branco, M., S. Neuenschwander & W. Singer. 1998. Synchronization of visual responses between the cortex, lateral geniculate nucleus, and retina in the anesthetized cat. J. Neurosci. 18, 6395-6410.

18. ↑ Crick, F & C. Koch, C. (1990) Towards a neurobiological theory of consciousness. Seminars in the Neurosciences, 2, 263-75

19. ↑ Weiskrantz, L. (1986) Blindsight: A Case Study and Implications. Oxford, Oxford University Press.

20. ↑ [20.0] [20.1] Weiskrantz, L. (1997) Consciousness Lost and Found. Oxford, Oxford University Press.

21. ↑ Banich, M. T. (2004) Cognitive Neuroscience and Neuropsychology (2nd ed). Boston: Houghton Mifflin Company

22. ↑ Levy, J., Heller, W., Banich, M.T. & Burton, L.A. (1983) Asymmetry of perception in free viewing of chimeric faces. Brain and Cognition, 2, 404-419

23. ↑ Weintraub, S. & Mesulam, M. (1987). Right cerebral dominance in spatial attention. Archives of Neurology, 44, 621-625.

24. ↑ Berti, A. & Rizzolatti, G. (1992). Visual processing without awareness: Evidence from unilateral neglect. Journal of Cognitive Neuroscience, 4, 345-351.

25. ↑ Damasio, A. (1999) The Feeling of what happens: Body, Emotion and the making of Consciousness. London: Heinemann.

26. ↑ Sacks, O. (1992) the last hippie. New York Review of Books 39 (26 March), 51-60

27. ↑ Kandel, E. R., Schwartz, J. H., Jessell, T. M. (2000). Principles of Neural Science, 4th edition. New York: McGraw-Hill

• Carruthers, P. & Chamberlain, A. (2001). Evolution and the Human Mind: Modularity, Language and Meta-Cognition.
• Gaulin, S. J. C. & McBurney, D. (2000). Psychology: An Evolutionary Approach
• Goldstein, E. B. (2005). Cognitive Psychology: Connecting Mind, Research and Everyday Experience. Belmont: Thomson Wadsworth
• Held, C. & Knauff, M. & Vosgerau, G. (2006). Mental Models and the Mind: Current Developments in Cognitive Psychology, Neuroscience, and Philosophy of Mind (Advances in Psychology). Amsterdam: Elsevier B.V.
• Sternberg, R. J. & Davidson, J. E. (1996). The Nature of Insight.

Links

• Evolution of Consciousness, by Olivia Moschetti
• Consciousness and the Binding Problem, by Prof. Dr. Wolf Singer
• Mental Models, by Philip N. Johnson-Laird

live version • discussion • edit lesson • comment • report an error

3 EVOLUTIONARY PERSPECTIVE ON SOCIAL COGNITIONS

live version • discussion • edit lesson • comment • report an error

Introduction

The term "social cognition" describes all abilities necessary to act adequately in a social system. The understanding of a social environment presupposes representations of the other agents as intentional and goal-directed. Social cognition is a common skill among various species, however we can observe distinct levels of complexity. As proposed by Tomasello (2004), we can distinguish between the following degrees (sorted by increasing sophistication):

Caricature of Charles Darwin himself

- Dyadic engagement: Sharing behavior and emotions; Direct interaction of two animate agents.
- Tryadic engagement: Sharing goals and perception; Some goal directed agents acting together towards some shared goal.
- Collaborative engagement: Joint intentions and attention; Two or more agents acting (in complementary roles), according to a coordinated action plan with mutual knowledge and the possibility of helping the other in his role.

The latter is considered to be the crucial difference between humans and all other species: Human beings possess a uniqe motivation to share psychological states with other persons.

When we describe psychological features of animals or humans, and we accept evolution as the process which designs everything in biosphere, the question arises whether psychological characteristics and their development are explainable in terms of genetic variation and natural selection. There are three main-theories of evolutionary development of the social structure of modern man:

1. group selection,
2. kin selection,
3. reciprocal altruism

From selection to sociality

While we behold development of life on earth, we soon take a evolutionary stance to explain the change of life over time. That means we try to reconstruct the way life developed on earth and also the modality of the processes that control these changes. In reference to social behaviour of creatures there are many evolutionary theories to explain this. As proposed by Gaulin and McBurney (see references below), we attend to three major theories: Group selection, an intuitive approach to describe social behaviour. Kin selection, a more advanced theory considering laws of genetics to cause social behaviour. Reciprocal alturism is a sophisticated approach to treat the individual in social barter-deals. These theories all have in common that the goal of the described agents is to pass on their genetic material into the next generations. And this common goal creates the social interaction we can observe.

Group Selection

Vero Wynne-Edwards (1906-1997) proclaimed this theory first in the 1960's. On an evolutionary perspective a group is a number of individuals who affect the fitness of each other. Notice that biological relatedness and periods of time are not taken into account with this definition. Group selection now means that if any of the individuals of a group is doing benefit to its group, the group is more likely to survive and pass its predisposition to the next generation. This again improves the chance of the individual to spread its genetic material. So in this theory an alturist is more likely to spread his alleles than a non-alturistic organism. The distinction to the „classical" theory of evolution is that not only the fittest individuals are likely to survive, but also the fittest groups, so to speak the ones with the most cooperation.

Let's consider an example: Take some bacteria in the human mouth. These bacteria are very slow moving. The first group of bacteria, which perform cell division as fast as possible, soon waste all their nutriments and have no resources left. Instead, they have to face their bordering bacteria colonies. So the first group is facing death very fast.

The second group of bacteria, which perform a more moderate cell division, leave more resources to their bordering colonies. Whereas first group offspring always have to compete for the resources with its neighbours, the second groups offspring have savings of resources and so survives more likely a longer time period. The altruism of the second group makes it fitter as a whole. In the case of bacteria swimming in a growing medium, in which the bacteria can move freely, the fast group always overwhelms the second group. This indicates the problem of the group selection theory: it needs certain circumstances to describe things properly. Additionally, every theory about groups should include the phenomenon of migration. So in this simple form, the theory is not capable in handling selfish behaviour of some agents in altruistic groups: Alturistic groups which include selfish members would turn into pure selfish ones over time, because alturistic agents would work for selfish agents, thereby increasing the cheaters' fitness while decreasing their own. So generally, group selection is a poor explanation for altruism and sociality.

Kin Selection

A more sophisticated approach to explain cooperative behaviour is kin selection. Kin selection theory is embedded in the natural selection theory and the inclusive fitness theory (the later one arose from kin selection), which we do not inspect further here. William D. Hamilton and John M. Smith puplished the kin selection theory in 1964. The improvment compared to group selection is, that not the individuals are seen as actor, but the genes are identified as the actual „players". The theory declares: An agent acts cooperatively, if the adressee is genetically related to him, because he wants the genetic material to spread which he has in common with the beneficiary. The more genetic material two agents have in common, the more they will cooperate. To help its own kin, an agent improves the chance its own genetic material to spread, at least the part he has in common with its kin.

As a rule of thumb we propose: "The relative benefit to the adressee of an altruistic action, has to be higher than the costs to the giver."

Hamiltons rule also considers the relatedness between giver and adressee of a favor, which he expressed in his famous formula:

$$r * B > C$$

where

> **r** is the relatedness (value between zero and one) - it shows how akin the actor and the beneficiary are;
> **B** is the benefit to the beneficiary;
> **C** are the costs to the giver

If the left value is greater than the costs of the right side, the behaviour increases the fitness of the giver and should therefore be done.

Reciprocal Alturism

In general reciprocal alturism is to do benefit to any organism in expectation of a reciprocation, so to speak a benefit pay-back. This behaviour establishes a system by which social interaction can be viewed as barter-deals. These barter-deals are concrete described by the prisoner's dilemma, which Albert W. Tucker formalized as follows:

> Two suspects, A and B, are arrested by the police. The police have insufficient evidence for a conviction, and, having separated both prisoners, visit each of them to offer the same deal: if one testifies for the prosecution against the other and the other remains silent, the betrayer goes free and the silent accomplice receives the full 10-year sentence. If both stay silent, the police can sentence both prisoners to only six months in jail for a minor charge. If each betrays the other, each will receive a two-year sentence. Each prisoner must make the choice of whether to betray the other or to remain silent. However, neither prisoner knows for sure what choice the other prisoner will make. So the question this dilemma poses is: What will happen? How will the prisoners act?

Enhanced prisoner's dilemma looks like this:

> Agents A and B making a barter-deal.
> If A cheats on B, whereas B cooperates with A, B gets no points, A gets more than average points.
> If A cooperates with B and vise versa, both get average points.
> If both cheat on each other, none of them gets points.

Iterated prisoner's dilemma reminds strongly on social interactions and many strategies for it were designed. A famous iterated prioner's dilemma strategie is tit for tat, which can be viewed as specification of reciprocal alturism. Among the „simple" stategies, it is the most effective one. Tit for tat means if an organisms cooperation is reciprocated, it keeps the cooperation running, otherwise it stops cooperating with the organism, who did not cooperate. Because it is often hard to determine who is cooperating and who only pretends to be reliable, but actually acts selfish, organisms developed mechanisms to detect cheaters and selfish agents in altruistic groups in order to withhold favors from them. The development of cognitive abilities to detect cheaters is important for altruistic groups to survive - as we have seen, migration of selfish agents into altruistic groups infects it which in the end leads in dying out of the altruistic allele. Therefore, to keep altruism efficient and still benefit from its advantages, complex organism have developed various social cognitive abilities.

Possible selection pressures favoring human sociality

From an evolutionary perspective, sociality is another adaptation of some species to their environment - just like eyes, pelt, legs and the like. We know that adaptations are constantly tested against their environment, and that those traits (genes) who increase the fitness of the bearer are more likely to get passed on to the next generation. So what are the benefits and costs of living-within-a-group in general? One of the first principal costs is of course increased competition in almost any area of life. Animals that live solitary don't have to fight for rare resources such as foods or possible mates with companions. In addition, groups tend to attract more predators, as you can imagine. However, these two issues also have a positive side: A group tends to be more successful in finding food and is more powerful in defense against mentioned predators: More eyes/ears simply see/hear more than fewer do. This leads us to the first conclusion (which in principal can be generalized for all adaptations): Selection favors social habits if the benefits of living in a group outweights the costs.

Knowing that, what were the conditions of our ancestors in the **Environment of Evolutionary Adaptedness (EEA)**? Of course nobody can exactly say how they lived, but by considering life of contemporary great apes and hunter-gatherer societies, we can make a reasonable guess on which we can draw some conclusions: Presumably, early humans inhabited more open, less forested country than the majority of primates, which certainly increased their exposure to predators. Also, open habitats typically contain herds of grazing animals. Thus, if our ancestors' diet depended on meat, cooperative hunters maybe were more successful than solitary ones. Other food than meat also may support living in a group: If resources are generally rich, but scattered over the landscape, the costs of sharing the found food with others is low - while the benefits of getting help in finding them in the first place are very high. Another possible pressure was revealed by observing social great apes like gorillas: Neither their food comes in patches (they eat leaf material and do never hunt), nor have they natural enemies after reaching adulthood. It seems that the standard reasons for sociality have not much force on them - but one aspect of their behaviour gives a hint anyway: Killing among members of their own species. Especially female apes are at risk of having their infants killed by males that did not father those infants, so female gorillas cluster around strong, powerful males that are capable of protecting their children. Life of chimpanzees also includes fatal violence, concentrated onto struggles between communities: Males invade other groups to kill infants of unfamiliar females or even other males, if the numerical advantage is sufficient. These kinds of risk clearly favor sociality over living in solitude.

So we get a small overview of the probable pressures on our ancestors that lead to sociality:

- inhibiting open country,
- hunting,
- gathering rich but scattered patches of food,
- hostilities/infanticide among neighbours.

Social Cognition

Having talked about various processes and theories about evolution, the further discussion in this chapter will require detailed elaboration on the term 'social cognition'. While 'cognition' for itself is already a rather complex term, 'social cognition' is even more specific. In order to make it accessible and to understand the general idea behind it, several main aspects and the respective vocabulary to talk about it need to be introduced. The suggestions of Tomasello et al 2004 will serve as a basis for this.

First of all it has to be said that, when talking about 'social cognition', we talk about human cognitive skills, for, as we will see, humans are the only species abilities in the respective sense evolved. Trying to find the reasons for this fact will go hand in hand with inquiring into the nature of social cognition as a species unique human faculty.

Drawing a rough sketch of the topic, what we are interested in is the ability to participate with others in collaborative actions with not only common but also shared goals. The term introduced to describe this aspect is called **shared intentionality**. This presupposes the ability to read the intentions of other **agents**, as well as a broad background of cultural learning during the development of a human being. Especially the latter is a strictly human phenomenon, since it arises from a unique motivation to share psychological states, which in turn needs unique forms of cognitive representation for doing so. Hence it is proposed that the creation of linguistic symbols is closely related, as well as the rise of social norms and the establishment of social institutions.

The human faculty of social cognition

Around a child's first birthday the capability emerges to understand the intentions of other people. Humans are by far the most skillful species at reading the minds of specimen, i.e. successfully guessing or reasoning about what other fellow humans perceive, intend, believe, know, desire, etc. - which is crucial in order to decide what someone else is doing in the first place. While the action might be quite the same, it is the respective intention according to which the action has to be judged. For example, seeing somebody breaking a window has to be judged differently if somebody has just lost his keys, if he tries to break in somewhere or if someone simply exerts wanton destruction. While reading the intentions of another agent is not a strictly human capability, humans also collaborate and interact culturally, that means we have complex collaborative activities, shared symbolic artifacts and social institutions that allow for communication and structure, which lead to powerful abstract levels and organizational concepts like societies, states, etc., and give the possibility to convey knowledge on these levels from one generation to another, hereby creating a vast complexity and variety over historical time.

It is proposed that reading intentions and cultural learning give rise to species unique processes of cultural cognition and evolution.

In order to explain the level of complexity found in human cultural and collaborative activities, we need the term of **shared intentionality**. Apparently it is a strictly human faculty to participate in collaborative actions that involve shared goals and socially coordinated action plans, which is also called **joint intentions**. This requires an understanding of the goals and perceptions of other involved agents, as well as sharing and communicating these, which again seems to be a strictly human behavior. This then may have brought forth elaborate cognitive representations for dialogs, like the human faculty for language, mathematics and the creation of social practices and institutions. For further discussion, the questions of how humans come to understand intentional action and how they participate in actions born of shared intentionality will have to be dealt with.

Understanding intentional action

For our purposes, we will consider intentional action as an organism's intelligent behavioral interaction with its environment and the factors that play a role in that.

According to cybernetic theory this presupposes an organizational structure consisting of three components:

1. a goal,
2. perceiving the environment,
3. acting towards the goal by changing the environment.

This is a circular organization that causes action, which in turn causes a change in perception, which again determines the action. In this way, the system is self-regulating. This model is used by Tomasello et al to describe human intentional action.

Let's look at an example: A closed box which a person wants open. The latter obviously is the goal state, however, apparently it is necessary to distinguish between an external goal, which is the actual state of an open box in the environment, and an internal goal, which is something like a mental representation of the goal state, that the person needs to operate towards that goal.

Furthermore, a sharp distinction is drawn between a goal and an intention. Whereas a goal describes merely the state desired by the person, an intention includes this goal and the means to achieve it, that is a sort of action plan the person decided for to achieve the goal. In the given example, this might be cutting the box open with a sharp knife or scissors. As mentioned earlier, since an intention includes the goal, the same action can have different intentional interpretations. As we saw with breaking a car window for example, it can either be a means to get to the keys, or merely an expression of wanton destruction.

The results of the action are a change in the state of the environment, which, according to a person's internal goal, can be a failed attempt, a success, where the state of the environment matches the internal goal, or an accident, which is in a way a failed attempt with unpredicted consequences in the environmental state. Since we are talking about a human person, the results of an action are usually accompanied by an emotional reaction, like happiness, sadness, anger or surprise.

On the part of perception, the term 'selective attention' is introduced to point out that the monitoring of the environment done by the organism is focused on the goals at hand, which means that only those facts that are relevant for opening the box in the example before are taken into active consideration. The color of the box, for example, plays an unimportant role in the action plan chosen to open the box.

Depending of the complexity of the goal, the means may include the creation of subgoals, or even a whole subplan. Also, the organism probably wants the box open for a reason, which would be in the context a higher level goal. Concerning the intention involving this potential higher level goal, the act of opening the box may itself be just a subgoal. Choosing appropriate subgoals is referred to as 'decision making' by Tomasello et al.

Finally, the action itself might be the actual goal, consider for example the act of jogging, of dancing or of singing, where the respective action is not meant to bring about some immediate goal but represents by itself already the desired state.

These are all considerations that have to be taken into account in order to understand the intentional action of other organisms, which, as was pointed earlier, is a crucial point for social cognition. Referring to children's understanding of intentional action, the latter can be divided into three groups representing more and more complex level of grasp.

The first one to be mentioned is the perception of animate action. This means that after a couple of months, babies can differentiate between motion that was caused by some external influence to some passive object, and actions that an object or organism has performed by itself, as animate being. At this stage, however, the child has not yet any understanding of potential goals the observed actor might have.

The next stage of comprehension includes the understanding that the organism acts with persistence towards achieving a goal, including trial and error, and is developed by children after about 9 months. This also means that the child knows that the person it observes has a certain perception. At this stage, a certain amount of predicting the behavior of the actor is possible. After one year of age, a child understands that an actor pursuing a goal may have a variety of action plans to achieve the goal, and is choosing between them. Furthermore a certain sense for the selective attention of the actor will have developed, and the child realizes that action and attention are directed towards a goal. This allows a broad variety of predictions of behavior of organisms in a certain environment.

By 14 months of age, children fully comprehend intentional action, including the basics of rational decision making. According to Tomasello et al, this leads to powerful forms of cultural learning, which is especially important since a child not only learns to predict behavior in an environment, but it also learns, foremost by imitation, how things are conventionally done in their culture.

Shared intentionality

According to Tomasello et al, shared intentionality might emerge whenever socially interacting agents in an environment understand each other as acting intentionally. What this means is that the agents work together towards a shared goal in collaborative interaction. Furthermore, they do that in coordinated action roles and mutual knowledge about them. The nature of the activity or its complexity is not important, as long as the action is carried out in the described fashion. It is important to mention that the notion of 'shared goals' means that the internal goals of each agent include the intentions of the others. If you take a group of apes on a hunt, for example, the apes appear to be acting in a collaborative fashion, however, it is reasonable to assume that neither do they have coordinated action roles, nor do they have a shared goal, but rather act as seen fit towards the same individual goal state. Summing up, the important characteristics of the behavior in question are that the agents are mutually responsive, have the goal of achieving something together, and coordinate their actions with distributed roles and action plans.

Tomasello et al argue that in complex social groups the repeated sharing of intentions in a particular interactive context leads to the creation of habitual social practices and beliefs, that may form normative or structural aspects of a society, like government, money, marriage, etc., which of course form the notion of society itself. Society might hence be seen as a product and an indicator of social cognition.

The social interaction that builds the ground for activities involving shared intentionality is proposed to be divided into three groups:

The first one is called 'dyadic engagement'. What is meant here is the simple sharing of emotions and behavior, by means of a direct mutual responsiveness, for example by expressing emotions. The motivation to share emotions, repeatedly, is already a key factor for social cognition and a main difference between humans and other species, as for example primates.

The next level is called 'triadic engagement', where two agents act together towards a shared goal, while monitoring the perception and goal-direction of the other agent. Sharing a goal is one step further than simply a direct responsiveness as in dyadic engagement.

The last supposed level is called 'collaborative engagement', which comprises, as introduced earlier, joint intentions and attention. At this point the agents share a goal, act in different, even complementary roles with a complex action plan and mutual knowledge about selective attention and intentions of one another. The latter aspect allows the agents to assist each other and reverse or take over roles.

These different levels of social engagement require the understanding of the different aspects of intentional action, as introduced above, and presuppose the uniquely human motivation to share psychological states with each other.

According to Tomasello et al, human infants develop very early in ontogeny the strong motivation to share emotions, goals and perception and participate in collaborative pretense activities in fictional environments.

The special motivation to share psychological states of course needs means to do so. These means have to be certain complex cognitive representations, especially for the joint intentions that require at least two sets of action plans, since in the spirit of shared goals those of the other one have to be represented as well for true shared intentionality. Since these representations have as content mostly social engagement, Tomasello et al make use of the term 'dialogic cognitive representations' at this point. Closely related with this is the communication and use of linguistic symbols. Dialogic cognitive representations allow in some sense a form of 'collective intentionality', which is important to construct social norms, conceptualize beliefs and, most importantly, share them. This gives rise to something like social rationality: by internalizing collective norms children learn to regulate their own behavior.

In this sense, social cognition is what enables us to create culture and lays the foundation for society. With this knowledge we can now return to the discussion of how and why this particular kind of human behavior may have evolved during evolution and in what way it is useful.

References

- M. S. Gazzaniga, R. B. Ivry, G. R. Mangun; Conitive Neuroscience, Norton & Company, 1998
- M. Tomasello; Understanding and sharing intentions: The origins of cultural cognition, Cambridge University Press, 2004
- Steven J. C. Gaulin, Donald H. McBurney; Psychology: An evolutionary approach, Prentice-Hall New Jersey, 2001

live version • discussion • edit lesson • comment • report an error

4 BEHAVIORAL AND NEUROSCIENCE METHODS

live version • discussion • edit lesson • comment • report an error

Introduction

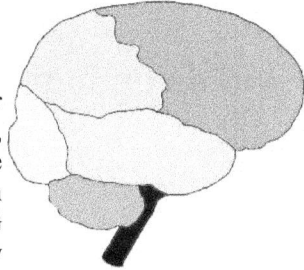

Lobes of the brain

Behavioral and Neuroscientific Methods are used to get a better understanding of how our brain influences the way we think, feel, and act. There are many different methods which help us to analyze the brain and as well to give us an overview of the relationship between brain and behaviour. Well-known technique are the EEG (Electroencephalography) which records the brain's electrical activity and the fMRI (functional magnetic resonance imaging) method which tells us more about brain functions. Other methods, such as the lesion method, are not as well-known but still very influential in today's neuroscientific research.

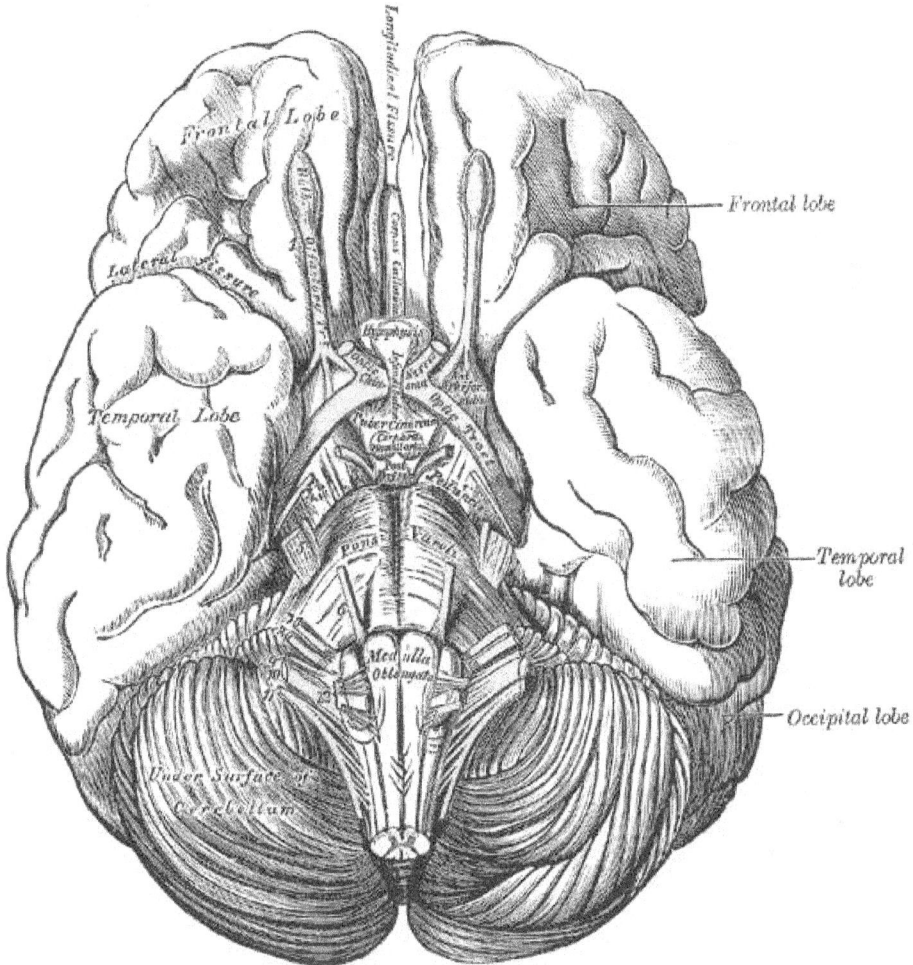

Methods can be summmed up in the following categories: There are techniques for assessing brain anatomy and others for assessing physiological functions. Furthermore there are techniques for modulating brain activity, analyzing behaviour or for modeling brain- behaviour relationships. In some cases, as in the lesion method, patients with brain damage are examined to determine which brain structures were damaged and to what extent this influences the patient's behaviour.

Studies on humans with brain damages

Lesion method

The brain is a complicated structure, composed of many structures. It seems obvious that any task a person performs needs the successful work of the brain's components. A long-standing method of the neurophysiologist has been to study how behaviour is altered by selectively removing one or more of these parts. If a neural structure contributes to a task, then rendering structure dysfunctional should impair the performance of that task. A lesion is an area of the brain that is damaged in both structure and function. If this damage of the brain region leads to an inability of performig a particular mental function, then this function and brain region must be correlated with each other. This means that the function depended on the brain region, and is called lesion method. Lesions can occur accidentally in the course of life events, or can be caused deliberately, in a laboratory. The lesion method relates the area of a lesion, to loss in behaviour. Put simply: If structure X is damaged, and changes in behavior Y occur, we can infer that structure X caused, or at least had to do with, behaviour Y.

Example: Paul Broca examined the brain of a patient who lost almost all his language ability. Broca found a lesion in the left frontal lobe. Based on several examples of this, he concluded that the ability to speak is at least partially controlled by this area, now referred to as Broca's area.

Because of the nature of non-laboratory settings, lesions such as these cannot be considered experimentally valid. So experimental lesioning occurs mainly with animals. Various animals are used for chemically inducing lesions in their brains, thereafter they are compared to various control groups in order to determine specifically where, and to what degree, a structure controls a behaviour.

Areas where it is used

The lesion method can be used as experimental probes to investigate hypotheses about the relationship between the brain and cognitive processes.In this field research is done a lot with animals, where lesions are created in a particular brain region, and then the effects on the behaviour of this lesion are observed. Humans obviously cannot be subjected to brain lesions to investigate their nervous sytem's function. Human neuropsychology requires patients with naturally occurring lesions, generally accidentally under particular circumstances. Because of this fact the researchers have no control over the location or extent of the lesion, and because of this research on humans is only rarely possible.

According to the goal of the researcher, he can choose between two approaches concerning the lesion method. One of the approach serves for investigation of neural systems, whereby the other approach accentuates cognitive processes. The approach of neural systems deals with the task to find out what functions are correlated with a specific brain region. Due to the fact that it is possible that a specific function is not only supported by one brain region, but can also be supported by other brain regions, it is important to do experiments with groups of patients who had damage in a brain region and because of this a loss of a specific function, but also to do experiments with groups of patients, who had damage in an other brain region. This allows the researchers to find out if a function is correlated with one specific brain region or also with other brain regions. This research enables inestimable information about the relationship between brain areas and cognitive functions, which in turn is useful for other medically related professionals, like neurosurgeons, clinical neuropsychologists etc.

The approach which distinguishes the cognitive processes fiddles with behavioral signs, where primarily the region of the brain damage plays little role. It is important that the group of patienst have the same behavioral deficit, so the researchers have the possibility to examine each patients damaged brain region. If the researchers determine that there is similarity in the location of the damages brain region, they can allege hypotheses, that a specific brain region supports a cognitive function. Research in this field allows to affect the location of the brain damage more closely, when patients show the same behavioral signs. This facilitates to say more about the particular neural structure of the damaged brain area and which loss of function results.

Problems which can occur

Even though the lesion method is an important method and so to say the cornerstone of cognitive neuroscience, because it enables to make hypotheses about the relationship between brain and behaviour, it has limitations. These limitations depend on the variableness of the properties of the brain damage, as well as on the variability of the attributes of the patients. For example the location and extent of the damage could be variable in the different cases of patients. And also the different characteristics of the patients make it difficult to give definitive conclusions about the correlation between a specific brain region and a particular cognitive function.

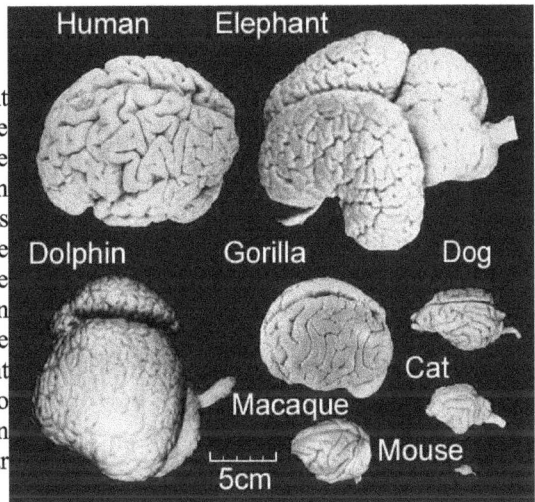

Comparative Brain Size

Experimental lesions done with animals, resemble in the accomplishment. Generally the animals for the experiments are raised in the same environment, have the same lesion at the same age, so their characteristics are near the same. Because of this resemblance in general the same behavioral deficits are observable after the lesion. Contrary to the lesions with animals, individuals with brain damages are absolutely different. They are not raised in the same environment, have different ages at time of the lesion and other differences. This fact makes it difficult to give definite statements about the correlation between specefic brain regions and cognitive fuctions. These difficulties can also result in improper conclusions. Moreover the lesions created in animals are more specific, because the researcher creates the lesion in a certain manner, and because of this has more control over the lesion, whereby lesions by humans are much less specific. The lesions vary in location, extent and origin, this complicates to make definite inferences about neural strucures and their influence on cognitive functions. Another limitation of the lesion mehtod reflects in the fact, that it is hardly possible to determine which function is supported by the damaged brain region. It is only possible to watch how the rest of the brain works without the damaged brain region. First of all, only the brain regions which are crucial for a specific function can be determined, but not the rest of the brain regions which may be as well important for that function. Furthermore it is not definitively find out, if a brain region is really crucial for a specific function, or if this brain region connects only other brain regions, which are important for the performance of this specific function. All in all one can say that the lesion method has two major limitations, which occur, because of the complex structure of the brain, and because it is never possible to determine definitively if the damaged brain region is the real reason for the loss of a cognitive function. These perceived limitations of the lesion method provided a strong incentive for the parallel development of functional imaging, which offered a new means of studying the dynamic neural correlates of cognitive processes in normal humans. Two key techniques were developed: positron-emission tomography (PET) and functional magnetic resonance imaging (fMRI).

single case studies

Perhaps the most famous single case study involving lesions occurred in the 19th century. A young man named Phineas Gage was working on railroad construction in 1848. One day, a 3ft, 7in (1.0922m) tamping iron (a long metal pole), 1.25in (0.381m) in diameter, was propelled through Gage's skull, through the left frontal lobe of his brain and out the other side of his head. Miraculously, Gage survived, but he was not the same. Phineas had previously been the foreman of the construction crew. He was well regarded as stable, well mannered, good handeling money. After his left frontal lobe was destroyed, his personality changed. He began to cuss inappropriately, gamble, drink. In other words, he exhibited personality changes dealing with self control.

Because his left frontal lobe was damaged in the accident, it can be inferred that that is the area of the brain that deals with personality traits and self control. Unfortunately, because this is a case study, and not a controlled experiment, any inferences can't be truly accepted, but this idea of connecting brain damage to behavioral changes is the core idea behind lesion experiments.

Techniques for Assessing Brain Anatomy

Are the art of creating images of the inside of an organism without (necessarily) killing it. There's a lot of complexity on the inside of something that you can't guess from the outside, to explore or create images of the inside of an organism e.g. brain without killing it or cutting it in slices CAT as well as MRI are imaging technique which use changes in electrically charged molecules when they are placed in a magnetic field to assess differences in cerebral activity in different regions of the brain. Both technologies are more precise than ordinary X-ray and help us "map" the brain regions associated with different behaviours, often by studying people with specific brain injuries. MRI images are clearer than CAT scans and don't use radiation; they show brain atrophy and increased cerebrospinal fluid

CAT

CAT scanning was invented in 1972 by the British engineer Godfey N. Hounsfield (later Sir Godfrey) and the South African (later American) physicist Alan Cromack.

CAT (computed axial tomography) is a painless test that uses multiple x-ray images, taken from different angles, to create three-dimensional images of body structures. Increasingly, CAT scans use digital x-rays to produce their images on a computer screen. The tomograms ``cuts`` for the CAT scan are usually made 5 or 10 mm apart. The CAT machine rotates 180 degrees around the patient's body;

hence, the term "axial." The machine sends out a thin X-ray beam at 160 different points. Crystals positioned at the opposite points of the beam pick up and record the absorption rates of the varying thicknesses of tissue and bone. The data are then relayed to a computer that turns the information into a 2-dimensional cross-sectional image. Risks

CT scan risks are similar to those of conventional X-rays. During the CT scan, you're briefly exposed to radiation. But scientists believe that CT scans provide enough valuable information to outweigh the associated risks. But if the subject or the patient: Pregnant it may be recommended to do another type of exam to reduce the possible risk of exposing his fetus to radiation. Have asthma or allergies. And the CT scan requires a contrast medium, there's a slight risk of an allergic reaction to the contrast medium. Have certain medical conditions. Diabetes, asthma, heart disease, kidney problems or thyroid conditions also increase the risk of a reaction to contrast medium.

MRI

Although CAT scanning was a breakthrough, in many cases it was substituted by Magnetic resonance imaging (also known as MRI) since magnetic resonance imaging is a method of looking inside the body without using x-rays, harmful dyes or surgery. Instead, **radio waves** and a **strong magnetic field** are used in order to provide remarkably clear and detailed pictures of internal organs and tissues.

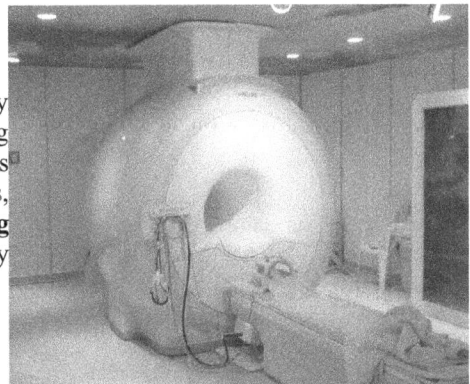
A full size MRI-Scanner. (GFDL – Kasuga Huang)

History and Development of MRI

MRI is based on a physics phenomenon, called nuclear magnetic resonance (NMR), which was discovered in1930s by Felix Bloch (working at Stanford University) and Edward Purcell(from Harvard University). In this resonance, magnetic fields and radio waves cause atoms to give off tiny radio signals. In the year 1970, Raymond Damadian, a medical doctor and research scientist, discovered the basis for using magnetic resonance imaging as a tool for medical diagnosis. Four years later a patent was granted, which was the worlds first patent issued in the field of MRI. In 1977, Dr. Damadian completed the construction of the first "whole-body" MRI scanner, which he called the "Indomitable". The medical use of magnetic resonance imaging has developed rapidly. The first MRI equipment in health were available at the beginning of the 1980s. In 2002, approximately 22000 MRI scanners were in use worldwide, and more than 60 million MRI examinations were performed.

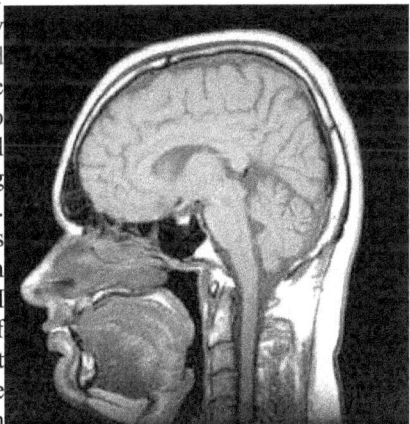
MRI head side (GFDL - TheBrain)

Common Uses of the MRI Procedure

Because of its detailed and clear pictures, MRI is widely used to diagnose sports-related injuries, especially those affecting the knee, elbow, shoulder, hip and wrist. Furthermore, MRI of the heart, aorta and blood vessels is a fast, non-invasive tool for diagnosing artery desease and heart problems. The doctors can even examine the size of the heart-chambers and determine the extent of damage, cause by a heart desease or a heart attack. Organs like lungs, liver or spleen can also be examined in high detail with MRI. Because no radiation exposure is involved, MRI is often the preferred diagnostic tool for examination of the male and female reproductive systems, pelvis and hips and the bladder.

Risks

An undetected metal implant may be affected by the strong magnetic field. MRI is generally avoided in the first 12 weeks of pregnancy. Scientists usually use other methods of imaging, such as ultrasound, on pregnant women unless there is a strong medical reason to use MRI.

Techniques for Assessing Physiological Function

PET

Positron emission tomography, also called PET imaging or a PET scan, is a diagnostic examination that involves the acquisition of physiologic images based on the detection of radiation from the emission of positrons. It is currently the most effective way to check for cancer recurrences. Positrons are tiny particles emitted from a radioactive substance administered to the patient. This radiopharmaceutical is injected to the patient and its emissions are measured by a PET scanner.

A PET scanner consists of an array of detectors that surround the patient. Using the gamma ray signals given off by the injected radionuclide, PET measures the amount of metabolic activity at a site in the body and a computer reassembles the signals into images. PET's ability to measure metabolism is very useful in diagnosing Altsheimer's desease, Parkinson's desease, epilepsy and other neurological conditions, because it can precisely illustrate areas where brain activity differs from the norm. It is also one of the most accurate methods available to localize areas of the brain causing epileptic seizures and to determine if surgery is a treatment option. PET is often used in conjunction with an MRI or CT scan through "fusion" to give a full three-dimensional view of an organ.

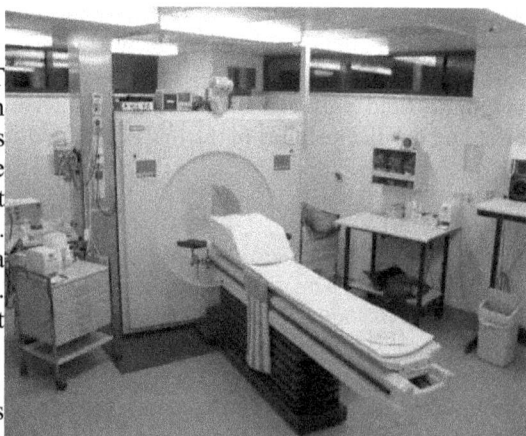

PET scanner

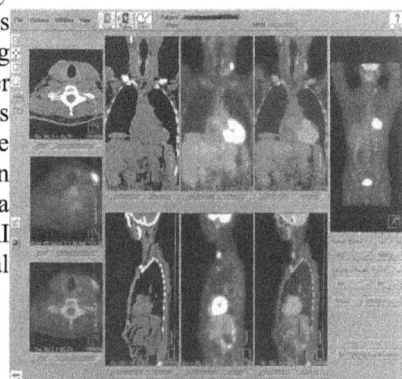

PET scan images

fMRI

fMRI (Functional Magnetic Resonance Imaging) is a technique for determining which parts of the brain are activated by different types of physical sensation or stimuli such as sight, sound or the movement of a subject's fingers. The brain mapping is done by setting up an MRI scanner in a special way so that the increased blood flow to the activated areas of the brain shows up on Functional MRI scans. Compared to MRI, fMRI does not depend on contrast agents although contrast agents enable far greater detection sensitivity than BOLD (Blood Oxygenation Level Dependent) signal. Higher BOLD signal intensities arise from decreases in the concentration of deoxygenated hemoglobin.

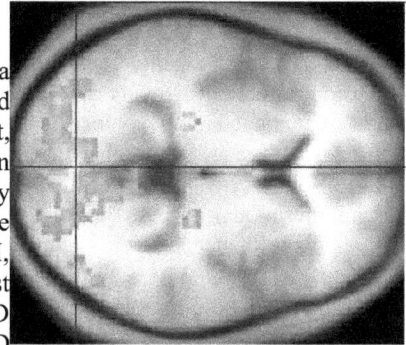

fMRI picture

An fMRI experiment usually lasts 1-2 hours. The subject will lie in the magnet and a particular form of stimulation will be set up and MRI images of the subject's brain are taken. In the first step a high resolution single scan is taken. This is used later as a background for highlighting the brain areas which were activated by the stimulus. In the next step a series of low resolution scans are taken over time, for example, 150 scans, one every 5 seconds. For some of these scans, the stimulus will be presented, and for some of the scans, the stimulus will be absent. The low resolution brain images in the two cases can be compared, to see which parts of the brain were activated by the stimulus.

The rest of the analysis is done using a series of tools which correct distortions in the images, remove the effect of the subject moving their head during the experiment, and compare the low resolution images taken when the stimulus was off with those taken when it was on. The final statistical image shows up bright in those parts of the brain which were activated by this experiment. These activated areas are then shown as coloured blobs on top of the original high resolution scan. This image can also be rendered in 3D.

fMRI has moderately good spatial resolution. However, the temporal response of the blood supply, which is the basis of fMRI, is poor relative to the electrical signals that define neuronal communication. Therefore, some research groups are working around this issue by combining fMRI with data collection techniques such as electroencephalography (EEG) or magnetoencephalography (MEG), which have much higher temporal resolution but rather poorer spatial resolution.

Electromagnetic Recording Methods

The methods we have mentioned up to now examine the metabolic activity of the brain. But there are also other cases in which one wants to measure electrical activity of the brain or the magnetic fields produced by the electrical activity. The methods we discussed so far do a great job of identifying where activity is occurring in the brain. A disadvantage of these methods is that they do not measure brain activity on a millisecond-by-millisecond basis. This measuring can be done for example by methods as the single-cell recording or the Electronencephalography (EEG). These methods can measure brain activity really fast and so they can give a best available temporal resolution.

Single cell

When using the single-cell method an electrode is placed into a region of the brain in which we focus our attention. Now, it is possible for the experimenter to record the electrical output of the cells that are contacted by the exposed electrode tip. The researchers' goal is to determine for example if the cells respond to information from only specific places in the sensory world or from broad regions of space. Next they want to determine whether the cells are sensitive to input in only one sensory modality or are multimodal in sensitivity. Furthermore they want to find out if the animal's attention directed to a stimulus influence in a cell's respond.

Single cell studies are not sufficient for studying the human brain, since it is too invasive to be a common method. Hence, this method is most often used in animals. There are just a few cases in which the single-cell recording is also applied in humans. People with epilepsy sometimes get removed the epileptic tissue. A week before surgery electrodes are implanted into the brain or get placed on the surface of the brain during the surgery to better isolate the source of seizure activity. So using this method one can decrease the possibility that useful tissues will be removed. Next one can find out which properties of a stimulus make cells in those regions fire. Due to the limitations of this method in humans there are other methods which measure electrical activity. Those we are going to discuss next.

EEG

One of the most famous techniques to study brain activity is probably the Electroencephalograhpy (EEG). Most people might know it as a technique which is used clinically to detect abberant activity such as that which accompanies epilepsy and disorders.

In an experimental way this technique is used to show the brain activity in certain psychological states, such as alertness or drowsiness. To measure the brain activity mental electrodes are placed on the scalp. Each electrode, also known as lead, acts as its own recording site. Next, a reference is needed which provides a baseline against which the activity at each of the other electrodes can compared.This electrode must not cover muscles, because its contractions are induced by electrical signals Usually this electrode is placed at the mastiod bone which is located behind the ear.

During the EEG electrodes are places like this. Over the right hemisphere electrodes are labeled with even numbers.Odd numbers are used for those on the left hemisphere. Those on the midline are labeled with a z. The capital letters stands for the location of the electrode(C=central, F=frontal, Fp= frontal pole, O= occipital, P= parietal and T= temporal).(see picture)

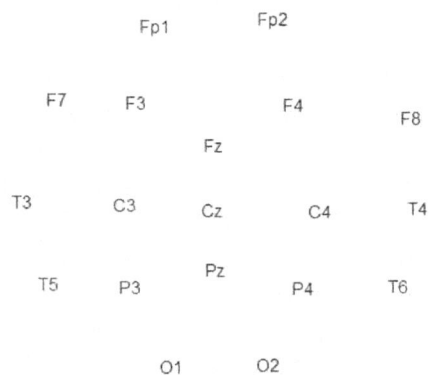

Fp1   Fp2

F7   F3   F4   F8

Fz

T3   C3   Cz   C4   T4

Pz

T5   P3   P4   T6

O1   O2

The right placement of the electrodes. (GFDL - Thekla Helmstedt)

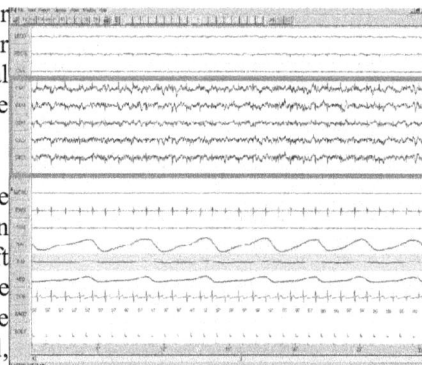

EEG Stage

After placing each electrode at the right position the electrical potential can be measured. This electrical potential has a particular voltage and furthermore a particular frequency. Accordingly, to a person's state the frequency and form of the EEG signal can differ. If a person is awake beta activity can be recognized, which means that the frequency is relatively fast. Just before someone falls asleep one can observe alpha activity, which have a slower frequency. The slowest frequencies are called delta activity, which occur during sleep.

Patients who suffer epilepsy show an increase of the amplitude of firing that can be observed on the EEG record. In addition EEG can also be used to help answering experimental questions. In the case of emotion for example, one can see that there is a greater alpha suppression over the right frontal areas than over the left ones, in the case of depression. One can conclude from this, that depression is accompanied by greater activation of right frontal regions than of left frontal regions.

ERP

Whereas EEG recordings provide a continuous measure of brain activity, event-related potentials (ERPs) are recordings which are linked to the occurrence of an event. A presentation of a stimulus would be such an event. When a stimulus is presented, the electrodes, which are placed on a person's scalp, record changes in the brain generated by the thousands of neurons under the electrodes.

By measuring the brain's response to an event we can learn how different types of information are processed. Representing the word eat or bake for example causes a positive potential at about 200msec. From this one can conclude, that our brain processes these words 200msec after presenting it. This positive potential is followed by a negative one at about 400msec. This one is also called N400 (whereas N stands for negative and 400 for the time). So in general one can say that there is a letter P or N to denote whether the deflection of the electical signal is positive or negative. And a number, which represent, on average, how many hundreds of milliseconds after stimulus presentation the component appears.

The event-related- potential shows special interest for researchers, because different components of the response indicate different aspects of cognitive processing. For example, presenting the sentences "The cats won't eat" and "The cat won't bake", the N400 response for the word eat is smaller than for the word bake. From this one can draw the conclusion that our brain needs 400msec to register information about a word's meaning. Furthermore, one can figure out where this activity occurs in the brain, namely if one looks at the position on the scalp of the electrodes that pick up the largest response.

MEG

Magnetoencephalography (MEG) is a related method to the EEG. But instead recording electrical potentials, it uses magnetic potentials at the scalp to index brain activity. To locate a dipole, the magnetic field can be used, because the dipole extreme high points of intensity of the magnetic field. By using devices called SQUIDs (superconducting quantum interference device) MEG can record these magnetic fields.

MEG is mainly used to localize the source of epileptic activity and to locate primary sensory cortices. This is helpful because by locating them they can be avoided during neurological intervention.

Furthermore, MEG can be used to understand more about the neurophysiology underlying psychiatric disorders such as schizophrenia. In addition, MEG can also be used to examine a variety of cognitive processes, such as language, object recognition and spatial processing among others, in people who were neurologically intact.

MEG has some advantage, because as well known, electrical currents conduct through different media to different degrees. The electrical current is also carried in different degrees through brain tissues, cerebral spinal fluid, the skull and the scalp. Magnetic fields instead are not so influenced by these variations. Another advantage is that the strength of the magnetic field which is recorded can also tell us information about how deep within the brain the source is located.

However, MEG also has some disadvantages. The magnetic field in the brain is 100 millionth the size of the earths' magnetic field. Due to this, shielded rooms, made out of aluminium, are required. Another disadvantage is that MEG cannot detect activity of cells with certain orientations within the brain. For example magnetic fields created by cells with long axes radial to the surface will be invisible.

Techniques for Modulating Brain Activity

Transcranical magnetic stimulation (TMS)

History and procedure

One important technique for modulating brain activity is the so called *transcranical magnetic stimulation*, better known as TMS. It is a relatively new technique for inducing small, localized, and reversible changes in living brain tissue. By using an electromagnet to produce a rapidly fluctuating magnetic field in the brain, TMS changes the electrical potential in brain tissue, which causes neuronal discharge.

Actually, the first modern TMS device was developed by Antony Baker in the year 1985 in Sheffield after 8 years of research. The field has developed rapidly since than with many researchers using TMS in order to study a variety of brain functions. It has been used, e.g., to block the perception of visual stimuli, in order to cause speech arrest, and to delay the onset of voluntary movements. The clinical effects of TMS have also been investigated in certain neuropsychiatric conditions. Several investigators have suggested the possible efficacy of TMS as a treatment for depression in human trials and animal models. Because of findings such as these, TMS has been considered as a possible alternative to antidepressant medication. (1, 2)

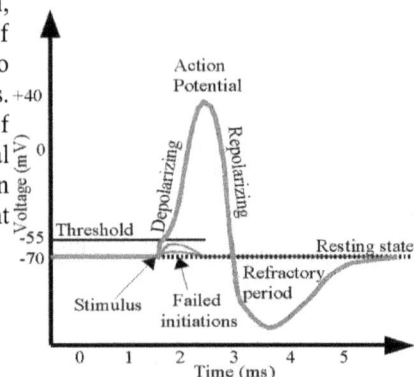

Action potential (GFDL - Chris 73)

Mechanisms

Although TMS is able to influence many brain functions,

including movement, visual perception, memory, attention, speech and mood, full knowledge of the neurobiological cascade of events remains unclear still. But studies combining TMS with other neurophysiological and neuroimaging techniques like EEG, PET and fMRI, are helping to explain how TMS achieves its effects.

TMS utilizes the principle of electromagnetic induction. It involves the discharge of very large current from a bank of capacitors, which rapidly flows through a simple LCR circuit and then though a copper-wire coil. A rapid time-varying magnetic field is induced at the level of the coil. When the coil is held to the head of subject, the magnetic field pulse penetrates the scalp and induces a small current in the brain, parallel to the plane of the coil. When the induced current is sufficient, depolarization of neuronal membranes occurs, and thus generation of action potentials are produced. (1)

Basic applications

One of the popular initial uses of TMS was the mapping of the motor cortex, because the effects of the stimulation could be easily measured by EMG of the motor evoked potential in peripheral muscles. Since even earlier researches were aware that TMS could cause suppression of visual perception, speech arrest, and parasthesias, TMS has been used to map specific brain functions in areas other than motor cortex. Several groups have applied TMS to the study of visual information processing, language production, memory, attention, reaction time and even more subtle brain functions such as mood and emotion.

Clinical applications

Although the potential utility of TMS as a treatment tool in various neuropsychiatric disorders is rapidly increasing, its use in depression is the most extensively studied clinical applications to date. For instance in the year 1994, George and Wassermann hypothesized that intermittent stimulation of important prefrontal cortical brain regions might also cause downstream changes in neuronal function that would result in an antidepressant response. In an initial open study it was reported that left prefrontal rTMS(repetitive transcranical magnetic stimulation) might be effective in the treatment of depression as well.

Moreover the transcranical magnetic stimulation shell decrease the frequency of the epileptic attacks. Targau & co could even achieve a decrease of attacks up to 80% in individual cases.

Future of TMS

Although it is too early at this point to tell whether TMS has long lasting therapeutic effects, this tool has clearly opened up new possibilities for clinical exploration and treatment of various psychiatric conditions. Further work understanding normal mental phenomena and how TMS affects these areas appears to be crucial for advancement. A critically important area that will ultimately guide clinical parameters is to combine TMS with functional imaging to directly monitor TMS effects on the brain. Since it appears that TMS at different frequencies has divergent effects on brain activity, TMS with functional brain imaging will be helpful to better delineate not only the behavioural neuropsychology of various psychiatric syndromes, but also some of the pathophysiologic circuits in the brain.

Nevertheless, TMS can be associated with other measures of brain activity as already mentioned above and such studies promise to further expand the application of TMS in the study of the pathophysiology of neuropsychiatric disorders. This new application of combining TMS and other neuroimaging techniques is already becoming popular in the field of cognitive neuroscience to investigate the brain-behavior relationship. (1)

Techniques for Analyzing Behaviour

Besides using methods to measure the brain's physiology and anatomy, it is also important to have techniques for analyzing behavior in order to get a better insight on cognition. There are various methods of clinical assessment of behavior, which aim at determining the impacts of brain damages on behavior. The goal of a neuropsychological assessment is to examine in what terms damage to the central nervous system influences cognitive abilities.

Test batteries

A neuropsychological assessment can be achieved, for instance, through the **test battery approach**, which gives an overview on a person's cognitive strengths and weaknesses by analyzing different cognitive abilities. A neuropsychological test battery is used by neuropsychologists to discover brain dysfunctions, arisen from neurological or psychiatric disorders. Such batteries do not only test various mental functions, but also the overall intelligence of a person.

The **Halstead-Reitan battery** is the most popular one, whereas the abilities tested range from basic sensory processing to tests that require complex reasoning. Furthermore, the Halstead-Reitan battery gives information concerning what caused the damage, the brain areas that were harmed, and it provides information about the stage the damage has reached. Such information is very helpful when it comes to propose a rehabilitation program. Another test battery, the **Luria-Nebraska battery**, is twice as fast to administer than the Halstead-Reitan, and the tests are ordered according to **twelve content scales** (e.g. motor functions, reading, memory etc.). This battery functions in accordance the view of the psychologist Alexander Luria about the brain, namely that there are three functional systems making up the brain (the brain-stem system, the anterior system and the posterior system), which all relate to one another. The purpose of these batteries is to find out if a person suffers from a brain damage or not, and they work well in discriminating persons with brain damage from neurologically impaired patients, but less well when it comes to discriminating them from persons with psychiatric disorders. In addition to that, test batteries do not only focus on the data results, which assesses the absolute level of performance, but beyond that, test batteries give attention to data on the qualitative manner of performance, and this is useful in gaining a better understanding of the cognitive impairment.

Customized neuropsychological assessment

The so called **customized neuropsychological assessment** is an alternative to the use test-batteries, in which an examiner develops, according to information from other tests (e.g. **WAIS-III** [Wechsler Adult Intelligence Scale]), a hypotheses about which cognitive abilities were influenced by brain damage. After the analysis of each hypothesis with a certain neuropsychological test, the hypothesis will either be kept on or it will be abandoned and a new hypothesis will be developed and the procedure will be repeated. In contrast to the test battery assessment, which is a standardized approach, the customized neuropsychological assessment requires a more experienced examiner.

Overall Intelligence tests

The most common used tests to estimate the intelligence of a person are the **Wechsler family intelligence tests**. These imply the WPPSI-R (Wechsler Preschool and Primary Scale of Intelligence) for children 3-7 years old, the WISC-III (Wechsler Intelligence Scale for Children) for children 6-16 years old, the WAIS-III (Wechsler Adult Intelligence Scale) and the WAIS-NI (Wechsler Adult Intelligence Scale as a Neuropsychological Instrument). Every test gives an estimation of the overall IQ (Full Scale IQ [FSIQ]) and provides two other subscale scores - a **Verbal IO** (VIQ) and a **Performance IQ** (PIQ). In the Verbal part of the test, for many subscales (e.g. Vocabulary) the relevant feature of the response is not the timing but that the answers are complete and correct. In the Performance part of the test, on the other hand, the points are given according to how long it takes to give an answer. The special feature of the WAIS-III test is that it gives a profile of certain abilities, in contrast to other tests that give just a single score, and its subtests are dived into four different index scores. Firstly, The Verbal Comprehension Index, which is assessed according to performance on vocabulary, similarities and information, secondly, the Perceptual Cortex Index analyzing non-verbal abilities (e.g. Visual-Motor Integration), thirdly, the Working Memory Index being evaluated according to a person's digit span, arithmetical performance and object assembly subtests, at last there is the Processing Speed Index according to digit symbol coding and letter-number sequencing. The WAIS-NI test on the other hand has the advantage that it supplies the examiner with information regarding the way the patient approaches problem-solving tasks. For instance, information about how the patient manipulates blocks on the Block Design test can be very useful. Sometimes individuals get quickly tired and overstrained doing a whole WAIS test - in such cases, it is better to let people do only a subset of the WAIS-III tests, as e.g. on similarities or Block Design.

Premorbid functioning

Test batteries and tests on the overall intelligence provide information on the functioning of cognitive abilities of a person. However, brain damage, of course, has an immense impact on the scores of such tests and it is quite difficult for a neurophysiologist to assess how well the functioning was before the brain damage occurred. In order to differentiate in such cases, psychologists try to come up with an estimate of premorbid functioning, which is a warrantable guess on the functioning of a person before the brain damage. Information about the person's educational background can be taken as such a standard - but it is not the appropriate approach in all cases. The test that is usually used to make an estimation on the premorbid functioning is the **Vocabulary subtest** of the WAIS-III, because it analyses abilities that do not seem to be influenced by brain damage. If the scores of the estimated premorbid intelligence are significantly higher than the current test scores, it is reasonable to assume that the brain damage caused a decrease in the intellectual strengths of an individual.

Techniques for Modeling Brain-Behaviour Relationships

Another major method, which is used in cognitive neuroscience, is the use of **neural networks** (computer modelling techniques) in order to simulate the action of the brain and its processes. These models help researchers to test theories of neuropsychological functioning and to derive principles viewing brain-behaviour relationships.

In order to simulate **mental functions** in humans, a variety of **computational models** can be used. The basic component of most such models is a "unit", which one can imagine as showing neuron-like behaviour. These units receive input from other units, which are summed to produce a net input. The net input to a unit is then transformed into that unit's output, mostly utilizing a sigmoid function. These units are connected together forming layers. Most models consist of an input layer, an output layer and a "hidden" layer as you can see on the right side.

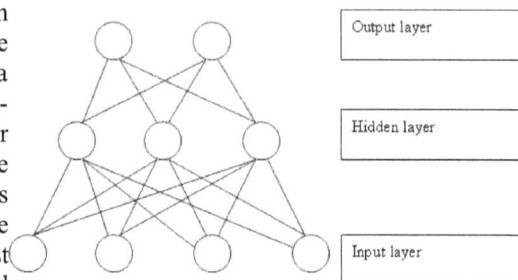

A basic neural network. (GFDL - Anna Schroeder)

The input layer simulates the taking up of information from the outside world, the output layer simulates the response of the system and the "hidden" layer is responsible for the transformations, which are necessary to perform the computation under investigation. The units of different layers are connected via connection weights, which show the degree of influence that a unit in one level has on the unit in another one.

The most interesting and important about these models is that they are able to "learn" without being provided specific rules. This ability to "learn" can be compared to the human ability e.g. to learn the native language, because there is nobody who tells one "the rules" in order to be able to learn this one. The computational models learn by extracting the regularity of relationships with repeated exposure. This exposure occurs then via "training" in which input patterns are provided over and over again. The adjustment of "the connection weights between units" as already mentioned above is responsible for learning within the system. Learning occurs because of changes in the interrelationships between units, which occurrence is thought to be similar in the nervous system.

References

- Banich,Marie T. (2004). Cognitive Neuroscience and Neuropsychology. Housthon Mifflin Company. ISBN 0618122109
- Gazzangia, Michael S.(2000). Cognitive Neuroscience. Blackwell Publishers. ISBN 0631216596

- (1) 4 April 2001 / Accepted: 12 July 2002 / Published: 26 June 2003 Springer-Verlag 2003. Fumiko Maeda • Alvaro Pascual-Leone. Transcranial magnetic stimulation: studying motor neurophysiology of psychiatric disorders
- (2) a report by Drs Risto J Ilmoniemi and Jari Karhu Director, BioMag Laboratory, Helsinki University Central Hospital, and Managing Director, Nexstim Ltd
- (3) Repetitive Transcranial Magnetic Stimulation as Treatment of Poststroke Depression: A Preliminary Study Ricardo E. Jorge, Robert G. Robinson, Amane Tateno, Kenji Narushima, Laura Acion, David Moser, Stephan Arndt, and Eran Chemerinski
- Moates, Danny R. An Introduction to cognitive psychology. B:HRH 4229-724 0
- © 1995-2006, Healthwise, Incorporated, P.O. Box 1989, Boise, ID 83701. Author: Jan Nissl, RN, BS.

live version • discussion • edit lesson • comment • report an error

5 MOTIVATION AND EMOTION

live version • discussion • edit lesson • comment • report an error

Introduction

Expression of emotions on the face
Several human face expressions connected to emotions (GFDL - Ddeunert)

Happiness, anger, love, sorrow, confusion and excitement. All these words describe some kind of abstract inner states in us, humans, many of them difficult for us to control. We usually call them feelings or emotions. But what is the reason that we are able to "feel"? Where do emotions come from and how are they caused? And are emotions and feelings the same thing? Or are we supposed to differenciate?

These are all questions that Cognitve Psychology deals with in *Emotion Research*. According to a scientific definition *feelings* are subjective experienced emotions, which are connected with motivation in what we want, need, and desire. It took quite long to get to such a brief definition, which is right now just a definition that separates these two terms. The roots of studying emotions go back until the very beginning of the history of Philosophy over 2000 years ago, where Philosophers like Plato already thought about the nature of emotions. Throughout the time it became more and more important in other scientific disciplines. Especially in psychology, where the term "feelings" got separated from the term "emotions".The psychologists tried to provide a definition and build theories to desribe it.

Among those, the most important ones are the "James-Lange theory", the "Canon-Bard theory" as well as the "Two factor theory" (see following chapter). The last theory will lead us to a further extend of disciplines involved in this research process. The increase of Neuroscience and especially its powerful tools, that were developed in the recent past, allow today's scientists to get a good picture of the brain, understand its complex processes better and try to discover the origin of emotions. But there is still a lot which we do not know or cannot explain in respect of emotions, even today. Nevertheless, research of emotions has made a big step towards understanding its essence, since the birth of Cognitive Science and especially Cognitive Psychology.

The following chapter gives an overview for a better understandíng of emotions. It provides information about theories and its functions, the causation of emotions in the human brain, its processes and their role in the human body in connection with motivation. We will try to show different points of view in the issue of emotions, the actual state of research, and some examples of psychologist experiments. In the end we will outline some application areas of scientific emotion research, especially concerning brain deseases.

Motivation - about drives and motives

Motivation is an extended notion, which refers to the starting, controlling and upholding of corporal and psychic activities. It is declared by inner processes and variables which are used to explain behavioural changes. Motivations are commonly separated into two types. *Drives* describe acts of motivation like thirst or hunger that have primarily biological purposes. The acts of *motives*, on the other hand, are driven by primarily social and psychological mechanisms. Motivation is an interceding variable, which means that it is a variable that is not directly observable. Therfore, in order to study motivation, one must approach it through variables which are measurable and observable:

1. Observable terms of variation (independent variables)
2. Indicators of behaviour (dependent variables), e.g.: rate of learning, level of activity, ...

There are two major methodologies used to manipulate drives and motives in experiments:

One method is *stimulation*. Aversive attractions could initiate motives such like shocks, heat, cold or loud noise. Sexual drives were also activivated by attractions which lead positive affective states.

Deprivation means that you prohibit the access of nutrition or water to an animal. As a result it leads it to motives or drives which are not common for this special situation. It is known that human for example try to avoid social deprivation. So everyone has the inherent motive to maintain the contact with other humans and be a part of a social structure. Nevertheless, a reader might imagine some people who desire to be alone and seek a life of isolation and reduced social contact. These people may be the exceptions to this hypothesis, but they may also have some other, more pressing, motives or drives which induce them to behave in this way. Think of the Russian mathematician Grigori Perelman(40) who seems to have recently proved the mathematical proof of Poincaré: "Everything without a hole is a sphere.". He prefers to stay alone and lessened his social contacts because of his belief (motive) that modern society is not ruled by ethical norms.

So, one may generalize that individuals are able to resist certain motives via personal cognitive states. The ablity of cognitive reasoning and willing is human like and the reason for much psychological deseases which indicates that the human is not able to handle all rising mental states. Humans are able to manipulate their motives which make sure that they have the motive to do so but the real emotional and psychlogical causales are unclear. This introduces the problem that the entity of consciousness, unconsciouness and what ever else could be take into account is pretty unknown. However it is not able to handle the discussion in this chapter so far. Motivation is the link from internal events to external one and could maybe bring light into it. A theory of motivations was conceived by Abraham Maslow in 1970 (Maslow's hierarchy of needs). He considered two kinds of motivation:

1. The defected motivation (Mangelmotivation) brings humans to reconsider their psychical and physical balance.
2. The other one is the adolescence motivation (Wachstumsmotivation) which get people to pass old events and states of their personal development.

Maslow argues that everyone has a hierarchy of needs.

Regarding to this, our innate needs could be ordered in a hierarchy, starting at the "basic" ones towards the most human one. The idea is, that the human is ruled by lower needs as long as they are not satisfied. If they are satisfied in a adequate manner he dealed with higher needs. Compare to Chapter Attention.

Transzendence	spiritual needs, to feel as one with the univers
Self Realization	the need to fullfill ones own potential and to have important goals to reach
Aesthetic Needs	needs of order and beauty
Cognitive Needs	needs of knowledge, understanding and new coherences
Self Worth	needs of trust, the feeling of to be someone and to obtain respect by others
Relationship	needs of affiliation, relation to others, to love and to be loved
Safeness	needs of safeness, cosiness, ease and to be free of anxieties
Biological Needs	needs of nutrition, water, oxygen, relaxation, and sexuality

Hierachy of Needs   according to Maslow, 1970

Hierachy of needs, Maslow (1970) (GFDL - Ddeunert)

In the following it is not intended to explain all facettes of motivation and behaviour and drives and motives. The framework of this part is going to state the relation between motivation, emotion and cognitve psychology.

What is an emotion?

Emotion is not something shameful,subordinate, second-rate; it is a supremely valid phase of humanity at its noblest and most mature. -- Joshua Loth Liebman

The very old question "What is an emotion?" can only be answered partially in this chapter,according to the results of current research, because the entire topic as itself is huge enough to write whole books about. First we should distinguish between feelings and emotions. f.e. The feeling of hunger is not an explicit emotion,more a recognition of sensory input. Emotions could be roughly described by the process of evaluation of such an event, namely become aware of that feeling. Awareness is close connected with changes in the environment or in the psychophysiological state. Why recognize changes rather than stable states? An answer could be that changes are an important indicator for our situation. They show that our situation is unstable. Pay attention or focus on that might increase the chance to survive. A change bears more information than repetitive events.This appears more exciting. Repitition reduces excitement. If we think that we got the most important information from a situation or an event,we become unaware of such an event or certain facts.

Current research in this field suggest that changes are needed to emerge emotions,so we can say that it is strong attention dependent. The event has to draw our attention.No recognition, no emotions. But do we have always an emotional evaluation, when we are aware of certain events? How has the change to be relevant for our recognition? Emotional changes are highly personal significant, saying that it needs a relation to our personal self. Significance presupposes order and relations.Relations are to meaning as colours are to vision: a necessary condition,but not its whal content. One determines the significance and the scope of a change by f.e. event´s impact (event´s strengh),reality,relevance and factors related to the background circumstances of the subject. We feel no emotion in response to change which we perceive as unimportant or unrelated. Roughly one can say that emotions express our attitude toward unstable significant objects which are somehow related to us. This is also always connected with the fact that we have greater response to novel experience. Something that is unexpected or unseen yet. When children get new toys, they are very excited at first, but after a while one can perceive,or simply remember the own childhood, that they show less interest in that toy. That shows, that emotional response declines during time. This aspect is called the process of adaptation. The threshold of awareness keeps rising if stimulus level is constant. Hence, awareness decreases. The organism withdraw its consciousness from more and more events. The person has the pip,it has enough. The opposite effect is also possible. It is known as the process of facilitation. In this case the threshold of awareness deminishes. Consciousness is focusing on increasing number of events. This happens if new stimuli are encountered. The process of adaptation might prevent us from endlessly repetitive actions. A human would not be able to learn something new, if got catched in an infinite loop. The emotional environment contains not only what is, and what will be, experienced but also all that could be, or that one desires to be, experienced ; for the emotional system, all such possibilities are posited as simultaneously there and are compared with each other. Whereas intellectual thinking expresses a detached and objective manner of comparison, the emotional comparison is done from a personal and interested perspective; intellectual thinking may be characterized as an attempt to overcome the personal emotional perspective. It is quite difficult to give an external description of something that is related to an intrinsic, personal perspective. But it is possible. In the following we will see the most popular theories, and an external view with focus on the neuronal networks responsible for emotions.

Functional Theories

James-Lange Theory

The James-lange theory states that a specific stimulus causes a certain emotion. f.e. When a person sees a spider he or she might experience fear. Alternatively, when a person sees a lovely dog, this person might experience happiness. One problem with this theory is that it is based on the experience of different bodily changes. That means that the stimuli causes a change in the bodily state of which the person is aware and hence relates the change experienced to the event and equates it with an emotion. However, people paralyzed from the neck down, who have little awareness of sensory input are still able to experience emotions. Also, research has shown, that the same physiological states occur across many different emotions. So, an extension of this theory was necessary. This leads us to the Cannon-Bard Theory

Cannon-Bard Theory

This theory states that emotions emerge when the thalamus percieves an event or an object. According to this theory, physiological changes in the body and the processing of information in the brain influence the experience of emotions, because the thalamus conveys information to the skeletal muscles and autonomic nervous system.Hence on the way from stimulus to an experienced emotion the thalamus is responsible for a physiological response and a cognitive evaluation. Furthermore this theory states, that the experience of emotions could be different in the same physiological state what fills the lack of the James-Lange Theory. The cerebral cortex plays an important role in evaluating the emotional significance of the stimulus.

Two Factor Theory

In this theory it is assumed that emotional experience is the outcome of physiological arousal in correlation to a cause for that arousal. Schachter and Singer (1962) did well known studies in this field of research. They induced a physiological arousal in their subjects by injection of a chemical substance. Given a situation, they changed the action of the experimenters in order to switch the emotional tone of the subject. According to their results, they claimed that one can manipulate a subject into different emotional states from a given state of physiological activation. The interpretation of a certain emotion depends on the physiological state in correlation

to the subjects circumstances. It is very context dependent.

More recent research has shown, that different emotions have certain physiological signatures. Patterns of heart rate, electrodermal response, and physiological changes in the brain have been associated with specific emotions.

The Neural Correlate of Emotion

Emotions are processed through several brain regions as you can see on the picture (Papez.jpg). This Network is called "Circuit of Papez", after James W. Papez. The contemporary interpretation of the roles of the different parts have changed, but the parts have remained the same.

There are 2 important pathways in the processing of emotions: the subcortical pathway, or "low road" and the cortical way, the "high road". The "low road" processes the sensory input "quick and dirty", that means it responds very fast but does not analyze the stimulus very well. It is responsible for quick reactions, like ducking if a you ride your bike and there is suddenly a tree limb in front of your head. The "high road" is responsible for the conscious, aware processing of the emotion. It is slower because there are a lot more neurons involved.(LeDoux)

Let's take a closer look at some important parts of Papez circuit:

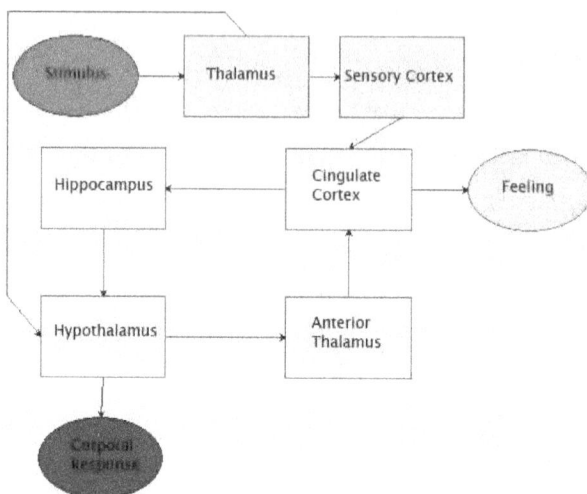

Circuit of Papez

Circuit of Papez (GFDL - Ddeunert)

The Hippocampus

Once seen as the Hub of Information processing, contemporary research has shown that the hippocampus plays a bigger role in memory, than in emotion processing. Nevertheless it is still important but instead of generating emotion it plays a modulatory role in the affective response to a stimulus. The hippocampus "puts thing in perspective" exerting a modulating effect on output from the amygdala, the real hub of emotion processing.

The Thalamus

The Cerebral Cortex

The cerebral cortex plays an important role in analyzing and understanding emotional behavior and expression. In contrast to the limbic system the cortex is responsible for cognitive emotional processing. Researchers use brain scanning or observe patients with known cortical damage to elucidate the function of the cerebral cortex in emotional processes. Link: chapter 4.

The prefrontal cortex (PFC)

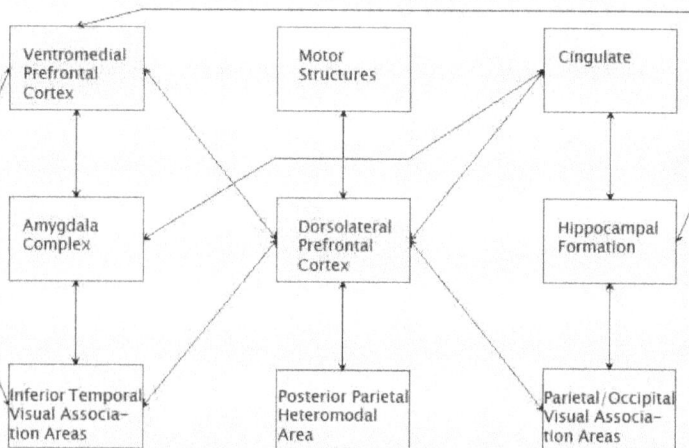

Connectivity between Prefrontal Cortex and other Brain Regions

Connectivity between the PFC and the brain. (GFDL - Ddeunert)

is well known for rational and analytical cognitive functions and can be seen as the analytical part of rational-emotional decision making.

The role the cortex plays in aspects of emotional functions can be summarized as follows:

1. the cognitive ability to interpret emotional information (perceiving, comprehending and recalling emotionally meaningful content)
2. the ability to express emotions (e.g. facial expression, gesture and tone of voice)
3. and the experience of emotions or emotional state

Today there are known many syndromes and deseases which describe lesions of the cerebral cortex. Anosognosia is attributed to lesions in the right hemiphere.

This syndrome is well described in detail by A. Damasio in his book called "Descartes' Error". People suffering from anosognosia are not aware of their inabilities. The inabilties could for example occur from strokes.

In further researches and experiments it was shown that lateral hemispherical damages causes different emotional impairments. As a result of it you can ascribe the left and the right hemisphere dedicated functions in emotional processing:

The right hemisphere is responsible for nonverbal skills and understanding of emotions. So patients with damages in their right hemisphere are according to the circumstances unable of Discriminate between emotional faces, neither there are able to name emotional scenes, nor matching emotional expressions or grouping both pictorially presented and written emotional scences and faces. Therefore those people suffer addional social interferences. To describe one situation you allowed to imagine a communication with such a person. Within the talk you might recognize queerly responses of your opponent. So it is possible that he or she make inappropriate turn within the your conversation, or gives inconsequential reasons for something. Futhermore it is typical for them to laugh at inproperly points of the talk.

The left hemisphere contains the main regions of language processing (Broca's , Wernicke's area). So it is not surprising that damages to this area and the lobes in general results in impairments of language processing. Researchers have discovered that the left hemisphere processes ideas about emotions and verbal emotional content.

The Amygdala

Anatomy

The amygdala is the most important part in the processing of emotion. It is a bilateral organized nuclei complex, located in the anterior, medial temporal lobe (Adolphs & Damasio, 2000; Nieuwenhuys, Voogd & Huijzen, 1991).

It can be subdivided into several nuclei with distinct functional traits: the centromedial nucleus, the cortical nucleus and the basolateral complex, which can be subdivided further into the lateral, the basal and the accessory basal nuclei.

The amygdalae send impulses to the hypothalamus for activation of the sympathetic nervous system, to the reticular nucleus for increased reflexes, to the nuclei of the trigeminal nerve and facial nerve for facial expressions of fear, and to the ventral tegmental area, locus ceruleus, and laterodorsal tegmental nucleus for activation of dopamine, norepinephrine and epinephrine.

The cortical nucleus is involved in the sense of smell and pheromone-processing. It receives input from the olfactory bulb and olfactory cortex. The lateral amygdalae, which send impulses to the rest of the basolateral complexes and to the centromedial nuclei, receive input from the sensory systems. The centromedial nuclei are the main outputs for the basolateral complexes, and are involved in emotional arousal in rats and cats.

Functions

In 1937 Heinrich Klüver and Paul Bucy described the behavoir of monkeys with large temporal lobe lesions. The affected monkeys showed extremely abnormal reactions to their environment. Namely a loss of fear of things they where afraid before the brain damage, attempts to engage in sexual behaviors with other species and to ingest things indiscriminately. They seemed to suffer a kind of "psychic blindness" which kept them from understanding the affective properties of the things they perceived. This put the amygdala in the center of emotion research. Today we know that the Amygdala is one of the most important brain regions for emotional processing. It plays a key role in the interpretation of social signals of emotion, emotional conditioning (especially fear) and the consolidation of emotional memories. We will discuss this now more in detail:

Processing social signals of emotion

Very famous experiments measure responses to emotional facial expressions. They give evidence that the amygdala is responsible for the recognition of facial expressed emotions. There are different methods to measure these responses. For example, single unit recording, which allows to measure the activity of only a few neurons. Single unit recording experiments on animals, showed that the amygdala neurons responded differently to different faces. Also, they responded selectively to dynamic social stimuli (like for example approach behavior) (1). There are also studies on people with amygdala lesions who suffered from difficulties in the processing of emotional facial expressions(2,3,4).

Neuroimaging studies also support these results (PET: Morris et al., fMRi: Breiter et al.) In addition, there are studies on responses to emotional vocal expressions, especially the vocal expression of fear, which give evidence that the amygdala is selective for certain emotions(5). Recapitulating we can say, that the amygdala is extremely important for the processing/understanding of emotional expressions and therefore for social life.

Emotional conditioning

We will explain using the example fear-conditioning. That means that a meaningless stimuli is combined with a naturally threatening event (e.g. a shock). If the stimulus appears alone after the conditioning it causes the same reaction. For example, a higher pulse. A big role in this phenomenon play the two different routes of emotion we discussed before:

- The direct thalamo-amygdala-route is responsible for the fast reaction to a stimulus. For

being fast it lacks on detailanalysis.
- The thalamo-cortico-amygdala pathway handles the more complex analysis of the situation.

The role of the amygdala in fear-conditioning is confirmed by several experiments with people who suffer from certain brain lesions. Angrilli and colleagues for example report about a man with extensive right amygdala damage showed reduced startle response to a sudden burst of white noise and was also relatively immune to fear conditioning. Bechara and colleagues report about a patient with bilateral amygdala damage. He also failed fear-conditioning to aversive stimuli, but he could report facts about the conditioning experience. Another patient suffered from hippocampal damage. He was successfully fear-conditioned but had no explicit memory of the conditioning procedure.

Emotional memories

There are different studies which indicate, that patients better memorize emotional aspects of stories. This is not the case for people who suffer from certain amygdala damage (6). If you want to learn more about memory please take a look in the memory chapter.

References

Books

- Zimbardo, Philip G. (1995, 12th edition). Psychology and Life. Inc. Scott, Foresman and Company, Glenview, Illinois.
ISBN 020541799X
- Banich,Marie T. (2004). Cognitive Neurosciene and Neuropsychology. Housthon Mifflin Company.
ISBN 0618122109
- Robert A. Wilson and Frank C. Keil. (2001). The MIT Encyclopedia of Cognitive Sciences (MITECS). Bradford Book.
ISBN 0262731444
- Antonio R. Damasio. (1994) reprinted (2005). Descartes' Error: Emotion, Reason and the Human Brain. Penguin Books.
ISBN 014303622X
- Antonio R. Damasio. (1999). The Feeling of what Happens. Body and Emotion in the Making of Consciousness. Harcourt Brace & Company.
ISBN 0099288761
- Aaron Ben-Ze'ev (Oct 2001).The Subtlety of Emotions.(MIT CogNet).
ISBN 0262523191

Journals

- The emotional brain. Tim Dalgleish.
- (1) Leonard, C.M., Rolls, E.T., Wilson, F.A.W. & Baylis, C.G. Neurons in the amygdala of the monkey with responses selective for faces.
Behav. Brain Res. 15, 159-176 (1985)
- (2)Adolphs, R., Tranel, D., Damasio, H. & Damasio, A. Impaired recognition of emotion in

facial expressions following bilateral damage of the human amygdala.
Nature 372, 669-672 (1994)

- (3)Young, A. W. et al. Face processing impairments after amygdalotomy.
Brain 118, 15-24 (1995)

- (4)Calder, A. J. et al. Facial emotion recognition after bilateral amygdala damage: Differentially severe impairment of fear.
Cognit. Neuropsychol. 13, 699-745 (1996)

- (5)Scott, S. K. et al. Impaired auditory recognition of fear and anger following bilateral amygdala lesions.
Nature 385, 254-257 (1997)

- (6)Cahill, L., Babinsky, R., Markowitsch, H. J. & McGaugh, J. L. The amygdala and emotional memory.
Nature 377, 295-296 (1995)

- (7)Wood, Jacqueline N. and Grafman, Jordan (02/2003). Human Prefrontal Cotex.
Nature Reviews/ Neuroscience

- (8)Brothers, L. , Ring, B. & Kling, A. Response of neurons in the macaque amygdala to complex social stimuli.
Behav. Brain Res. 41, 199-213 (1990)

Links

- Dana Foundation and the Dana Alliance: The Site for Brain News
- Brain Facts: PDF
   live version • discussion • edit lesson • comment • report an error

live version • discussion • edit lesson • comment • report an error

Introduction

Memory is "the capacity of the nervous system to acquire and retain usable skills and knowledge, which allows living organisms to benefit from experience." (source: www.wwnorton.com)

Today's memory is stuffed with faces, birthdays, telephone numbers, meetings, mathematical functions and the like - we may call these things informations. But how is this information stored, accessed and manipulated? Or, on the other side, why or how do we forget? Can we influence this process to save information or can we store more information in less time? It is indisputable that the process of saving and retrieving informations has affected human life until now. If, for example, our ancestors had not been able to memorize the location and the edibility of certain roots and berries, the development of crafts, house building, in short, of civilization, would surely have been a rather complicated and slow process.

First we are going to give an basic overview on how memory works. First of all we will approach the question "What is Memory?". We will discuss three types of memory - the Sensory Memory, the Short Term Memory and the Long Term Memory.

We will also mention memory models, like the "Atkinson's & Shiffrin's Memory Model", are going to be introduced and advance with Baddeley's "Working Memory Model". Further we will compare declarative and implicit memory (different types of Long Term Memory, LTM).

Finally, we will turn to another interesting phenomenon related to our topic, errors. By examining the occurrence of errors we will be able to introduce the designated functions of the memory parts in the brain.

What is Memory

What ability enables us to learn new things and thereby helps us survive? The answer to this question is: memory. Without memory we would not have been able to develop into what we now are, without memory we would probably have died out in the early years of human life. We would not have known which berries to collect, which ones were good and healthy and which ones were poisonous. Or how to find our way home without getting lost, or how to start a fire. We most probably would not be what we are now: a technologically advanced society that rules the planet and explores the universe. So how does this amazing thing called memory work? What is it? Where is it?

What is memory?

Memory is the ability of an organism to store, retain, and subsequently recall information. Although traditional studies of memory began in the realms of philosophy, the late nineteenth and early twentieth century put memory within the paradigms of cognitive psychology. In the recent decades, it has become one of the principal pillars of a new branch of science that represents a marriage between cognitive psychology and neuroscience, called cognitive neuroscience. There are several ways of classifying memories, based on duration, nature and retrieval of information. From an information processing perspective there are three main stages in the formation and retrieval of memory: encoding (processing and combining of received information), storage (creation of a permanent record of the encoded information), retrieval/recall (calling back the stored information in response to some cue for use in some process or activity). We can classify memory also by: duration, information type, temporal direction

Classification by duration

A basic and generally accepted classification of memory is based on the duration of memory retention, and identifies three distinct types of memory: sensory memory, short term memory, and long term memory. The sensory memory corresponds approximately to the initial moment that an item is perceived. Some of this information in the sensory area proceeds to the sensory store, which is referred to as short-term memory. Sensory memory is characterized by the duration of memory retention from milliseconds to seconds and short-term memory from seconds to minutes. These stores are generally characterized as of strictly limited capacity and duration, whereas in general stored information can be retrieved in a period of time which ranges from days to years; this type of memory is called long-term memory. It may be that short-term memory is supported by transient changes in neuronal communication, whereas long-term memories are maintained by more stable and permanent changes in neural structure that are dependent on protein synthesis. Some psychologists, however, argue that the distinction between long- and short-term memories is arbitrary, and is merely a reflection of differing levels of activation within a single store. If we are given a random seven-digit number, we may remember it only for a few seconds and then forget (short-term memory). On the other hand, we can remember telephone numbers for many years (assuming we use them often enough). Those long-lasting memories are said to be stored in long term memory. Additionally, the term working memory is used to refer to the short-term store needed for certain mental tasks - it is not a synonym for short-term memory, since it is defined not in terms of duration, but rather in terms of purpose. Some theories consider working memory to be the combination of short-term memory and some attentional control. For instance, when we are asked to mentally multiply 45 by 4, we have to perform a series of simple calculations (additions and multiplications) to arrive at the final answer. The ability to store the information regarding the instructions and intermediate results is what is referred to as working memory.

Classification by information type

Long-term memory can be divided into declarative (explicit) and procedural (implicit) memories. Declarative memory requires conscious recall, in that some conscious process must call back the information. It is sometimes called explicit memory, since it consists of information that is explicitly stored and retrieved. Declarative memory can be further sub-divided into semantic memory, which concerns facts taken independent of context; and episodic memory, which concerns information specific to a particular context, such as a time and place. Semantic memory allows the encoding of abstract knowledge about the world, such as "Paris is the capital of France". Episodic memory, on the other hand, is used for more personal memories, such as the sensations, emotions, and personal associations of a particular place or time. Autobiographical memory - memory for particular events within one's own life - is generally viewed as either equivalent to, or a subset of, episodic memory. Visual memory is part of memory preserving some characteristics of our senses pertaining to visual experience. We are able to place in memory information that resembles objects, places, animals or people in sort of a mental image. Visual memory can result In priming and it is assumed some kind of perceptual representation system or PRS underlies this phenomenon. In contrast, procedural memory (or implicit memory) is not based on the conscious recall of information, but on implicit learning. Procedural memory is primarily employed in learning motor skills and should be considered a subset of implicit memory. It is revealed when we do better in a given task due only to repetition - no new explicit memories have been formed, but we are unconsciously accessing aspects of those previous experiences. Procedural memory involved In motor learning depends on the cerebellum and basal ganglia.. So far, nobody has successfully been able to isolate the time dependence of these suggested memory structures.

Classification by temporal direction

A further major way to distinguish different memory functions is whether the content to be remembered is in the past, retrospective memory, or whether the content is to be remembered in the future, prospective memory. Thus, retrospective memory as a category includes semantic memory and episodic/autobiographical memory. In contrast, prospective memory is memory for future intentions, or remembering to remember. Prospective memory can be further broken down into event- and time-based prospective remembering. Time-based prospective memories are triggered by a time-cue, such as going to the doctor (action) at 4pm (cue). Event-based prospective memories are intentions triggered by cues, such as remembering to post a letter (action) after seeing a mailbox (cue). Cues do not need to be related to the action (as the mailbox example is), and lists, sticky-notes, or string around the finger are all examples of cues that are produced by people as a strategy to enhance prospective memory.

Most important brain structures responsible for memory

Amygdale
The amygdale also are involved in the modulation of memory consolidation. Following any learning event, the long term memory for the event is not instantaneously formed. Rather, information regarding the event is slowly assimilated into long-term storage over time, a process referred to as memory consolidation, until it reaches a relatively permanent state.
During the consolidation period, the memory can be modulated. In particular, it appears that emotional arousal following the learning event influences the strength of the subsequent memory for that event. Greater emotional arousal following a learning event enhances a person's retention of that event. Experiments have shown that administration of stress hormones to individuals immediately after they learn something enhances their retention when they are tested two weeks later.
The amygdale, especially the basolateral nuclei, are involved in mediating the effects of emotional arousal on the strength of the memory for the event. There were experiments conducted by James McGaugh on animals in a special laboratories. These laboratories have trained animals on a variety of learning tasks and found that drugs injected into the amygdala after training affect the animals' subsequent retention of the task. These tasks include basic Pavlovian tasks such as inhibitory avoidance, where a rat learns to associate a mild footshock with a particular compartment of an apparatus, and more complex tasks such as spatial or cued water maze, where a rat learns to swim to a platform to escape the water. If a drug that activates the amygdale is injected into the amygdale, the animals had better memory for the training in the task. If a drug that inactivates the amygdale is injected, the animals had impaired memory for the task.

Despite the importance of the amygdale in modulating memory consolidation, however, learning can occur without it, though such learning appears to be impaired, as in fear conditioning impairments following amygdale damage.

Evidence from work with humans indicates that the amygdale plays a similar role. Amygdale activity at the time of encoding information correlates with retention for that information. However, this correlation depends on the relative "emotionalness" of the information. More emotionally-arousing information increases amygdalar activity, and that activity correlates with retention.

Hippocampus

Psychologists and neuroscientists dispute the precise role of the hippocampus, but, in general, agree that it has an essential role in the formation of new memories about experienced events (episodic or autobiographical memory). Some researchers prefer to consider the hippocampus as part of a larger medial temporal lobe memory system responsible for general declarative memory (memories that can be explicitly verbalized — these would include, for example, memory for facts in addition to episodic memory).

Some evidence supports the idea that, although these forms of memory often last a lifetime, the hippocampus ceases to play a crucial role in the retention of the memory after a period of consolidation. Damage to the hippocampus usually results in profound difficulties in forming new memories (anterograde amnesia), and normally also affects access to memories prior to the damage (retrograde amnesia). Although the retrograde effect normally extends some years prior to the brain damage, in some cases older memories remain - this sparing of older memories leads to the idea that consolidation over time involves the transfer of memories out of the hippocampus to other parts of the brain. However, experimentation has difficulties in testing the sparing of older memories; and, in some cases of retrograde amnesia, the sparing appears to affect memories formed decades before the damage to the hippocampus occurred, so its role in maintaining these older memories remains controversial.

Damage to the hippocampus does not affect some aspects of memory, such as the ability to learn new skills (playing a musical instrument, for example), suggesting that such abilities depend on a different type of memory (procedural memory) and different brain regions. And there is some evidence to suggest that patient HM (who had his medial temporal lobes removed bilaterally as a treatment for epilepsy) can form new semantic memories.

Types of Memory

In the following section we will discuss the three different types of memory and their respective characteristics: Sensory Memory, Short Term (STM) or Working Memory and Long Term Memory (LTM).

Sensory Memory

This type of memory has the shortest duration time, only 0.5 to 2.0 seconds. Roughly, Sensory Memory can be subdivided into two kinds: iconic and echoic memory. The first is concerned with visual input, the latter with auditory input. (It should be noted, though, that according to the Atkinson and Shiffrin model of memory, only iconic memory is equal to sensory memory. The addition of echoic memory to the level of sensory memory is due to research done by Darwin and others (1972).) Let us consider the following intuitive example for iconic memory: probably we all know the phenomenon that it seems possible to draw lines, figures or names with lighted sparklers by moving the sparkler fast enough in a dark environment. Physically, however, there are no such things as lines of light. So how come we can nevertheless see such figures? This is due to iconic memory. Roughly speaking, we can think of this subtype of memory as a kind of photographic memory, but one which only lasts for a very short time. The image of the light of a sparkler remains in our memory (persistence of vision) and thus makes it seem to us like the light would leave lines in the dark. The same effect occurs, e.g., if we watch a sprinkler and we think that we can see a ring of water drops. As for echoic memory, as the name already suggests, it is meant to apply to auditory input. Here the persistence time is a little longer as with iconic memory (up to 4 seconds). At the level of sensory memory no manipulation of the incoming information occurs, it is simply transferred to, e.g., short term memory (at least the information that is somehow important at the time of perception is transferred).

Short Term Memory

The term "short term memory" stems from the modal model approach to memory by Atkinson and Shiffrin. In more modern approaches the idea of short term memory has been further investigated and there seems to be evidence that also short term memory consists of several separated, but of course closely related, subparts. Baddeley (2000) introduced the nowadays most often used term "working memory". We will first look at the modal model approach and then go on to the concept of working memory.

Short Term Memory

As the name suggests, information is stored in short term memory for a rather short period of time (15-20 seconds). If we look up a phone number in the phone book and memorize it long enough until we dialed that number, it is stored in short term memory. (Unless we want to remember that phone number for a longer period of time, it will most probably not be stored in long term memory.) Now we know how long information can be stored in short term memory, but what about the question about how much can be stored? George Miller in his seminal paper (1956) proposed "the magical number seven, plus minus two". He showed that between 5 and 9 items can usually be stored in short term memory at a time. The term "item" might strike one as a little vague, all of the following are considered items: single digits or letters, whole words or even sentences, and the like. It has been shown by experiments also done by Miller that chunking is a useful method to memorize more than just single items. Gobet et al. defined a chunk as "a collection of elements that are strongly associated with one another but are weakly associated with other chunks" (p. 157 in Goldstein). A famous experiment was conducted by Chase and Simon (1973) with amateur and experienced chess players. When asked to remember certain arrangements of chess pieces on the board, the experts performed significantly better that the amateurs. However, if the pieces were arranged arbitrarily, i.e. not corresponding to possible game situations, both the experts and the amateurs performed equally bad. This shows that chunking (as done by experienced chess players) enhances the performance in such memory tasks.

Problems with the Modal Model Approach: According to the memory-model proposed by Atkinson and Shiffrin, all information has to pass the STM in order to be stored in LTM. However, cases have been reported where patients can form long term memories even though their STM-abilities are severely reduced. This clearly poses a problem to the modal model approach. It was suggested by Shallice and Warrington (1970) that there must be another possible way for information to enter LTM than via STM. Baddeley and Hitch (1974) drew attention to another problem. Under certain conditions it seems to be possible to do two different tasks simultaneously, even though STM, as suggested by Atkinson and Shiffrin, should be regarded as a single, undivided unit. An example for the performance of two tasks simultaneously would be the following: a person is asked to memorize 4 numbers and then read a text (unrelated to the first task). Most people are able to recall the 4 numbers correctly after the reading task, so apparently both memorizing numbers and reading a text carefully can be done at the same time. According to Baddeley and Hitch the result of this experiment indicates that the number-task and the reading-task are handled by two different components of short term memory. So they coined the term "working memory" instead of "short term memory".

Working Memory

Working memory is defined by Baddeley (2000) as follows: "Working memory is a limited capacity system for temporary storage and manipulation of information for complex tasks such as comprehension, learning and reasoning" (p. 162 in Goldstein). What is interesting here is that (a) the system is limited in its capacity (the same limitations hold as for short term memory) and (b) that the task of working memory is not only storage, but also manipulation of incoming information. Working memory consists of three parts: the **phonological loop**, the **visuospatial sketch pad** and the **central executive**. We will consider each subpart in turn. Let us begin with the phonological loop.

The phonological loop is responsible for auditory and verbal information, such as phone numbers, person's names or general understanding of what other people are talking about. We could roughly say that it is a system specialized for language. This system can again be subdivided into an active and a passive part. The storage of information belongs to the passive part and fades after 2 second if the information is not rehearsed explicitly. Rehearsal, on the other hand, is regarded as the active part of the phonological loop. The repetition of information deepens the memory. There are three well-known phenomena that support the idea that the phonological loop is specialized for language: the phonological similarity effect, the word-length effect and articulatory suppression. When words that sound similar are confused, we speak of the phonological similarity effect. The word-length effect refers to the fact that it is more difficult to memorize a list of long words and better results can be achieved if a list of short words should be memorized. Let us consider the phenomenon of articulatory suppression in a little more detail. Consider the following experiment: participants are asked to memorize words while saying "the, the, the ..." out loud. What we find is that, with respect to the word-length effect, the difference in performance between lists of long and short words is levelled out. Both lists can be memorized equally well. The explanation given by Baddeley et al. (1984), who conducted this experiment, is that the constant repetition of the word "the" prevents the rehearsal of the words in the lists, independent of whether the list contains long or short words. The findings become even more drastic if we compare the memory-performance in the following experiment (also conducted by Baddeley and his co-workers in 1984): participants were again asked to say out loud "the, the, the ...". But instead of memorizing words from a list of short or long words, their task was to remember words that were either spoken to them or shown to them written on paper. The results indicated that the participant's performance was significantly better if the words were presented to them and not read out aloud. Baddeley concluded from this fact that the performance in a memory task is improved if the two stimuli can be dealt with in distinct components of the working memory. In other words, because the reading of words is handled in the visuospatial sketch pad, whereas the saying of "the" belongs to the phonological loop, the two tasks do not "block" each other. The rather bad performance of hearing words while speaking could be explained by the fact that both hearing and speaking are dealt with in the phonological loop and thus the two tasks conflict with each other, decreasing the performance of memorization.

In **the visuospatial sketch pad** visual and spatial information is stored. As we have seen above, performance decreases if two tasks that are dealt with in the same component are to be done simultaneously. Let us consider a further example that illustrates this effect. Brandimonte and co-workers (1992) conducted an experiment where participants were asked to say out loud "la, la, la ...". At the same time they were given the task of subtracting a partial image from a given whole image. The subtraction had to be done mentally because the two images were presented only for a short time. The interesting result was that not only did the performance not decrease while saying "la, la, la ..." when compared to doing the subtraction-task alone, but the performance even increased. According to Brandimonte this was due to the fact that the subtraction task was easier if handled in the visuospatial sketch pad as opposed to the phonological loop (both the given and the resulting pictures were such that they could also be named, i.e. verbalized, a task that belongs to the phonological loop). In principle, the participants could freely choose whether they did the subtraction-task verbally or visually. But because the phonological loop was already occupied by saying "la, la, la ..." and would therefore have been overloaded if the subtraction-task had been done verbally as well, the participants were forced to do the task visually. As mentioned above, because of the fact that the subtraction of a partial image from a whole given image is easier if done visually, the performance increased if participants were forced to visually perform that task, i.e. if they were forced to use the component that is suited best for the given task. We have seen that the phonological loop and the visuospatial sketch pad deal with rather different kinds of information which nonetheless have to somehow interact in order to do certain tasks. The component that connects those two systems is the central executive.

The central executive co-ordinates the activity of both the phonological loop and the visuospatial sketch pad. Imagine the following situation: you are driving a car and your friend in the passenger seat has the map and gives you directions. The directions are given verbally, i.e. they are handled by the phonological loop, while the perception of the traffic, street lights, etc. is obviously visual, i.e. dealt with in the visuospatial sketch pad. If you now try to follow the directions given to you by your friend it is necessary to somehow combine both kinds of information, the verbal and the visual information. This important connection of the two components is done by the central executive. (It also links the working memory to long term memory, we will discuss long term memory below.) Currently, research is being done in order to find out how the central executive solves the complex task of co-ordinating and controlling the other components. Unfortunately, we do not know much about the operation of the central executive yet. Let us hope that the research will be as fruitful as it has been so far with respect to other parts of memory.

Long Term Memory

As the name already suggest, long term memory is the system where memories are stored for a long time. "Long" in this sense means something between a few minutes and several years or even decades. Similar to working memory, long term memory can again be subdivided into different types. Two major distinctions are being made between declarative (conscious) and implicit (unconscious) memory. Those two subtypes are again split into two components each: episodic and semantic memory with respect to declarative memory and priming effects and procedural memory with respect to implicit memory. In contrast to short term or working memory, the capacity of long term memory is theoretically infinite. The magic number seven obviously does not apply here, because, as mentioned above, information can be stored for a very long time and is not restricted to a few items. The opinions as to whether information remains in long term memory for ever, or whether information can get deleted differ. The main argument for the latter opinion is that apparently not all information that ever got stored in LTM can be recalled. However, theories that regard long term memories as not being subject to deletion emphasize that there might be a useful distinction between the existence of information and the ability to retrieve or recall that information at a given moment. An example for the inability to retrieve a particular memory would be a situation in which someone tries to remember a name, but cannot come up with it. The saying of something like "I have it on the tip of my tongue..." indicates that the speaker is sure that the information is still existent in his memory, but that the retrieval is somehow blocked. It such situations the circumstances (in a rather broad sense) might enhance the retrieval of information. An example would be that someone helps the aforementioned speaker by giving the first letter of the name or something similar. Or another enhancement might be that in order to better recall memories about the childhood, it could be helpful to visit the places or people that are connected to childhood, like the kindergarten or an elementary school teacher.

Declarative Memory

Let us now consider the two types of declarative memory. As noted above, those two types are episodic and semantic memory. Episodic memory refers to memories for particular events that have happened to someone. Typically, those memories are connected to specific times and places. Semantic memory, on the other hand, refers to knowledge about the world that is not connected to personal events. Vocabulary, concepts, numbers or facts would be stored in semantic memory. The two types are usually closely related to one another, i.e. memory of facts might be enhanced by interaction with memory about personal events and vice versa. For example, the answer to the factual question of whether people put vinegar on their chips might be answered positively by remembering the last time you saw someone eating fish and chips. The other way around, good semantic memory about certain things such as football can contribute to more detailed episodic memory of a particular personal event, like watching a football match. A person that barely knows the rules of that game will most probably have a less specific memory for the personal event of watching the game than a football-expert will.

Implicit Memory

We now turn to the different types of implicit memory. As the name suggests, both types are usually active when unconscious memories are concerned. This becomes most evident for procedural memory, though it must be said that the distinction between both types is not as clearly cut as in the case of declarative memory and that often both categories are collapsed into the single category of procedural memory. But if we want to draw the distinction between priming effects and procedural memory, the latter category is responsible for highly skilled activities that can be performed without much conscious effort. Examples would be the tying of shoelaces or the driving of a car, if those activities have been practiced sufficiently. As regards the priming effect, consider the following experiment conducted by T.J. Perfect and C. Askew (1994). Participants were asked to read a magazine without paying attention to the advertisements. After that, different advertisements were presented to them, some had occurred in the magazine, others had not. The participants were told to rate the presented advertisement with respect to different criteria such as how appealing, how memorable or eye-catching they were. The result was that in general those advertisements that had been in the magazine received higher rankings than those that had not been in the magazine. Additionally, when asked which advertisements the participants had actually seen in the magazine, the recognition was very poor (only 2.8 of the 25 advertisements were recognized). This experiment shows that the participants performed implicit learning (as can be seen from the high rankings of advertisements they had seen before) without being conscious of it (as can be seen from the poor recognition rate). This is an example of the priming effect.

Errors in Memory

Finally we arrive at the errors or disorders. A definition of Memory: "Memory is the ability of an organism to store, retain, and subsequently recall information." So we are on our way to discover what blocked processes or defective mechanisms of the brain are leading to what kind of disfunction. We like to divide the errors in biochemical and hardware. (like a brain injury or operation).

Biochemical

A biochemical error is for example alzheimer where patients show a depletion of acetylcholine and glutamate. *"Alzheimer disease is a neurodegenerative disease characterized by progressive cognitive deterioration together with declining activities of daily living and neuropsychiatric symptoms or behavioral changes."* Alzheimer - Wikipedia

But there are many more Neurodegenerative Diseases. Commonly known are Parkinson, Multiple sclerosis and Creutzfeld-Jakob. A Neurodegenerative Disease is a *"disease caused by the irreversible deterioration of essential cell and tissue components of the nervous system."*. So the basis gets lost and the brain loses its cognitive functions.

Hardware Errors

Structure of a Typical Neuron

The most studied patient with a so called hardware error is Henry M. H.M.'s History A man who had as child a bicycle accident and suffered from epilepsy. In an experimental surgery Dr. William Scoville removed H.M.'s hippocampus and other parts of the brain. Good for Henry was that the frequency of the epilepsy was reduced, bad was that he was not able to store any new memories. By the way, his Short Term Memory was normal. Corkin showed in 1968 that he could learn new simple tasks. So he concluded that his procedural memory was working. H.M. is suffering from Anterograde amnesia. Amnesia - Wikipedia

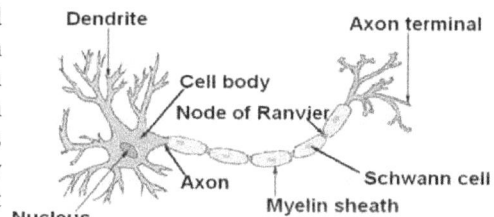

Diagram of basic features of a neuron.

Sources

- E. Bruce Goldstein: *Cognitive Psychology: Connecting Mind, Research, and Everyday Experience.* Thomson Wadsworth, USA 2005 ISBN 0-534-57726-1
- Lyle E. Bourne and Bruce R. Ekstrand: *Einführung in die Psychologie.* (4. Auflage). Verlag Dietmar Klotz GmbH, Eschborn 2005 ISBN 3-88074-500-5

live version • discussion • edit lesson • comment • report an error

7 MEMORY AND LANGUAGE

live version • discussion • edit lesson • comment • report an error

Introduction

"You need memory to keep track of the flow of conversation" [1]

This chapter deals with the correlation of language and memory which is divided into two main parts, namely acquisition of natural language and speech production. Both are strongly connected to memory. Acquisition of language describes the act of learning not only the mother tongue (in childhood) but also additional languages, whereas speech production consists of the physical and mental processes. However, only the latter is part of our field of interest.

Basically, language is processed in the higher hemisphere of the brain (Broca Region). The dependencies between speech processes like recall, search and decision problems are localised within different memory specifications (long term memory, short term memory, working memory and sensory memory). Therefore if one of the these parts are affected by specific diseases (Anterior Aphasia) it causes problems of understanding language, building complex sentences or even remembering simple words. Although interacting of language and memory does not seem to be mentionable at first, by regarding it closer it exposed to be the most important interaction which is necessary of being conversational.

Definition

Language

Language is one of the most important ability of human beings which allows them to communicate with each other. Language processing and comprehension occurs in the left hemisphere in the **Broca's area** *(especially for processing/production)* and in the **Wernicke's area** *(especially for comprehension)*. The sounds and written language (based on phonemes, letters and symbols) need to be structured with the help of a specific grammar, which indicates the syntax and its semantics. That construction is the condition of sharing and conveying information about thoughts, knowledge and feelings with other human beings. Primitive species (other than human beings) do not have such a complex and mature communication system. On that score human's communication is unique. However, if the specific areas in the brain are damaged or suffer from a specific disease, it leads to a limitation of its function.

(For further information see also chapter : **Comprehension**)

Memory

Memory can basically be seen as a collection of a versatile memory system. That multilateral system has many-sided storage processes for each individual constituent. Every component varies fundamentally in its specific functions. All of them play an important role in guiding human's life and behavior by encoding and storing information, which was received over sensory stimuli in the past, for later usage. For instance, if humans would not have such a storage system, communication (language processing, which is very important for this chapter) would not function to some extent. Due to the fact that memory and its abilities are very voluminous, the discriminative types are allocated in many regions of the brain. Nonetheless the temporal lobe is the most important area for memory storage.

(For further information see also the previous chapter : **Memory**)

Brain regions

Language-related areas in the human brain basically are located in the left hemisphere. The processing of language requires a more complex network of interacting brain areas as previously assumed. In addition to Broca's and Wernicke's areas, several cortical and subcortical regions seem to be involved in normal language processing. Broca's (adjacent to motor cortex) and Wernicke's (posterior superior temporal lobe) areas are joined by the arcuate fasciculus, a bidirectional pathway, and are part of the implementation system - one of three functional language systems (implementation, mediational, and conceptual system)

(For further information see also chapter : **Comprehension**)

Memory

Short term/long term Memory

The distinction between long-term memory (LTM) and short-term memory (STM) is necessary since experiments have shown that they are functioning independently. Experiments with patients having brain lesions and as a consequence either a poor LTM and a functioning STM, or vice versa have shown that there is a double dissociation of LTM and STM. This means that one can infer that they are independent and served by different mechanisms.

The STM holds information only 15-30 seconds after the initial stimulus and the informations get lost after this time span if they are not transferred into LTM. Therefore the STM is meant to provide the information that is just being worked with. The information in the STM is most commonly coded phonologically, which means that it is represented by its sound (in contrast to visual or semantic coding), this was shown by an experiment of Conrad (1964, Acoustic confusion in Immediate Memory).

The LTM in contrast, can hold information for long periods of time, up to decades. The information gets most commonly encoded semantically, with respect to its meaning, although as in STM all three types of coding occur. Within the LTM there are two different types of memories; declarative/conscious memories and implicit/unconscious memories. The declarative memory gets also divided into two different subtypes. The episodic memory, which is responsible for storing specific autobiographic events, and the semantic memory, which holds general world knowledge (not in an personal context). The implicit memory is, as said before unconscious. This means that experiences of the past may affect a persons future behaviour without explicit knowledge about the reasons. A good example for this kind of memory is shown by the propaganda effect, which states that a person is more likely to evaluate a statement as true if the statement was heard before, even if the person does not consciously remember. This class of phenomena is referred to as the priming effect. Practical skills, such as used for motor or cognitive tasks are also part of the implicit memory and stored in the procedural memory.

(For more detailed information see chapter 6 Memory)

Working Memory

Working memory consists of a number of parts which help human beings to manipulate information for solving complex cognitive tasks such as thinking *(also decision making)* , comprehension, learning and reasoning. It is a temporal storage and works parallel to the long term memory. Both share most of their cortical structures. It basically means that both structures communicate very closely with each other. If a sensory stimulus is retained in the working memory it activates a cortical network which encodes its past associative context from the storage of long term memory while the working memory contemporaneously encodes that stimulus also. Working memory could be seen as a system recalling explicit knowledge for a specific task which needs to be solved.

The activity of working memory is localized between the prefrontal cortex and associative areas of the posterior cortex.

Researchers such as Alan Baddeley leads to the assumption that working memory consists of three components (**Baddeley's model of working memory**). One of it is the phonological loop which is an important part for language. It holds information about verbal and auditory stimulus. Another one is the visuospatial sketch pad that upholds the visual and spatial information. The last and probably the most complex and important one of the three components is the central executive. It dovetails the information which is stored in the long term memory and the information of the other two components with regard to the specific parts of the task which has to be solved. Therefore the central executive part could be understood as being the responsible one for the attentional control to some specific portions of the task. Due to that fact long term memory and working memory should be seen as a parallel working system whereas the latter is the on-line processing part. It is called „on-line processing" because the working memory is able to sustain information as long as it is needed to reach a goal, understand and comprehend a sentence or a complex story, or to be able to dail a telephone number after looking it up in a telephone book. This chapter will focus on the role which working memory plays in reading, learning and comprehension of language is the important one to focus on. Hence without working memory human beings would be incapable of recognizing words and consequently understand and comprehend the syntax of spoken language or a text. It is not possible to hold on phonemes, letters, sentences and numbers in another storage system long enough to comprehend the context of the information which was just been written, heard, spoken or read. A small limit of the capacity of working memory is already sufficient to give trouble in syntax comprehension.

Sensory Memory

Sensory memory functions as an unconscious, huge collection of all sensory impressions or stimuli a person gets exposed to. Sensory memory can register a very large amount of information but this information gets lost very rapidly. It is only retrievable within seconds or sometimes only fractions of a second after the initial stimulus.

From today's point of view sensory memory is considered to be important for several purposes. First of all, it is important for collecting all the information that is potentially processed later on. Then it functions as a temporary storage while processing is going on. Additionally, sensory memory is important for filling in gaps if a stimulus gets interrupted, as will be discussed later on.

There are three types of sensory memory Iconic memory or visual icon, memory for visual stimuli, *echoic memory*, memory for auditory stimuli and *haptic memory*, memory for touch. The two types of sensory memory that are most investigated in are the iconic memory and the echoic memory.

A very common example for iconic memory is the light beam that for example a pocket lamp leaves behind when it is moved rapidly through the dark night. The apparently real light beam is only created by the images one retrieves and stores in the sensory memory while the pocket lamp moves (*persistence of vision*). Another, maybe more common example where iconic memory is important is watching a movie. The movie is broadcast with 25 to 30 images per second. This is sufficient to give the illusion of a fluently moving movie because the gaps or interruptions that occur between the images get filled in with the information from the sensory memory.

The time how long a visual stimulus is kept in iconic memory was first investigated in by George Sperling (1960). In his experiment Sperling flashed an array of 12 letters (in three rows) on a screen for a total time of 50 milliseconds. He distinguished between a *whole-report procedure* and a *partial-report procedure*. Participants of the first group had to recall as many words as possible from the array after the stimulus was presented. In the partial-report procedure, Sperling indicated the exact row participants had to recall by a tone that was presented right after the stimulus. The results of this experiment showed that participants from the whole-report group were able to report only 4 or 5 of the 12 letters, while participants from the partial-report group were able to recall an average of 3.3 of the 4 letters. Therefore the percentage of recalled letters was much higher for the partial-report group. Sperling concluded from these results that after reporting the first 4 or 5 letters from the array the rest had already faded away and was therefore no longer recallable for his participants. To determine the exact time-span it takes for a iconic memory to decay, Sperling repeated the experiment with the partial-report procedure only and delayed the tone after the stimulus representation. He found out that already after one second delay the participant could only recall 1 out of the 4 letters and therefore performed equivalent to the participants of the whole-report group. Sperling concluded that the information stored in the iconic memory fades away in less than one second.

Darwin et al. (1972) replicated the Sperling experiment in order to investigate the echoic memory. Their participants had to wear headphones and Darwin et al. simultaneously presented nine letters, three to the left ear, three to the right ear and three to both ears. Afterwards a bar on a screen indicated which letters the participants had to recall. The results this experiment showed were closely related to the results of Sperling's experiment. The differences they found is that echoic memory lasts a bit longer than iconic memory, two to four seconds, and that not as much information gets stored as in the iconic memory. One commonality echoic and iconic memory have is that there is a lot more information stored than could be retrieved in the shored time it is available.

Sensory memory is neither a kind of short term memory, since these memories last longer, nor any kind of long term memory. Because of its huge capacity and short duration Sensory Memory can be seen as a accumulator and filter for sensory information.

Semantic Memory

Semantic memory is a form of declarative long-term memory and stands in contrast to episodic memory (particular,personal time and place related events) as first suggested by Tulving (1972).

Semantic memory holds the general knowledge about the world. This can be for example in the form of facts, skills, concepts or vocabulary and is therefore not related to emotions. Wheeler, Stuss and Tulving (1997) specified the differences between episodic and semantic memory more concrete in terms of their retrieval. Whereas episodic memory depends on a special kind of awareness, autonoetic or self-knowing, which is experienced when people think back to a certain moment of their life-time and remember former states of time, semantic memory only involves knowing or noetic awareness, because people think without emotions or personal relation, and therefore objectively about what they know.

In addition Wheeler et al. (1997) pointed out that semantic and episodic memory are closely connected and that, due to the similar encoding, it is not possible to store some event (e.g. knowing a new vocabulary) in semantic memory without encoding some kind of subjective experience in the episodic memory. This holds also for the opposite direction.

There are different views concerning the brain regions that play an important role for semantic memory. The two major opinions are first, that semantic memory is processed or stored by the same brain regions as episodic memory (medial temporal lobes, hippocampal formation) and , opposing to this, that these brain regions do not plain a role for semantic memory. Researchers supporting the second opinion propose different alternatives. Some claim that the episodic memory gets encoded in the neocortex, and others claim that the different aspects of one fact or concept are represented in different brain, so for example sounds in the auditory cortex and visual representations in the visual cortex.

Correlation between Language and Memory

Acquisition of language

According to Chomsky (1959) a child possesses innate neural circuitry specifically dedicated to the acquisition of language. However, many psychologists and linguists believe that language is neither entirely innate nor only acquired by learning.

Children possess an **innate capacity for language** and they acquire the language without special training or feedback. Normally, babies start to speak the first words around their first birthday and produce fluent grammatical sentences at the age of two or three. In contrast, other species fail to learn at all. Children have the instinctive tendency to speak as babbling of babies show. In their first month they are even able to discriminate speech sounds that are not discriminated in their parent's language. Thereby, children perform a sophisticated acoustic and grammatical analysis of its parent's speech, rather than correlating sounds with meaning or merely imitating speech. Although language is more specific than general intelligence, it is not a specific system for language but rather a general capacity to learn patterns: Every child will learn any language it is exposed to. Thus, there seems to be neural system that analyzes communicative signal from other people according to the design of language.

Speech production

Speech production processing is a more complex activity than one might think and requires several skills. We have to think about what to say, then to select the right words, to order these words grammatically finally express the sentence in actual speech. The speaker eases for the listener to understand him by using prosodic clues as rhythm, stress and intonation. Generally, syntactic boundaries (e.g. the ends of sentences) or grammatical junctures (e.g. the ends of phrases) are signalled by hesitations or pauses.

Since speech is normally way too fast it is hard to identify processes involved in speech production. Therefore, research focuses on **speech errors** in spoken language that can reveal how this complex system might work. There exist several types of speech errors while selecting the correct word. One kind of this lexical selection is *semantic substitution* where a word is replaced by another with a similar meaning, and normally of the same form class (e.g. "week" instead of "day"). *Blending* is the joining part of a word (or sentence) on to part of another (e.g. "breakfast" and "lunch" becomes "brunch"). In the case of the *word-exchange error* two words switch their places. If inflections or suffixes are attached to the wrong word, it is call *morpheme-exchange error* (e.g. "buyed"). *Spoonerism* is switching the initial letters of two or more words. Consonants are always exchanged with consonants and vowels with vowels, and often similar phonemes are switched. Mostly, letters within the same clause are switched which shows that a clause is an important unit in a sentence.

On the base of speech errors several theories have been developed. There is a strong similarity among these theories and most of them agree on the following points: Pre-production planning of speech, series of processing stages and procedure from the general to the specific. The **spreading-activation** theory by Dell et al. is based on the assumption that a representation is formed at the semantic, the syntactic, the morphological and the phonological level. Processing occurs at all four levels, and is both parallel and interactive. So-called categorical rules define categories at each level and dictate the required word. Nodes of the lexicon (network containing concepts, words, morphemes and phonemes) become activated. The most activated node of the appropriate category is then selected by insertion rules. A further approach is the theory by **Levelt** assumes that there is a network containing three levels. The levels represent lexical concepts, lemmas or abstract words, and morphemes. Activation proceeds only forwards and, the speech production involves a series of six processing stages: Conceptual preparation (potential concepts are activated), lexical selection (lemma is selected), morphological encoding (basic word form activated), phonological encoding (syllables of the word are computed), phonetic encoding (speech sounds are prepared) and articulation. The theory is to show that the word production proceeds from meaning to sound.

Diseases

The research on patients with brain lesions gives important evidence to the structure of the brain and thus, to the function of certain brain regions. By these dysfunctions existing theories about memory or language production can be tested or new hypothesises developed. **Amnesia** describes the loss of memory and can among others be caused by a bilateral stroke, closed head injury or the Korsakoff's syndrome (chronic alcohol abuse). Since brain damage is often widespread the function of a certain area in the brain is problematic to determine. A further result of brain damage is **aphasia**, which is the impairment of language abilities. There are several forms of aphasia, e.g. patients with Wernicke's (or fluent) aphasia suffer from impaired language comprehension while patients with Broca's (or non-fluent) aphasia are not able to speak properly.

(For further information read the chapter Neuroscience of Language comprehension)

References

1. ↑ E. G. Goldstein, "Cognitive Psychology - Connecting Mind, Research, and Everyday Experience", page 137, THOMSON WADSWORTH TM 2005

External resources

Books

- "Cognitive Psychology: A Student's Handbook", fourth edition, M. Eysenck, 2000
- "Cognitive Psychology – Connecting Mind, Research, and Everyday Experience", E. Bruce Goldstein (University of Pittsburgh), Thomson Wadsworth, 2005
- "Neuropsychology - The Neural Bases of Mental Function", Marie T. Banich (University of Illinois at Urbana-Champaign), Houghton Mifflin Company, 1997
- "PRINCIPLES OF NEURAL SCIENCE", fourth Edition, international Edition, Erik R. Kandel, James H. Schwartz, Thomas M Jessell, McGraw-Hill, 2000

Links

- http://www.almaden.ibm.com/institute/agenda.shtml (*Almaden Institute;* **Joaquin Fuster**, UCLA: *Cortical Dynamics of Working Memory*, 2006)
- http://www.brainconnection.com/topics/?main=fa/memory-language (**Maxine L. Young**, 2000)
- http://io.uwinnipeg.ca/~epritch1/sensmem.htm (*University of Winnipeg;* **Prof. Evan Pritchard, PhD** *Attention & Memory*, 2006)
- http://library.thinkquest.org/C0110291/science/research/basics/sensory.php (**ThinkQuest Team**)

- http://www.physiol.ox.ac.uk/~kk3/PP%2002%20Sensory%20Memory.ppt(*University of Oxford, Department of Physiology, Anatomy and Genetics;* **Kristofer Kinsey PhD**)
- http://www-static.cc.gatech.edu/classes/cs6751_97_winter/Topics/human-cap/memory.html(*Georgia Tech, College of Computing;* **Harish Kotbagi**, *Human Capabilities(Memory)*, 1997)
- http://www.mtsu.edu/~sschmidt/Cognitive/sensory_store/sensory.html(*Middle Tennessee State University;* **Stephen R. Schmidt**, *Copgnitive Psychology*)

live version • discussion • edit lesson • comment • report an error

live version • discussion • edit lesson • comment • report an error

8 IMAGERY

Introduction

Mental imagery (varieties of which are sometimes colloquially refered to as "visualizing," "seeing in the mind's eye," "hearing in the head," "imagining the feel of," etc.) is quasi-perceptual experience; it resembles perceptual experience, but occurs in the absence of the appropriate external stimuli. It is also generally understood to bear intentionality (i.e., mental images are always images of something or other), and thereby to function as a form of mental representation. Traditionally, visual mental imagery, the most discussed variety, was thought to be caused by the presence of picture-like representations (mental images) in the mind, soul, or brain, but this is no longer universally accepted.

Very often, imagery experiences are understood by their subjects as echoes, copies, or reconstructions of actual perceptual experiences from their past; at other times they may seem to anticipate possible, often desired or feared, future experiences. Thus imagery has often been believed to play a very large, even pivotal, role in both memory (Yates, 1966; Paivio, 1986) and motivation (McMahon, 1973). It is also commonly believed to be centrally involved in visuo-spatial reasoning and inventive or creative thought. Indeed, according to a long dominant philosophical tradition, it plays a crucial role in all thought processes, and provides the semantic grounding for language. However, in the 20th century vigorous objections were raised against this tradition, and it is now widely repudiated.

The Imagery Debate

What is it about?

Visual imagery is a flow of thoughts you can see, hear, feel, smell, or taste. Visual imagery is a window on your inner world, a way of viewing your own ideas, feelings, and interpretations. But it is more than a mere window ---why---It is a means of transformation and liberation from distortions in this realm that may unconsciously direct your life and shape your health.

Imagination, in this sense, is not sufficiently valued in our culture.

Without imagination, humanity would be long extinct.

Visual imagery is probably best known for its direct effects on physiology. Through imagery, you can stimulate changes in many body functions usually considered inaccessible to conscious influence.

How is it?

The original imagery debate is concerned with the question how cognitive mechanisms in the brain function when imagining pictures. First attempts at explaining these processes simply dealt with how during real visual stimuli the light (photons) hits the retina where the picture is decomposed and reassembled again in the brain. Similar processes occur in the brain in the absence of visual stimuli during the act of imagery. Pictures are produced in our mind without an actual visaul input. Modern cognitive psychologists rather deny the production of pictures in the brain because then, there has to be something (Homunculus) that continuously looks at the pictures and interprets them. Because of the lack of reasonable explanations a behaviourist theory arose that opposed the view that pictures are actually projected into the brain.

Today's imagery debate is mainly influenced by two opposing theories: (1) Zenon Pylyshyn's propositional theory and (2) Stephen Kosslyn's depictive representation theory of imagery processing. Pylyshyn idea is that information is stored in the brain in a propositional manner. The sentences "the sun is shining" and "it's the case that the sun is shining" have the same proposition, namely "*shining (sun)*" which is stored in a Meta language (all propositions are of the form predicate(arguments)). Contradicting Kosslyn states that there has to be some kind of spatial image representation. His image-scanning experiments discovered that we actually create a mental picture of scenes while trying to solve small cognitive tasks. Kosslyn argued that the responsible mechanisms involve a spatial representation which is similar to the way we conceive things by actually perceiving them. Other advocates of the depictive representation of scenes in our mind, Shepard and Metzler, developed the mental rotation task. Two objects are presented to a participant in different angles and his job is to decide whether the objects are identical or not. The result shows that the reaction times increases linearly with the rotation angle of the objects. This phenomenon can't be explained by a propositional model, but instead implies that participants mentally rotate the objects in order to match the objects to one another. This process is called mental chronometry.

The actual difference between imagery and perception occurs in their distinct processing behaviour. Perception is a bottom-up process that originates with an image on the retina, whereas imagery is a top-down mechanism which originates when activity is generated in higher visual centers without an actual stimulus. Another distinction can be made by saying that perception occurs automatically and remains relatively stable, whereas imagery needs effort and is fragile.

Biological reasoning of debate

Partially imagery is represented by certain neurons in our medial temporal lobe which might respond to one image, but not to another (category-specific neurons). Lesion techniques have advanced the research on the representation of imagery in our brain. For example, the size of our mental images decreases when our primary visual cortex is damaged. There are also such phenomena as unilateral neglect where the patient simply neglects half of his visual field. This occurs both when perceiving and when imagining an object or a scene. The deficit, also called hemi-neglect, is usually due to a lesion in the right hemisphere (most likely the superior temporal gyrus).

Spatial Representation

Abstract

This target article reviews evidence for the functional equivalence of spatial representation of observed enviroment and environments described in discourse. It is argued that people possess a spatial representation system that constructs mental spatial models on the basis of perceptual and linguistic information. Evidence for a distinct spatial system is reviewed.

Introduction

1.1 Space can be understood through perception and language, but are the mental representations of space the same in both cases? Evidence for this position comes from a number of areas, including mental imagery , such representations appear to be equivalent in form and operation to representations of observed environments.

1.2 A number of empirical effects observed in spatial learning studies can be obtained when subjects do not study a map or physical route but instead read a description of an environment.

1.3 People's spatial representations of descriptions can be seen to interact with perceptual spatial systems.

1.4 Further evidence that spatial descriptions are represented in a spatial format comes from the study of mental models. People generally represent texts in mental models rather than by retaining the linguistic structure of the text

1.5 Although most research on mental models has focussed on text comprehension, researchers generally believe that mental models are perceptually based .Indeed, people have been found to use spatial frameworks like those created for texts to retrieve spatial information about observed scenes (Bryant, 1991). Thus, people create the same sorts of spatial memory representations whether they read about an environment or see it themselves.

What is it?

People create the same sorts of cognitive maps and mental spatial models from verbal descriptions and direct observations. This suggests that people have a distinct spatial representation system that creates spatial models from disparate sources of input and is independent of memory systems for other domains of knowledge. The primary role of the SRS is to organize spatial information in a general form that can be accessed by either perceptual or linguistic mechanisms. The SRS provides the coordinate frameworks in which to locate objects, thus creating a model of a perceived or described environment. The advantage of a coordinate representation is that it is directly analogous to the structure of real space and captures all possible relations between objects encoded in the coordinate space. These frameworks also reflect differences in the salience of objects and locations in accord with properties of the environment and the ways in which people interact with it . Thus, the SRS creates representations that are models of the physical and functional aspects of the environment.

How is spatial knowledge encoded?

What, then, can be said about the primary components of cognitive spatial representation? Certainly, the distinction between the external world and our internal view of it is key, and it is helpful to explore the relationship between the two further from a process-oriented perspective.

The classical approach assumes a complex intern al representation in the mind that is constructed through a series of specific perceived stimuli, and that these stimuli generate specific internal responses. Research dealing specifically with geographic-scale space has worked from the perspective that the macro-scale physical environment is extremely complex and essentially beyond the control of the individual. This research, such as that of Lynch and of Golledge and his colleagues, has shown that there is a complex of behavioral responses generated from correspondingly complex external stimuli, which are themselves interrelated. Moreover, the results of this research offers a view of our geographic knowledge as a highly interrelated external/internal system. Using landmarks encountered within the external landscape as navigational cues is the clearest example of this interrelationship.

The rationale is as follows: We gain information about our external environment from different kinds of perceptual experience; by navigating through and interacting directly with geographic space as well as by reading maps, through language, photographs and other communication media. With all of these different types of experience, we encounter elements within the external world that act at symbols. These symbols, whether a landmark within the real landscape, a word or phrase, a line on a map, or a building in a photograph, trigger our internal knowledge representation and generate appropriate responses. In other words, elements that we encounter within our environment act as knowledge stores external to ourselves.

Each external symbol has meaning that is acquired through the sum of the individual perceiver's previous experience. That meaning is imparted by both the specific cultural context of that individual and by the specific meaning intended by the generator of that symbol. Of course, there are many elements within the natural environment not "generated" by anyone, but that nevertheless are imparted with very powerful meaning by cultures (e.g., the sun, moon and stars). Manmade elements within the environment, including elements such as buildings, are often specifically designed to act as symbols as at least part of their function. The sheer size of downtown office buildings, the pillars of a bank facade and church spires pointing skyward are designed to evoke an impression of power, stability or holiness, respectively.

These external symbols are themselves interrelated, and specific groupings of symbols may constitute self-contained external models of geographic space. Maps and landscape photographs are certainly clear examples of this. Elements of differing form (e.g., maps and text) can also be interrelated. These various external models of geographic space correspond to external memory.

From the perspective just described, the sum total of any individual's knowledge is contained in a multiplicity of internal and external representations that function as a single, interactive whole. The representation as a whole can therefore be characterized as a synergistic, self-organizing and highly dynamic network.

Propositional Representation

Theory

The theory of Propositional Representation was founded by Dr. Zenon Pylyshyn who invented it in 1973. He described it as an epiphenomenon which accompanies the process of imagery, but is **not** part of it. Mental images do not show us how the mind works exactly. They only show us that something is happening. Just like the display of a compact disc player. There are flashing lights that display that something happens. We are also able to conclude what happens, but the display does not show us how the processes inside the compact disc player work. Even if the display would be broken, the complact disc player would still continue to play music.

Representation

The basic idea of Propositional Representation is that relationships between objects are representated by symbols and not by spatial mental images of the scene. For example: A bottle under a table would be represented by a formula made of symbols like **'UNDER(BOTTLE,TABLE)'** and not by an image which shows a bottle under a table.

Complex objects

According to the theory of spatial representation, complex objects would appear as a mental image of an object, for example a ship. This mental image would consist of all properties which are remembered. Maybe it would look like this:

Even those complex objects can be generated and described by propositional representation. A complex object like a ship would consist of a structure of nodes which represent the objects properties and the relationship of this properties. A propositional representation of a ship may look like this:

Proofs for propositional representation

As we have seen, even complex objects can be represented propositionally by a symbolic structure of nodes. This indicates that people would need a short time to "travel" mentally from one node to an adjacent node and would need much more time to "travel" from one node to another one if they would have to pass many nodes on the way.

Imagery and Perception

Size and the Visual Field

If an object is observed from different distances, it is harder to perceive details if the object is far away because the objects fills only a small part of the visual field. Kosslyn made an experiment in 1973 in which he wanted to find out if this is also true for mental images. He told participants to imagine objects which are far away and objects which are near. After asking the participants about details, he supposed that details can be observed better if the object is near and fills the visual field. He also told the participants to imagine animals with different sizes near by another. For example an elephant and a rabbit. The elephant filled much more of the visual field than the rabbit and it turned out that the participants were able to answer questions about the elephant more rapidly than about the rabbit. After that the participants had to imagine the small animal besides an even smaller animal, like a fly. This time, the rabbit filled the bigger part of the visual field and again, questions about the bigger animal were answered faster. The result of Kosslyns experiments is that people can observe more details of an object if it fills a bigger part of their visual field. This provides evidence that mental images are represented spatial.

Current state of imagery debate

It seems hard to decide, which position has the stronger arguments, since both give good explanations. The development of the recent years shows that the use of modern techniques of neuroscience, like magnetic resonance imaging, was stronger involved in experiments on visual imagery. But the results are not as clear as one could expect: The regions in the brain which are activated during the processing of mental images are the same which are also important for normal visual processing(especially the visual cortex). On the other hand, there are so-called double dissociations between visual images and visual processing, that means that both can be distorted independently from each other. The experimentators concluded that there are different mechanisms involved. Recapitulating, it can be said that there is no definite answer on the debate up until now, but this is also due to the different formulations of the two sides, for example, the propositions of Pylyshyn can probably not be found by applying methods of neuroscience.

Imagery and memory

The loci of imagery effects in several domains are clarified by separating issues related to the storage of information in memory and its use following retrieval. Empirical findings from studies of memory for word and sentence lists, language comprehension and memory, and symbolic comparisons are discussed. These consistently indicate a functional role for imagery in human cognition but provide no data necessitating the storage of perceptual information related to verbal materials in an analog form. Instead, concreteness effects in memory appear to result from differential processing of relational (shared) and item-specific (distinctive) information for high- and low-imagery materials. The available evidence suggests that verbal and imaginal processing systems may operate in conjunction with a more generic semantic memory, the form of which is not an issue here, yielding apparently contradictory findings in support of both dual-code and common-code theories.

References

Ashwin Ram Kenneth Moorman (1999) Understanding Language Understanding - chapter 5

Bertram F. Malle Louis J. Moses Dare A. Baldwin (2001) Intentions and Intentionality - chapter 9

Emmanuel Dupoux . Language, Brain, and Cognitive Development - chapter7

E.Bruce Goldstein, Cognitive Psychology, Connecting Mind, Research, and Everyday Experience (2005) - ISBN: 0-534-57732-6.

John H. Holland, Keith J. Holyoak, Richard E. Nisbett, Paul R. Thagard (1986) Induction Johnson-Laird, P. N. (1983). Mental models: Towards a cognitive science of language, inference, and consciousness. Cambridge, MA: Harvard University Press.Anderson, J. R. (1978). "Arguments Concerning Representations for Mental Imagery." Psychological Review 85(4): 249-276.

Bryant, D. J., B. Tversky, et al. (1992). "Internal and External Spatial Frameworks for Representing Described Scenes." Jornal of Memory and Language 31: 74-98.

Downs, R. (1985). The Representation of Space: Its Development in Children and in Cartography. The Development of Spatial Cognition. R. Cohen. Hillsdale, NJ, Lawrence Erlbaum Associates: 323-344.

Franklin, N. (1992). "Spatial Representation for Described Environments." Geoforum 23(2): 165-174.

Garling, T., A. Book, et al. (1984). "Cognitive Mapping of Large-Scale Environments." Environment and Planning 16(1): 3-34.

Hayward, W. G. and M. J. Tarr (1995). "Spatial Language and Spatial Representation." Cognition 55: 39-84.

Ioerger, T. R. (1994). "The Manipulation of Images to Handle Indeterminacy in Spatial Reasoning." Cognitive Science 18: 551-593.

Kuipers, B. (1978). "Modeling Spatial Knowledge." Cognitive Science 2: 129-153.

Montello, D. R. (1992). The Geometry of Environmental Knowledge. International Conference GIS - From Space to Territory: Theories and Methods of Spatio-Temporal Reasoning. A. U. Frank, I. Campari and U. Formentini. Pisa, Italy, Springer-Verlag.

Portugali, J., Ed. (1996). The Construction of Cognitive Maps. The GeoJournal Library. Dordrecht, Kluwer Academic Publishers.

Taylor, H. and B. Tversky (1992). "Descriptions and Depictions of Environments." Memory & Cognition 20(5): 483-496.* Clahsen, Harald: Lexical Entries and Rules of Language: A Multidisciplinary Study of German Inflection.

Further Reading

- Cherney, Leora (2001): Right Hemisphere Brain Damage
- Grodzinsky, Yosef (2000): The neurology of syntax: Language use without Broca's area.
- Müller, H.M. & Kutas, M. (1996). What's in a name? Electrophysiological differences between spoken nouns, proper names and one's own name.NeuroReport 8:221-225.
- Müller, H. M., King, J. W. & Kutas, M. (1997). Event-related potentials elicited by spoken relative clausesCognitive Brain Research 4:193-203.

Links - german

- University of Bielefeld:
    - Müller, H. M., Weiss, S. & Rickheit, G. (1997). Experimentelle Neurolinguistik: Der Zusammenhang von Sprache und GehirnIn: Bielefelder Linguistik (Hrsg.) Aisthesis-Verlag, pp. 125-128.
- Müller, H.M. & Kutas, M. (1997). Die Verarbeitung von Eigennamen und Gattungsbezeichnungen: Eine elektrophysiologische Studie. In: G. Rickheit (Hrsg.). Studien zur Klinischen Linguistik - Methoden, Modelle, Intervention. Opladen: Westdeutscher Verlag, pp. 147-169.

- Müller, H.M., King, J.W. & Kutas, M. (1998). Elektrophysiologische Analyse der Verarbeitung natürlichsprachlicher Sätze mit unterschiedlicher Belastung des Arbeitsgedächtnisses. **Klinische Neurophysiologie**

Links

Cognitive Psychology Osnabrück

Dr. Rolf A. Zwaan's Homepage with many Papers

live version • discussion • edit lesson • comment • report an error

9 COMPREHENSION

live version • discussion • edit lesson • comment • report an error

Introduction

"Language is the way we interact and communicate, so, naturally, the means of communication and the conceptual background that's behind it, which is more important, are used to try to shape attitudes and opinions and induce conformity and subordination. Not surprisingly, it was created in the more democratic societies." - Chomsky

Language is a central part of everyday life and communication a natural human necessity. For those reasons there has been a high interest in their properties. However describing the processes of language turns out to be quite hard.

We can define language as a system of communication through which we code and express our feelings, thoughts, ideas and experiences.[1]

Already Plato was concerned with the nature of language in his dialogue "Cratylus", where he discussed first ideas about nowadays important principles of linguistics namely morphology and phonology. Gradually philosophers, natural scientists and psychologists became interested in features of language.

Since the emergence of the cognitive science in the 50's and Chomsky´s criticism on the behaviourist view, language is seen as a cognitive ability of humans, thus incorporating linguistics in other major fields like computer science and psychology. Today, psycho-linguistics is a discipline on its own and its most important topics are acquisition, production and comprehension of language.

Especially in the 20th century many studies concerning communication have been conducted, evoking new views on old facts. New techniques, like CT, MRI and fMRI or EEG, made it possible to observe brain during communication processes in detail.

Later on an overview of the most popular experiments and observed effects is presented. But in order to understand those one needs to have a basic idea of semantics and syntax as well as of linguistic principles for processing words, sentences and full texts.

Finally some questions will arise: How is language affected by culture? Or more philosophical, the development of discussions about the relationship between language and thoughts has to be examined.

Language as a cognitive ability

Historical review on Psycholinguistics & Neurolinguistics

Starting with philosophical approaches, the nature of the human language had ever been a topic of interest. Galileo in the 16th century saw the human language as the most important invention of humans. Later on in the 18th century the **scientific study** of language began by psychologists. Wilhelm

Wundt (founder of the first laboratory of psychology) saw language as the mechanism by which thoughts are transformed into sentences. The observations of Wernike and Broca (see chapter 9) were milestones in the studies of language as a cognitive ability. In the early 1900s the behaviouristic view influenced the study of language very much. In 1957 B.F.Skiner published his book "Verbal Behaviour", in which he proposed that learning of language can be seen as a mechanism of reinforcement. Noam Chomsky (quoted at the beginning of this chapter) published in the same year "Syntactic Structures". He proposed that the ability to invent language is somehow coded in the genes, what lead him to the idea, that the underlaying basis of language is similar across cultures. There might be some kind of universal grammar as a base, independent of what kind of language (also sign language) might be used by humans. Further on Chomsky published a review of Skinner's "Verbal Behaviour" in which he presented arguments against the behaviouristic view. There are still some scientists who are convinced that it does not need a mentalist approach like Chomsky proposed, but in the meantime most agree that human language has to be seen as a cognitive ability.

Todays goals of Psycholinguistics

A natural language can be analysed at a number of different levels. In linguistics we differ between phonology (sounds), morphology (words), syntax (sentence structure), semantics (meaning), and pragmatics (use). Linguists try to find systematic descriptions capturing the regularities inherent in the language itself. But a description of natural language just as a abstract structured system, can not be enough. Psycholinguists rather ask, how the knowledge of language is represented in the brain, and how it is used. Todays most important research topics are:

1. comprehension: How humans understand spoken as well as written language, how language is processed and what interactions with memory are involved.
2. speech production: Both the physical aspect of speech production, and the mental process that stands behind the uttering of a sentence.
3. acquisition: How people learn to speak and understand a language.

Characteristic features

What is a language? What kinds of languages do exist? Are there characteristic features that are unique in human language?

There are plenty of approaches how to describe languages. Especially in computational linguistics researchers try to find formal definitions for different kinds of languages. But for psychology other aspects are of central interest. Language is also a tool we use for social interactions starting with the exchange of news up to the identification of social groups by their dialect. We use it for expressing our feelings, thoughts, ideas etc. But aboveall it is a system of communication.

Although there are plenty ways to communicate (see Non-Human-Language) humans expect their system of communication - the human language to be unique. But what is it that makes the human language so special and unique?

Four major criteria were proposed by Professor Schmalhofer from the University of Osnabrück. The first criterion he names is **semanticity** which means the usage of symbols. Symbols can either refer to objects or to relations between objects. In the human language words are the basic form of symbols. For example the word "book" refers to an object made of paper on which something might be written. A relation symbol is the verb "to like" which refers to the sympathy of somebody to something or someone. Not only objects or relations at presence can be described but there are also symbols which refer to objects in another time or place which is the **criterion of displacement**. The word "yesterday" refers to day before and objects mentioned in a sentence with "yesterday" refer to objects from another time than the present one. Displacement is about the communication of events which had happened or will happen and the objects belonging to that event.

Having a range of symbols to communicate these symbols can be newly combined. **Creativity** is the probable most important feature. Our communication is not restricted to a fixed set of topics or predetermined messages. The combination of a finite set of symbols to an infinite number of sentences and meaning. With the infinite number of sentences the creation of novel messages is possible. How creative the human language is can be illustrated by some simple examples like the process that creates verbs from nouns. New words can be created, which do not exist so far, but we are able to understand them:

> leave the boat on the *beach* -> *beach* the boat
> keep the aeroplane on the *ground* -> *ground* the aeroplane
> write somebody an *e-mail* -> *e-mail* somebody

Creative systems are also found in other aspects of language, like the way sounds are combined to form new words. i.e. *prab, orgu, zabi* could be imagined as names for new products. To avoid an arbitrary combination of symbols without any regular arrangement "true" languages need **structure dependency**. Combining symbols the syntax is relevant. A change in the symbol order might have an impact on the meaning of the sentence.

Non-Human Language - Animal Communication

To dicuss the issues of language we first have to know what language is about and what it is that makes the human communication system so unique and different to other communication system. Human language is just one of quite a number of communication forms. Different forms of communication can be found in the world of animals. From a little moth to a giant whale, all animals appear to have the use of communication.

Forms of Communication

First of all there is the *non-vocal communication*. A well known non-verbal communication method is the *facial expression*. Not only humans use facial expression for stressing utterances or feeling, facial expressions can be found among apes. The expression, for example "smiling" indicates cooperativeness and friendliness in both the human and the ape world. On the other hand an ape showing teeth indicates the willingness to fight.

Another way of communication is the *gesture* as an active posturing. Humans shake hands as a greeting or agreement after a bargain. Dogs wave their tail when they are excited and cats start purring when they feel relaxed. Besides gestures sometimes involve the whole body and its pose. That is called *posture*. Posture is a very common communicative tool among animals. Lowering the front part of the body and extending the front legs is a sign of dogs that they are playful whereas lowering the full body is a dog's postural way to show its submissiveness. Postural communication is known in both human and non-human primates.

However there are other not that obvious ways to communicate. Facial expression, gesture and posture are found in human communication. Furthermore there are other communicative devices which are either just noticeable by the sub-consciousness of humans like scent or cannot be found amongst humans like light, colour and electricity. *Scent* is a chemically based type of communication. The chemicals which are used for a communicative function are called pheremones. Those pheremones are used to mark territorial or to signal its reproductive readiness. For animals scent is a very important tool which predominates their mating behaviour. Humans are influenced in their mating behaviour by scent as well but there are more factors to that behaviour so that scent is not predominating.

Light is a communicative device mainly used by insects like the firefly and the lightning bug which can be found in North America. The insects use species-dependent light patterns to signal identity, sex and location. Another device which cannot be found in human communication but just among some eels in the Amazon River is *electricity*. With the help of electrical impulses at various frequencies those eels are able to communicate about their territory and their presence. Furthermore *colour* plays an important role among animals to identify members of their species and other animals. For example the octopus changes colour for signalling territorial defence and mating readiness. In the world of birds colour is wide spread, too. The male peacock has colourful feathering to impress female peahens as a part of mating behaviour. These ways of communication help to live in a community and survive in nature.

Characteristic Language Features in Animal Communication

As mentioned above there are four criteria (semanticity, displacement, creativity and structural dependency) which are important devices in the human language to form a clear communication between humans. To see if these criteria exist in animal communication - i.e. if animals possess a "true" language - several experiments with non-human primates were performed. Non-human primates were taught American Sign Language (ASL) and a specially developed token language to detect in how far they are capable of linguistic behaviour. Can semanticity, displacement, creativity and structure dependence be found in non-human language?

Experiments

Viki

In 1948 two psychologists tried to teach English words to a chimpanzee named Viki. The chimpanzee was wanted to speak easy English words like "cup". The experiment failed since with the supralanyngal anatomy and the vocal fold structure that chimpanzees have it is impossible for them to produce human speech sounds. The failure of the Viki experiment made scientists wonder how far are non-human primates able to communicate linguistically.

Washoe

From 1965 to 1972 the first important evidence showing rudiments of linguistic behaviour was "Washoe", a young female chimpanzee. The experimenters Allen and Beatrice Gardner conducted an experiment where Washoe learned 130 signs of the American Sign Language within three years. Showing pictures of a duck to Washoe and asking WHAT THAT? she combined the symbols of WATER and BIRD to create WATER BIRD as she had not learned the word DUCK (the words in capital letters refer to the signs the apes use to communicate with the experimenter).

It was claimed that Washoe was able to arbitrarily combine signs spontaneously and creatively. Some scientists criticised the ASL experiment of Washoe because they claimed that ASL is a loose communicative system and strict syntactic rules are not required. Because of this criticism different experiments were developed and performed which focus on syntactic rules and structure dependency as well as on creative symbol combination.

Sarah

A young female chimp called "Sarah" was trained by Premack in 1972. Sarah learned 100 symbols and she was asked to produce simple sentences like MARY GIVE BANANA SARAH. The production of a correctly structured sentences were rewarded. She also was able to deal with more abstract words like IF/THEN.

Kanzi

Another non-human primate named "Kanzi" was trained by Savage-Rumbaugh in 1990. Kanzi was able to deal with 256 geometric symbols and understood complex instructions like GET THE ORANGE THAT IS IN THE COLONY ROOM. Again the experimenter worked with rewards. A question which arose was whether these non-human primates were able to deal with human-like linguistic capacities or if they were just trained to perform a certain action to get the rewarded.

Can the characteristic language features be found in non-human communication?

Creativity seems to be present in animal communication as amongst others Washoe showed with the creation of WATER BIRD for DUCK. Although some critics claimed that creativity is often accidental or like in the case of Washoe's WATER BIRD the creation relays on the fact that water and bird were present. Just because of this presence Washoe invented the word WATER BIRD. In the case of Kanzi a certain form of syntactic rules was observed. In 90% of Kanzi's sentences there was first the invitation to play and then the type of game which Kanzi wanted to play like CHASE HIDE, TICKLE SLAP and GRAB SLAP. The problem which was observed was that it is not always easy to recognise the order of signs. Often facial expression and hand signs are performed at the same time. One ape signed the sentence I LIKE COKE by hugging itself for "like" and forming the sign for "coke" with its hands at the same time. Noticing an order in this sign sentence was not possible.

A certain structural dependency could be observed at Kanzi's active and passive sentences. When Matata, a fellow chimpanzee was grabbed Kanzi signed GRAB MATATA and when Matata was performing an action such as biting Kanzi produced MATATA BITE. It has not yet been proved that symbolic behaviour is occurring. Although there are plenty evidences that creativity and displacement occur in animal communication some critics claim that these evidences can be led back to dressage and training. It was claimed that linguistic behaviour cannot be proved as it is more likely to be a training to correctly use linguistic devices. Apes show just to a little degree syntactic behaviour and they are not able to produce sentences containing embedded structures. Some linguists claim that because of such a lack of linguistic features non-human communication cannot be a "true" language. Although we do not know the capacity of an ape's mind it does not seem that the range of meanings observed in ape's wild life approach the capaciousness of semanticity of human communication. Furthermore apes seem not to care to much about displacement as it appears that they do not communicate about imaginary pasts or futures.

All in all non-human primate communication consisting of graded series of communication shows little arbitrariness. The results with non-human primates led to a controversial discussion about linguistic behaviour. Many researchers claimed that the results were influenced by dressage. However human lack certain communicative devices as well. Humans are not able to follow scent trails or change their colour if they are in danger or in love. Humans are not even able to interpret posture and subtle gesture as precise as a dog or a horse might interpret it.

Language is a communication form for humans suited to the patterns of human life. Other communication systems are better suited for fellow creatures and their mode of existence.

Now that we know what we know that there is a difference between animal communication and human language we will see detailed features of the human language.

Language Comprehension & Production

Language features – Syntax and Semantics

In this chapter the main question will be "how do we understand sentences?". To find an answer to that problem it is necessary to have a closer look at the structure of languages. The most important properties every human language provides are rules which determine the permissible sentences and a hierarchical structure (phonemes as basic sounds, which constitute words, which in turn costitute phrases, which consitute sentences, which consitute stories). These feature of a language enable humans to create new unique sentences. Due to this fact that all human languages have a common ground even if they developed completely independent from one another the very interesting conclusion can be drawn that the ability to speak a language must be innate. Another evidence of a inborn universal grammar is that there were observations of deaf children who were not taught a language and developed there own form of communication which provided the same basic constituents. Two basic abilities human beings have to communicate is to interpret the syntax of a sentence and the knowledge of the meaning of single words, which in combination enables them to understand the semantic of whole sentences. Many experiments have been done to find out how the syntactical and semantical interpretation is done by human beings and how syntax and semantics works together to construct the right meaning of a sentence. Physiological experiments had been done in which for example the event-related potential (ERP) in the brain was measured as well as behavioristic experiments in which mental chronometry, the measurement of the time-course of cognitive processes, was used. Physiological experiments showed that the syntactical and the semantical interpretation of a sentence takes place separately from each other.

Physiological Approach

Semantics

The exploration of the semantic sentence processing can be done by the measurement of the event-related potential (ERP) when hearing a semantical correct sentence in comparison to a semantical incorrect sentence. For example there was done an experiment in which three reactions to sentences were compared:

Semantically correct: "The pizza was too hot to eat."
Semantically wrong: "The pizza was too hot to drink."
Semantically wrong: "The pizza was too hot to cry."

In such experiments the ERP evoked by the correct sentence is considered to show the ordinary sentence processing. The variations in the ERP in case of the incorrect sentences in contrast to the ERP of the correct sentence show at what time the mistake is recognized. In case of semantic incorrectness there was observed a strong negative signal about 400ms after perceiving the critical word which did not occure if the sentence was semantically correct. These effects were observed mainly in the paritial and central area. There was also found evidence that the N400 is the stronger the less the word fits semantically. The word "drink" which fits a little bit more in the context caused a weaker N400 than the word "cry". That means the intensity of the N400 correlates with the degree of difficulty of the semantic mistake. The more difficult it is to search for a semantic interpretation of a sentence the higher is the N400 response.

Syntax

To examine the syntactical aspects of the sentence processing a quite similar experiment as in the case of the semantic processing was done. There were used syntactical correct sentences and incorrect sentences, such as (correct:)"The cats won´t eat..." and (incorrect:)"The cats won´t eating...". When perceiving an syntactical incorrect sentence in contrast to an syntactical correct sentence the ERP changes significantly on two different points of time. First of all there a very early increased response to syntactical incorrectness after 120ms. This signal is called the 'early left anterior negativity' because it occurs mainly in the left frontal lobe. This advises that the syntactical processing is located amongst others in the Broca-area which is located in the left frontal lobe. The early response to syntactical mistakes also gives a hint that the syntactical mistakes are detected earlier than semantic mistakes.

The other change in the ERP when perceiving a syntactical wrong sentence occurs after 600ms in the paritial lobe. The signal is increasing positively and is therefore called P600. Possibly the late positive signal is reflecting the attempt to reconstruct the grammatical problematic sentence to find a possible interpretation.

Summing up... There are three important ERP-components. First of all there occurs the ELAN at the left frontal lobe which shows a violation of syntactical rules. After it follows the N400 in central and paritial areas as a reaction to a semantic incorrectness and finally there takes place a P600 in the paritial area which probably means a reanalysis of the wrong sentence.

Behavioristic Approach – Parsing a Sentence

Behavioristic experiments about how human beings parse a sentence often use syntactically ambiguous sentences. Because it is easier to realize that sentence-analysing mechanism called parser takes place when using sentences in which we cannot automatically constitute the meaning of the sentence. There are two different theories about how humans parse sentences. One of these theories clames that syntax plays the main part whereas semanitcs has only a supporting role, the syntax-first approach, the other theory states that both syntax and semantics work together to determine the meaning of a sentence, the interactionist approach.

The Syntax-First Approach of Parsing

The syntax-first approach concentrates on the role of syntax when parsing a sentence. That humans infer the meaning of a sentence with help of its syntactical structure (Kako and Wagner 2001) can easily be seen when considering Lewis Carroll's poem 'Jabberwocky':

"Twas brillig, and the slithy toves Did gyre and gimble in the wabe: All mimsy were the borogoves, And the mome raths outgrabe."

Although most of the words in the poems have no meaning one is able to understand the poem somehow because of its syntactical structure.

There are many different syntactic rules that are used when parsing a sentence. One important rule is the principle of late closure which means that a person assumes that a new word he perceives is part of the current phrase. That this principle is used for parsing sentences can be seen very good with help of a so called garden-path sentence. Experiments with garden-path sentences have been done by Frazier and Fayner 1982. One example of a garden-path sentence is: "Because he always jogs a mile seems a short distance to him." When reading this sentence one first wants to continue the phrase "Because he always jogs" by adding "a mile" to the phrase, but when reading further one realizes that the words "a mile" are the beginning of a new phrase. This shows that we parse a sentence by trying to add new words to a phrase as long as possible. Garden-path sentences show that we use the principle of late closure as long it makes syntactically sense to add a word to the current phrase but when the sentence starts to get incorrect semantics are often used to rearrange the sentence. The syntax-first approach does not disregard semantics. According to this approach we use syntax first to parse a sentence and semantics is later on used to make sense of the sentence.

There have not only been done experiments which show how syntax is used for parsing sentences but also how semantics can influence the sentence processing. One important experiment about that issue has been done by Daniel Slobin in 1966. He showed that passive sentences are understood faster if the semantics of the words allow only one subject to be the actor. Sentences like "The horse was kicked by the cow." and "The fence was kicked by the cow." are grammatically equal and in both cases only one syntactical parsing is possible. Nevertheless the first sentence semantically provides two subjects as possible actors and therefore it needs longer to parse this sentence. By measuring this significant difference Daniel Slobin showed that semantics play an important role in parsing a sentence, too.

The Interactionist Approch of Parsing

The interactionist approach ascribes a more central role to semantics in parsing a sentence. In contrast to the syntax-first approach, the interactionist theory clames that syntax is not used first but that semantics and syntax are used simultanuasly to parse the sentence and that they work together in clearifying the meaning. There have been made several experiments which provide evidence that semantics are taking into account from the very beginning reading a sentence. Most of these experiments are working with the eye-tracking techniques and compare the time needed to read syntactical equal senences in which critical words cause or prohibit ambiguitiy by semantics. One of these experiments has been done by John Trueswell and coworkers in 1994. He measured the eye movement of persons when reading the following two sentences:

The defendant examined by the lawyer turned out to be unreliable. The evidence examined by the lawyer turned out to be unreliable.

He observed that the time needed to read the words "by the lawyer" took longer in case of the first sentence because in the first sentence the semanics first allow an interpretation in which the defendant is the one who examines, while the evidence only can be examined. This experiment shows that the semantics also play a role while reading the sentence which supports the interactionist approach and argues against the theory that semantics are only used after a sentence has been parsed syntactically.

Situation Model

A situation model is a mental representation of what a text is about. This approach proposes that the mental representation people form as they read a story does not indicate information about phrases, sentences, paragraphs, but a representation in terms of the people , objects, locations, events described in the story (Goldstein 2005, p. 374)

For a more detailed description of situation models, see [Situation Models]

Using Language

Conversations are dynamic interactions between two or more people(Garrod &Pickering, 2004 as cited in Goldstein 2005). The important thing to mention is that conversation is more than the act of speaking. Each person brings in his or her knowledge and conversations are much easier to process if participants bring in shared knowledge. In this way, participants are responsible of how they bring in new knowledge.

H.P. Grice proposed in 1975 a basic principle of conversation and four "conversational maxims." His cooperative principle states that "the speaker and listener agree that the person speaking should strive to make statements that further the agreed goals of conversation." The four maxims state the way of how to achieve this principle.

1. **Quantity**: The speaker should try to be informative, no over-/underinformation.
2. **Quality**: Do not say things which you believe to be false or lack evidence of.
3. **Manner**: Avoiding being obscure or ambiguous.
4. **Relevance**: Stay on topic of the exchange.

An example of a rule of conversation incorporating three of those maxims is the *given-new-contract*. It states that the speaker should construct sentences so that they include given and new information. (Haviland & Clark, 1974 as cited in Goldstein, 2005). Consequences of not following this rule were demonstrated by Susan Haviland and Herbert Clark by presenting pairs of sentences (either following or ignoring the given-new-contract) and measuring the time participants needed until they fully understood the sentence. They found that participants needed longer in pairs of the type:

We checked the picnic supplies.
The beer was warm.

Rather than:

We got some beer out of the trunk.
The beer was warm.

The reason that it took longer to comprehend the second sentence of the first pair is that inferencing has to be done (beer has not been mentioned as being part of the picnic supplies). (Goldstein, 2005, p.377-378)

Language, Culture and Cognition

In the parts above we saw that there has been a lot of research of language, from letters through words and sentences to whole conversations. Most of the research described in the parts above was processed by English speaking researchers and the participants were English speaking as well. Can those results be generalised for all languages and cultures or might there be a difference between English speaking cultures and for example cultures with Asian or African origin?

This part is concerned with culture and its connection to language. Culture, not necessarily in the sense of "high culture" like music, literature and arts but culture is the "know-how" a person must have to tackle his or her daily life. This know-how might include high culture but it is not necessary.

Culture and Language

Scientists wondered in how far culture affects the way people use language. In 1991 Yum studied the indirectness of statements in Asian and American conversations. The statement "Please shut the door" was formulated by Americans in an indirect way. They might say something like "The door is open" to signal that they want to door to be shut. Even more indirect are Asian people. They often do not even mention the door but they might say something like "It is somewhat cold today". Another cultural difference affecting the use of language was observed by Nisbett in 2003 in observation about the way people pose questions. When American speaker ask someone if more tea is wanted they ask something like "More tea?". Different to this Asian people would ask if the other one would like more drinking as for Asians it seems obvious that tea is involved and therefore mentioning the tea would be redundant. For Americans it is the other way round. For them it seems obvious that drinking is involved so they just mention the tea.

This experiment and similar ones indicate that people belonging to Asian cultures are often relation orientated. Asians focus on relationships in groups. Contrasting, the Americans concentrate on objects. The involved object and its features are more important than the object's relation to other objects. These two different ways of focusing shows that language is affected by culture.

A experiment which clearly shows these results is the mother-child interaction which was observed by *Fernald and Morikawa* in 1993.They studied mother-child talk of Asian and American mothers. An American mother trying to show and explain a car to her child often repeated the object "car" and wants the child to repeat it as well. The mother focuses on the features of the car and labels the importance of the object itself. The Asian mother shows the toy car to her child, gives the car to the child and wants it to give the car back. The mother shortly mentions that the object is a car but concentrates on the importance of the relation and the politeness of giving back the object.

Realising that there are plenty differences in how people of different cultures use language the question arises if languages affects the way people think and perceive the world.

What is the connection between language and cognition?

Sapir-Whorf Hypothesis

In the 1950's Edward Sapir and Benjamin Whorf proposed the hypothesis that the *language of a culture affects the way people think and perceive*. The controversial theory was question by Elenor Rosch who studied colour perception of Americans and Danis who are members of an stone-age agricultural culture in the Iran. Americans have several different categories for colour as for example blue, red, yellow and so on. Danis just have two main colour categories. The participants were ask to recall colours which were shown to them before. That experiment did not show significant differences in colour perception and memory as the Sapir-Whorf hypothesis presumes.

Categorical Perception

Nevertheless a support for the Sapir-Whorf hypothesis was Debi Roberson's demonstration for *categorical perception* based on the colour perception experiment by Rosch. The participants, a group of English-speaking British and another group of Berinmos from New Guinea were ask to name colours of a board with colour chips. The Berinmos distinguish between five different colour categories and the denotation of the colour names is not equivalent to the British colour denotation. Apart from these differences there are huge differences in the organisation of the colour categories. The colours named *green* and *blue* by British participants where categorised as *nol* which also covers colours like *light-green, yellow-green,* and *dark blue*. Other colour categories differ similarly.

The result of Roberson's experiment was that it is easier for British people to discriminate between green and blue whereas Berinmos have less difficulties distinguishing between Nol and Wap. The reaction to colour is affected by language, by the vocabulary we have for denoting colours. It is difficult for people to distinguish colours from the same colour category but people have less trouble differentiating between colours from different categories. Both groups have categorical colour perception but the results for naming colours depends on how the colour categories were named. All in all it was shown that categorical perception is influenced by the language use of different cultures.

These experiments about perception and its relation to cultural language usage leads to the question whether thought is related to language with is cultural differences.

Is thought dependent on, or even caused by language?

Historical theories

An early approach was proposed by J.B. Watson's in 1913. His peripheralist approach was that thought is a tiny not noticeable speech movement. While thinking a person performs speech movements as he or she would do while talking. A couple year later, in 1921 Wittgenstein poses the theory that the limits of a person's language mean the limits of that person's world. As soon as a person is not able to express a certain content because of a lack of vocabulary that person is not able to think about those contents as they are outside of his or her world. Wittgenstein's theory was doubted by some experiments with babies and deaf people.

Present research

To find some evidence for the theory that language and culture is affecting cognition Lian-hwang Chiu designed an experiment with American and Asian children. The children were asked to group objects in pairs so that these objects fit together. On picture that was shown to the children there was a cow, a chicken and some grass. The children had to decided which of the two objects fitted together. The American children mostly grouped cow and chicken because of group of animals they belong to. Asian children more often combined the cow with the grass as there is the relation of the cow normally eating grass.

In 2000 Chui repeated the experiment with words instead of pictures. A similar result was observed. The American children sorted their pairs taxonomically. Given the words "panda", "monkey" and "banana" American children paired "panda" and monkey". Chinese children grouped relationally. They put "monkey" with "banana". Another variation of this experiment was done with bilingual children. When the task was given in English to the children they grouped the objects taxonomically. A Chinese task caused a relational grouping. The language of the task clearly influenced on how to group the objects. That means language may affects the way people think.

The results of plenty experiments regarding the relation between language, culture and cognition let assume that culture affects language and cognition is affected by language. *Our way of thinking is influenced by the way we talk and thought can occur without language but the exact relation between language and thought remains to be determined.*

References

1. ↑ E. B. Goldstein, "Cognitive Psychology - Connecting Mind, Research, and Everyday Experience" (2005), page 346

Books

- O'Grady, W.; Dobrovolsky, M.; Katamba, F.: Contemporary Linguistics. Copp Clark Pittmann Ltd. (1996)
- Banich, Marie T. : Neuropsychology. The neural bases of mental function. (1997)
- Goldstein, E.B.: Cognitive Psychology: Connecting Mind, Research and Everyday Experience. (2005)
- Akmajian, A.; Demers, R. A.; Farmer, A. K.; Harnish R. M.: Linguistics - An Introductin to

Language and Communication, fifth Edition; the MIT Press Cambridge, Massachusetts, London, England; (2001)
  • Yule, G.: The study of language, second edition, Cambridge University Press; (1996)

Journals

  • MacCorquodale, K.: On Chomsky´s Review of Skinner´s verbal Behavior. Journal of experimental analysis of behaviour. (1970) Nr.1 Chap. 13, p.83-99,
  • Stemmer, N: Skinner's verbal behaviour, Chomsky's review, and mentalism. Journal of experimental analysis of behaviour. (1990) Nr.3 Chap. 54 , p.307-315

live version • discussion • edit lesson • comment • report an error

10 NEUROSCIENCE OF COMPREHENSION

live version • discussion • edit lesson • comment • report an error

Introduction

What is happening inside my head when I listen to a sentence? How do I *process* written words? Our brain is not a black box any more - in this chapter, we will take a closer look at processes of the brain concerned with language comprehension. Dealing with natural language understanding, we distinguish between the neuroscientific and the psycholinguistic approach. As text understanding spreads through the broad field of cognitive psychology, linguistics, and neurosciences, our main focus will lay on the intersection of two latter, which is known as neurolinguistics.

Different brain areas need to be examined in order to find out how words and sentences are being processed. Since there are only limited possibilities of acquiring knowledge about brain states under natural conditions, we are restricted to draw conclusions from certain brain lesions to the functions of corresponding brain areas.

Hence, much research is done on those brain lesions that cause speech processing deficiencies (aphasiae). One of the most famous examples is Broca's aphasia, which is caused by a lesion of the frontal brain region. A typical symptom is telegraphese speech without grammar, while speech understanding is mainly unaffected. In contrast, persons suffering from Wernickes aphasia, an also well-known disruption of a more posterior brain region, speak very fluently, using neologisms (building of new words not belonging to the language) as well as phonematic and semantic paraphrasiae (substitution of a phoneme of the word by another one) but have a heavily impaired language understanding.

To examine these brain lesions, techniques for brain imaging and ERP-measurement have been established during the last 40 years. These devices contribute to the acquired data more and more adequate: The possibly best established brain imaging technique is the so called PET (positron emission tomography) scan, which was introduced in the 1970s. It maps the bloodflow in brain areas of interest onto colored "brain-activity-pictures" by measuring the activity of a radioactive tracer injected into the living person's blood. An analogous principle we find at fMRI-scans (functional magnetic resonance imaging). This (newer) method of brain imaging works without the use of radioactivity and is therefore non-intrusive and less injurious. Therefore it can be applied on a patient repetitivley as it might be needed for follow up studies. This technique works with the blood's substances responding to magnetic fields. EEG (Electroencephalography) records the electrical activity in the brain by placing electrodes on the scalp. Unlike PET and fMRI, it does not produce images, but istead waves which precisely show the size of activity for a given stimuli.

Scientific studies on these phenomena are generally divided into research on *auditory* and *visual language comprehension*; we will discuss both and have a glance at their differences and similarities. And not to forget is that it is not enough to examine English: To understand language processing in general, we have to look at non-Indoeuropean and other language systems like sign language also.

Today there are several theories about the roles of different brain domains in language understanding. For there is still a lot to do in this exciting field of current research.

Lateralization of language

Lateralization of language has frequently been ascribed to a specific side of the brain. There is a lot of evidence that each brain hemisphere has its own distinct functions. Most often, the right hemisphere is referred to as the non-dominant hemisphere and the left is seen as the dominant hemisphere. This has lead to the assumption that the right side of the brain may only be important for receiving sensory information from the left side and for controlling motor movement of the left half of the body. Yet, though it appears that it does not possess many language abilities, but is rather necessary for spatial tasks and non-verbal processing, this does not mean that both brain halves do not work together, in order to achieve maximal function. On the contrary, if interhemispheric transport is not hindered in some way or another, both halves can effectively interact with one another.

Anatomical differences between left and right hemisphere

Initially we will consider the most apparent part of a differentiation between left and right hemisphere: Their differences in shape and structure. As visible to the naked eye there exists a clear asymmetry between the two halves of the human brain: The right hemisphere typically has a bigger, wider and farther extended frontal region than the left hemisphere, whereas the left hemisphere is bigger, wider and extends farther in it's occipital (backward) region (M. T. Banich,"Neuropsychology", ch.3, pg.92). Significantly larger on the left side in most human brains is a certain part of the temporal lobe's surface, which is called the planum temporale. It is localized near Wernicke's area and other auditory association areas, wherefore we can already speculate that the left hemisphere might be stronger involved in processes of language and speech treatment. In fact such a leftlaterality of language functions is evident in 97% of the population (D. Purves, „Neuroscience", ch.26, pg.649). But actually the percentage of human brains, in which a „left-dominance" of the planum temporale is traceable, is only 67% (D. Purves, „Neuroscience", ch.26, pg.648). Which other factors play a role here, and lead to this high amount of human brains in which language is lateralized, is simply not clear.

Functional asymmetry

A rarely performed but popular surgical method to reduce the frequency of epileptic seizures in hard cases of epilepsy is the so called corpus callosotomy. Here a radical cut through the connecting „communication bridge" between right and left hemisphere, the corpus callosum, is done; the result is a „split-brain". For patients whose corpus callosum is cut, the risk of accidental physical injury is mitigated, but the side-effect is striking: Due to this eradicative transection of left and right half, these two are not longer able to communicate adequately. They function for their owns, separated and disjoined. This situation provides the opportunity to study the functionality of the two hemispheres independently. First experiments with split-brain patients were performed by Roger Sperry and his colleagues at the California Institute of Technology in 1960 and 1970 (D. Purves, „Neuroscience", ch.26, pg.646). They lead researchers to sweeping conclusions about laterality of speech and the organization of the human brain in general.

In split-brain experiments it is typically made use of the laterality of the visual system: A visual stimulus, located within the left visual field, projects onto the nasal (inner) part of the left eye's retina and onto the temporal (outer) part of the right eye's retina. As images on the temporal retinal region are to be processed in the visual cortex of the same side of the brain (ipsilateral), whereas nasal retinal information is mapped onto the opposite half of the brain (contralateral), the stimulus within the left visual field will completely arrive in the right visual cortex to be processed and worked up. In „healthy" brains this information furthermore attains the left hemisphere via the corpus callosum and can be integrated there. In split-brain patient's brains this current of signals is interrupted; the stimulus remains „invisible" for the left hemisphere.

Now in such an experiment a visual stimulus is often produced for only one half of the brain (that is, within one –the opposite- half of the visual field), while the participant is instructed to name the seen object, and to blindly pick it out of an amount of concrete objects with the contralateral hand. It can be shown that a picture, for example the drawing of a die, which was only been presented to the left hemisphere, can be namend by the participant („I saw a die"), but is not selectable with the right hand (no idea which object to choose from the table). Contrarily the participant is unable to name the die, if it was seen by the right hemisphere, but easily picks it out of the heap of objects on the table with the help of the left hand.

These outcomes are clear evidence of the human brain's functional asymmetry. The left hemisphere seems to dominate functions of speech and language processing, but is unable to handle spatial tasks like vision-independent object recognition. The right hemisphere seems to dominate spatial functions, but is unable to process words and meaning. In a second experiment it can be shown that a split-brain patient can only follow a written command (like „get up now!"), if it is presented to the left hemisphere. The right hemisphere can only „understand" pictorial instructions. The following table (D. Purves, „Neuroscience", ch.26, pg.647) gives a distinction of functions:

Left Hemisphere	Right Hemisphere

• analysis of right visual field
• language processing
   • writing
   • speech
	• analysis of left visual field
	• spatial tasks
	• visuospatial tasks
	• object and face recognition

It is important to keep in mind that these distinctions comprise only functional dominances, no exclusive competences. In cases of unilateral braindamage, often one half of the brain takes over tasks of the other one; full effectiveness of the two hemispheres is only reached during constructive interaction of both. So, it would be a fallacy to conclude the right hemisphere to have completely no influence on speech and language processing. One of the next sections will go into this point.

Cognitive functioning is most often ascribed to the right hemisphere of the brain. When damage is done to the this part of the brain or when temporal regions of the right hemisphere are removed, this can lead to cognitive-communication problems, such as impaired memory, attention problems, and poor reasoning (L. Cherney, 2001). Investigations lead to the conclusion that the right hemisphere processes information in a gestalt and holistic fashion, with a special emphasis on spatial relationships. Here, an advantage arises for differentiating two distinct faces because it examines things in a global manner and it also reacts to lower spatial, and also auditory, frequency. The former point can be undermined with the fact that the right hemisphere is capable of reading most concrete words and can make simple grammatical comparisons (M. T. Banich,"Neuropsychology", ch.3, pg.97). But in order to function in such a way, there must be some sort of communication between the brain halves. Since 1990, research suggests that the hemispheres do not have a single way of interacting with each other but can do so in a variety of ways. The corpus callosum, as well as some subcortical comissures serve for interhemispheric transfer. Both can simultaneously contribute to performance, since they use complement roles in processing.

Handedness

An important issue, when exploring the different brain organization, is handedness, which is the tendency to use the left or the right hand to perform activities. Throughout history, left-handers, which only comprise about 10% of the population, have often been considered being something abnormal. They were said to be evil, stubborn, defiant and were, even until the mid 20th century, forced to write with their right hand. An example that shows their initial position in society is the latin word sinistra, which means left, as well as unlucky, or an indian tradition, where the left hand is reserved for bathroom functions (M.T.Banich, "Neuropsychology", ch.3, pg. 117). There are many negative connotations associated with the phrase "being left-handed", e.g. being clumsy, awkward, insincere, malicious, etc.

One most commonly accepted idea, as to how handedness affects the hemispheres, is the brain hemisphere division of labor. Since both speaking and handiwork require fine motor skills, its presumption is that it would be more efficient to have one brain hemisphere do both, rather than having it divided up. Since in most people, the left side of the brain controls speaking, right-handedness predominates. The theory also predicts that left-handed people have a reversed brain division of labor.

In right handers, verbal processing is mostly done in the left hemisphere, whereas visuospatial processing is mostly done in the opposite hemisphere. Therefore, 95% of speech output is controlled by the left brain hemisphere, whereas only 5% of individuals control speech output in their right hemisphere. Left-handers, on the other hand, have a heterogeneous brain organization. Their brain hemisphere is either organzied in the same way as right handers, the opposite way, or even such that both hemispheres are used for verbal processing. But usually, in 70% of the cases, speech is controlled by the left-hemisphere, 15% by the right and 15% by either hemisphere. When the average is taken across all types of left-handedness, it appears that left-handers are less lateralized.

After, for example, damage occurs to the left hemisphere, it follows that there is a visuospatial deficit, which is usually more severe in left-handers than in right-handers. Dissimilarities may derive, in part, from differences in brain morphology, which concludes from asymmetries in the planum temporale. Still, it can be assumed that left-handers have less division of labor between their two hemispheres than right-handers do and are more likely to lack neuroanatomical asymmetries (M.T.Banich, "Neuropsychology", ch.3, pg. 123).

There have been many theories as to find out why people are left-handed and what its consequences may be. Some people say that left-handers have a shorter life span or higher accident rates or autoimmune disorders. According to the theory of Geschwind and Galaburda, there is a relation to sex hormones, the immune system, and profiles of cognitive abilities that determine, whether a person is left-handed or not. Concludingly, many genetic models have been proposed, yet the causes and consequences still remain a mystery (M.T.Banich, "Neuropsychology", ch.3, pg. 119).

Auditory Language Processing

Broca   Wernicke

For understanding how language is organized neurologically and what its fundamental components are, brain lesions, namely aphasiae, are examined. We will first consider the neurological perspective of work with aphasia and then turn to the psychological perspective later on in the chapter.

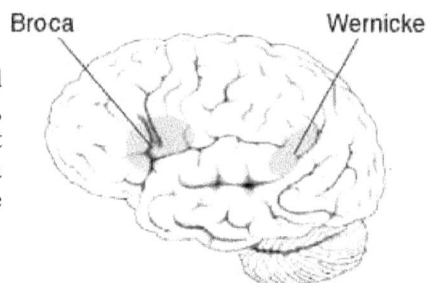

Broca's and Wernicke's area

Neurological Perspective

One of the most well-known aphasiae is **Broca`s aphasia**, that causes patients to be unable to speak fluently, but rather have a great difficulty producing words. Comprehension, however, is relatively intact in those patients. Because these symptoms do not result from motoric problems of the vocal musculature, a region in the brain that is responsible for linguistic output must be lesioned. Broca found out that the brain region causing fluent speech is responsible for linguistic output, must be located ventrally in the frontal lobe, anterior to the motor strip. Recent research suggested that Broca`s aphasia results also from subcortical tissue and white matter and not only cortical tissue.

Another very famous aphasia, known as **Wernicke`s aphasia**, causes the opposite syndromes as described above. Patients suffering from Wernicke`s aphasia usually speak very fluently, words are pronounced correctly, but they are combined senselessly – "word salad" is the way it is most often described. Understanding what patients of Wernicke`s aphasia say is especially difficult, because they use *paraphasiae* (subsitution of a word in verbal paraphasia, of word with similar meaning in semantic paraphasia, and of a phoneme phonemic paraphasia) and neologisms.With Wernicke`s aphasia comprehending simple sentences is a very difficult task. Thus their ability to process auditory language input but also written language is impaired. Concluding from this, one can say that the area that causes Wernicke`s aphasia, is situated at the joint of temporal, parietal and occipital regions, near *Heschl`s gyrus* (primary auditory area), because all the areas receiving and interpreting sensory information (posterior cortex), and those connecting the sensory information to meaning (parietal lobe) are likely to be involved.

Wernicke did not only detect the brain region responsible for comprehension, but also concluded that with an impairment of the brain region betwenn Wernicke`s and Broca`s area, speech could still be comprehended and produced, but repeating just heard sentences could not be possible, because the input received could not be conducted forwarded to Broca`s area to be reproduced. Thus the damage in this part of the brain is called **conduction aphasia**. Research has shown that damage to a large never fibre tract, the *arcuate fasciculus*, the connection between the two intact brain regions, causes this kind of aphasia. That is why conduction aphasia is also regarded as a *disconnection syndrome* (behavioural dysfunction because of a damage to the connection of two connected brain regions).

Transcortical motor aphasia, another brain lesion caused by a connection disruption, is very similar to Broca`s aphasia, with the difference that the ability to repeat is kept. In fact people with a transcortical motor aphasia often suffer from echolalia, the need to repeat what they just heard. Usually patients` brain is damaged outside Broca`s area, sometimes more anterior and sometimes more superior. Individuals with **transcortical sensory aphasia** have similar symptoms are those suffering from Wernicke`s aphasia, except that they show signs of echolalia.

Lesions in great parts of the left hemisphere lead to **global aphasia**, and thus to an inability of both comprehending and producing language, because not only Broca`s or Wenicke`s area is damaged. (Barnich, 1997, pp.276-282)

Type of Aphasia	Spontaneous Speech	Paraphasia	Comprehension	Repetition	Naming
• Broca`s   • Wernicke`s • Conduction • Transcortical motor • Transcortical sensory • Global	• Nonfluent • Fluent • Fluent • Nonfluent • Fluent • Nonfluent	• Uncommon • Common (verbal) • Common (literal) • Uncommon • Common • Variable	• Good • Poor • Good • Good • Poor • Poor	• Poor • Poor • Poor • Good (echolalia) • Good (echolalia) • Poor	• Poor • Poor • Poor • Poor • Poor • Poor

(Adapted from Benson, 1985,p.32 as cited in Barnich, 1997, p.287)

Psychological Perspective

Examining from the psychological perspective, brain lesions are used to understand which parts of the brain play roles for the linguistic features phonology, syntax and semantics.

Phonology

Examining which parts are responsible for phonetic representation, patients with Broca`s or Wernicke`s aphasia can be compared. As the speech characteristic for patients with Broca`s aphasia is non-fluent, i.e. they have problems prodcuing the correct phonetic and phonemic representation of a sound, and people with Wernicke`s aphasia do not show any problems speaking fluently, but also have problems producing the right phoneme. This indicates that Broca`s area is mainly involved in phonological production and also, that phonemic and phonetic representation do not take place in the same part of the brain. Scientists examined on a more precise level of speech production, on the level of the distinctive features of phonemes, to see in which features patients with aphasia made mistakes. Results show that in fluent as well as in non-fluent aphasia patients usually mix up only one distinctive feature, not two. In general it can be said that errors connected to the place of articulation are more common than those linked to voicing. Interestingly some aphasia patients are well aware of the different features of two Phoneme phonemes, yet they are unable to produce the right sound. This suggests that though patients have great difficulty pronouncing words correctly, their comprehension of words is still quite good. This is characteristic for patients with Broca`s aphasia, while those with Wernicke`s aphasia show contrary symptoms: they are able to pronounce words correctly, but cannot understand what the words mean. That is why they often utter phonologically correct words (neologisms), that are not real words with a meaning.

Syntax

Humans in general usually know the syntax of their mother tongue and thus slip their tongue if a word happens to be out of order in a sentence. People with aphasia, however, often have problems with parsing of sentences, not only with respect to the production of language but also with respect to comprehension of sentences. Patiens showing an inability of comprehension and production of sentences usually have some kind of anterior aphasia, also called **agrammatical aphasia**. This can be revealed in tests with sentences, these patients cannot distinguish between active and passive voice easily if both agent and object could play an active part. For example patients do not see a difference between "The boy saw the girl" and "The girl was seen by the boy", but they do understand both "The boy saw the apple" and "The apple was seen by the boy", because they can seek help of semantics and do not have to rely on syntax alone. Patients with posterior aphasia, like for example Wernicke's aphasia, do not show these symptoms, as their speech is fluent. Comprehension by mere syntactic means would be possible as well, but the semantic aspect must be considered as well.

Semantics

It has been shown that patients suffering from posterior aphasia have severe problems understanding simple texts, although their knowledge of syntax is intact. The semantic shortcoming is often examined by a Token Test, a test in which patients have to point to objects referred to in simple sentences. As might have been guessed, people with anterior aphasia have no problems with semantics, yet they might not be able to understand longer sentences because the knowledge of syntax then is involved as well.

In general studies with lesioned people have shown that anterior areas are needed for speech output and posterior regions for speech comprehension. As mentioned above anterior regions are also more important for syntactic processing, while posterior regions are involved in semantic processing. But such a strict division of the parts of the brain and their responsibilities is not possible, because posterior regions must be important for more than just sentence comprehension, as patients with lesions in this area can neither comprehend nor produce any speech. On the whole these studies have revealed that the human brain is divided into two subsystems, one more important for comprehension, the other for production.(Barnich,1997, pp.283-293)

Visual Language Processing

The question whether there is one processing unit in the brain for language as a whole is mostly answered by "no". Reading and writing respectively rely on vision whereas spoken language is first mediated by the auditory system. Language systems responsible for written language processing have to interact with a sensory system different from the one involved in spoken language processing.

Visual language processing in general begins when the visual forms of letters ("c" or "C" or "c") are mapped onto abstract letter identities. These are then mapped onto a word form and the corresponding semantic representation (the "meaning" of the word, i.e. the concept behind it). Observations of patients that lost a language ability due to a brain damage led to different disease patterns that indicated a difference between perception (reading) and production (writing) of visual language just like it is found in non-visual language processing.

Alexic patients possess the ability to write while not being able to read whereas patients with agraphia are able to read but cannot write. Though alexia and agraphia often occur together as a result of damage to the angular gyrus, there were patients found having alexia without agraphia (e.g.

Greenblatt 1973, as cited in M. T. Banich,"Neuropsychology", p. 296) or having agraphia without alexia (e.g. Hécaen & Kremin, 1976, as cited in M. T. Banich,"Neuropsychology", p.296). This is a double dissociation that suggests separate neural control systems for reading and writing.

But even language production and perception respectively are thought to subdivide into separate neural circuits, since double dissociations found in phonological and surface dyslexia suggest so called direct and phonological routes.

The phonological route

In essence, the phonological route means making use of grapheme-to-phoneme rules. Grapheme-to-phoneme rules are a way of determining the phonological representation for a given grapheme. A grapheme is the smallest written unit of a word (e.g. "sh" in "shore") that represents a phoneme. A phoneme on the other hand is the smallest phonological unit of a word distinguishing it from another word that otherwise sounds the same (e.g. "bat" and "cat"). People learning to read often use the phonological route to arrive at a meaning representation. They construct phonemes for each grapheme and then combine the individual phonemes to a sound pattern that is associated with a certain meaning. An example would be:

```
         h a t →    /h/ / a / /t/              → "hat"
  individual graphemes → phonological representation → meaning representation
```

The direct route

The direct route is supposed to work without an intermediary phonological representation, so that print is directly associated with word-meaning. A situation in which the direct route has to be taken is when reading an irregular word like "colonel". Application of grapheme-to-phoneme rules would lead to an incorrect phonological representation.

According to Taft (1982, as referred to in M. T. Banich,"Neuropsychology", p.297) and others, the phonological route is used by people who are learning to read or by skilled readers when encountering unknown words. The direct route is supposed to be faster since it does not make use of a "phonological detour" and is therefore said to be used for known words. However, this is just one point of view and others, like Chastain (1987, as referred to in M. T. Banich,"Neuropsychology", p.297), postulate a reliance on the phonological route even in skilled readers.

The processing of written language in reading

Several kinds of alexia could be differentiated, often depending on whether the phonological or the direct route was impaired. Patients with brain lesions participated in experiments where they had to read out words and non-words as well as irregular words. Reading of non-words for example requires access to the phonological route since there cannot be a "stored" meaning or a sound representation for this combination of letters.

Patients with a lesion in temporal structures of the left hemisphere (the exact location varies) suffer from so called surface alexia. They show the following characteristic symptoms that suggest a strong reliance on the phonological route: Very common are regularity effects, that is a mispronunciation of words in which the spelling is irregular like "colonel" or "yacht". These words are pronounced according to grapheme-to-phoneme rules, although high-frequency irregularly spelled words may be preserved in some cases. Furthermore, the would-be pronunciation of a word is reflected in reading-comprehension errors. When asked to describe the meaning of the word "bear", people suffering from surface alexia would answer something like "a beverage" because the resulting sound pattern of "bear" was the same for these people as that for "beer". This characteristic goes along with a tendency to confuse homophones (words that sound the same but are spelled differently and have different meanings associated). However, these people are still able to read non-words with a regular spelling since they can apply grapheme-to-phoneme rules to them.

In contrast, phonological alexia is characterised by a disruption in the phonological route due to lesions in more posterior temporal structures of the left hemisphere. Patients can read familiar regular and irregular words by making use of stored information about the meaning associated with that particular visual form (so there is no regularity effect like in surface alexia). However, they are unable to process unknown words or non-words. Word class effects and morphological errors are common. Nouns, for example, are read better than function words and sometimes even better than verbs. Affixes which do not change the grammatical class or meaning of a word (inflectional affixes) are often substituted (e.g. "farmer" instead of "farming"). Furthermore, concrete words are read with a lower error rate than abstract ones like "freedom" (concreteness effect).

Deep Alexia shares many symptomatic features with phonological alexia such as an inability to read out non-words. Just as in phonological alexia, patients make mistakes on word inflections as well as function words and show visually based errors on abstract words ("desire" → "desert"). In addition to that, people with deep alexia misread words as different words with a strongly related meaning ("woods" instead of "forest"), a phenomenon referred to as semantic paralexia. Coltheart (as referred to in the "Handbook of Neurolinguistics",ch.41-3, p.563) postulates that reading in deep dyslexia is mediated by the right hemisphere. He suggests that when large lesions affecting language abilities other than reading prevent access to the left hemisphere, the right-hemispheric language store is used. Lexical entries stored there are accessed and used as input to left-hemisphere output systems.

The processing of written language in spelling

Just like in reading, two separate routes –a phonological and a direct route- are thought to exist. The phonological route is supposed to make use of phoneme-to-grapheme rules while the direct route links thought to writing without an intermediary phonetic representation. It should be noted here that there is a difference between phoneme-to-grapheme rules (used for spelling) and grapheme-to-phoneme rules in that one is not simply the reverse of the other. In case of the grapheme "k" the most common phoneme for it is /k/. The most common grapheme for the phoneme /k/, however, is "c".

Phonological agraphia is caused by a lesion in the left supramarginal gyrus, which is located in the parietal lobe above the posterior section of the Sylvian fissure (M. T. Banich,"Neuropsychology",p.299). The ability to write regular and irregular words is preserved while the ability to write non-words is not. This, together with a poor retrieval of affixes (which are not stored lexically), indicates an inability to associate spoken words with their orthographic form via phoneme-to-grapheme rules. Patients rely on the direct route, which means that they use orthographic word-form representations that are stored in lexical memory

Lesions at the conjunction of the posterior parietal lobe and the parieto-occipital junction cause so called lexical agraphia that is sometimes also referred to as surface agraphia. As the name already indicates, it parallels surface alexia in that patients have difficulty to access lexical-orthographic representations of words. Lexical agraphia is characterised by a poor spelling of irregular words but good spelling for regular and non-words. When asked to spell irregular words, patients often commit regularization errors, so that the word is spelled phonologically correct (for example, "whisk" would be written as "wisque").

Evidence from Advanced Neuroscience Methods

In the past, most of the data in neurolinguistic experiments came from patients with brain lesions that caused disabling of particular linguistic functions. By evaluating which damage caused what kind of dysfunction, researchers could sketch a map of the different brain regions involved in language processing.

Measuring the functions of both normal and damaged brains has been possible since the 1970s, when the first brain imaging techniques were developed. With them, we are able to "watch the brain working" while the subject is e.g. listening to a joke. These methods (further described in chapter 4) show whether the earlier findings are correct and, when they are, how precise. Today, language can be localised better than ever.

Generally, imaging shows that certain functional brain regions are much smaller than estimated in brain lesion studies, and that their boundaries are more distinct (cf. Banich p.294). The exact location varies individually, therefore bringing the results of many brain lesion studies together caused too big estimated functional regions before. For example, stimulating brain tissue electrically (during epilepsy surgery) and observing the outcome (e.g. errors in naming tasks) led to a much better knowledge where language processing areas are located.

Left hemisphere dominance

The first thing to examine was the suspected dominance of the left hemisphere in auditory language processing. (The differences in visual processing are considered below.) From electric stimulation studies and PET studies like described above and in chapter 4, there was a lot of evidence for such a dominance: In right-handers, language functions were normally lateralized. The so-called Wada technique tests which hemisphere is responsible for speech output.

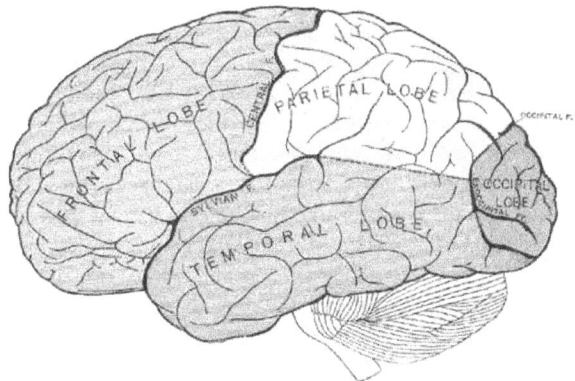

A view of the left hemisphere, green: temporal lobe; blue: frontal lobe; yellow: parietal lobe; red: occipital lobe

it is usually used in epilepsy patients during surgery. It is not a brain imaging technique, but simulates a brain lesion. One of the hemispheres is anesthetized by injecting a barbiturate (sodium amobarbital) in one of the patient's carotid arteries. Then he is asked to name a number of items on cards. When he is not able to do that, despite the fact that he could do it an hour earlier, the concerned hemisphere is the one responsible for speech output. This test must be done twice, for there is a chance that the patient produces speech bilaterally. The probability for that is not very high, in fact, according to Rasmussen & Milner 1997a (as referred to in Banich, p.293) it occurs only in 15 % of the left-handers and none of the right-handers. (It is still unclear where these differences in left-handers' brains come from.)

That means that in most people, only one hemisphere "produces" speech output – and in 96% of right-handers and 70% of left-handers, it is the left one. The findings of the brain lesion studies about assymmetry were confirmed here: Normally (in healthy right-handers), the left hemisphere controls speech output.

Besides left-handers, brain imaging techniques have shown that other examples of bilateral language processing: According to ERP studies (by Bellugi et al. 1994 and Neville et al. 1993 as cited in E. Dabrowska, "Language, Mind an Brain" 2004, p.57), people with the Williams' syndrome (WS) also have no dominant hemisphere for language. WS patients have a lot of physical and mental disorders, but show, compared to their other (poor) cognitive abilities, very good linguistic skills. And these skills do not rely on one dominant, but both hemispheres contribute equally. So, the majority of the population has a dominant left hemisphere for language processing. But what does it mean that in some individuals' brains there are other ways to do that? That there are different "organisation possibilities" in our brains? Dabrowska (p.57) suggests that the organisational structure in the brain could be less innate and fixed as it is commonly thought.

Different roles of posterior and anterior regions

In the left hemisphere, both anterior ("face side") and posterior ("back side" of the head) regions contribute to language processing and are strongly connected. For example, Broca's area is located more anterior and Wernicke's area more posterior. It is often generally said that the difference is speech production (Broca) versus language comprehension (Wernicke). PET studies (Fiez & Petersen, 1993, as cited in Banich, p.295) have shown that in fact both anterior and posterior regions were activated in both tasks, but with different strengths – in agreement with the lesion studies. The more active speech production is reqired in experiments, the more frontal is the main activation: For example, when the presented words must be repeated.

Another result (Raichle et al. 1994, as referred to in Banich, p.295) was that the familiarity of the stimuly plays a big role. When the subjects were presented well-known stimuli sets in well-known experimental tasks and had to repeat them, anterior regions were activated. Those regions were known to cause conduction apahsia when damaged. But when the words were new ones, and/or the subjects never had to do a task like this before, the activation was recorded more posterior. That means, when you repeat an unexpected word, the heaviest working brain tissue is about somewhere under your upper left earlap, but when you knew before this word would be the next to repeat, it is a bit nearer to your left eye.

Visual versus Auditory Language Processing

As indicated by the fact that the responsible damages for aphasiae are located in other brain regions than damages causing agraphia, these different types of language comprehension do not take place in the same regions. Reading, no matter if it is words or nonsense syllables, activates an area at the backward border of the

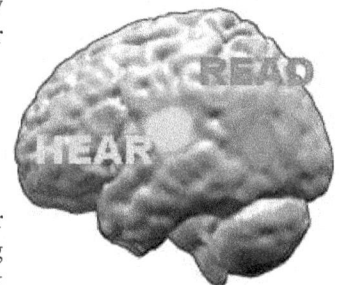

Main activation areas: Hearing and Reading

temporal lobe, that is somewhat backwards of the earlap. Hearing a word or thinking about how a written word sounds takes place at the upper border of the left temporal lobe, under the part of the skull that is located above the ear (Petersen et al. 1988, as cited in Banich, p. 300). That matches with the findings of the lesion studies described above.

When we look at visual language processing, many findings of PET-studies (Banich, p. 301) suggest that the right hemisphere first recognizes a written word as letter sequences, no matter how exactly they look like. Then the language network in the left hemisphere builds up an abstract representation of the word, not dependent on the visual form - e.g. case or whether it is handwriting or bold. In reading, the brain regions for recognizing symbols and the language areas work together hand in hand.

Beyond words

On the word level, the current studies are mostly consistent with each other and with findings from brain lesion studies. But when it comes to the more complex understanding of whole sentences, texts and storylines, the findings are split. According to E. C. Ferstl's review "The Neuroanatomy of Text Comprehension. What's the story so far?" (2004), there is evidence for and against right hemisphere regions playing the key role in pragmatics and text comprehension. On the current state of knowledge, we cannot exactly say how and where cognitive functions like building situation models and inferencing (see next chapter) work together with "pure" language processes.

Researchers hope to find out many more facts about the functional neuroanatomy of language with those neuroimaging methods. Their goal is to verify disprove psychological thories about comprehension. Many questions are to be answered, for it is e.g. still unclear wether there is a distinct language module (that you could cut out without causing anything in other brain functions) or not. As Evely C. Ferstl points out in her review, the next step after exploring distinct small regions responsible for subtasks of language processing will be to find out how they work together and build up the language network.

Findings from other language systems

Most neurolinguistic research is for obvious reasons concerned with production and comprehension of english language, either written or spoken. Currently there is a clear focus on investigating how the meaning of single words is being processed and less on sentence meaning. However looking at different language systems from a neuroscientific perspective can substantiate as well as differentiate acknowledged theories of language processing.

English, as well as all other indo-european languages, is a alphabetic (phonological) system: Each symbol represents one phoneme, either a consonant or a vowel. Other systems include

- logographic systems, where a symbol represents a whole morpheme (such as hieroglyphs and Chinese hanzi)
- syllabic systems, such as Japanese kana
- Abjad, in which only consonants are represented, such as Arabic or Hebrew

Sign language

A very special case among phonological systems are sign languages, which as we will see share many features of 'spoken' phonological language systems from a linguistic perspective but still differ in some ways from a neuroscientific point of view and are hence worth some consideration.

Contrary to popular belief, there is no universal sign language but many regionally bound languages with each a distinct grammar and lexicon. As said before, sign languages are phonological languages in a way that every meaningful sign is made of several phonemes (which used to be called cheremes (Greek χερι: Hand) in sign language until it's cognitive equivalence to phonemes in spoken languages was realized) that carry no meaning as such. A symbol in turn consists of five distinct features:

- Handshape
- Palm orientation
- Place of articulation
- Movement
- Non-manual markers (such as facial expressions)

Sign language grammar

Some neuroscientifically relevant principles of most sign language's grammars (including American Sign Language (ASL), Deutsche Gebärdensprache (DGS) and several other major sign languages) are:

Rich morphosyntactical properties
Elaboration of the manner of actions or the properties of objects that would lead to the introduction of many additional words to the discourse in spoken languages can be expressed within the base word by different movements or non-manual markers, e.g. "The flight was long and I did not enjoy it" is the single sign for "flight" with the past tense marker, moved in a way that represents the attribute "long" combined with the facial expression of disaffection. To that respect sign language is closer to Japanese language than to indo-european ones.

Setting up of nouns
Once signed, nouns can be 'linked' to a point in space, e.g. by pointing beneath one's head. Later in discourse the nouns can be retrieved from there by pointing to that spot again. This is functionally related to pronouns in English.

Chronologically sequenced ordering
Whereas English can order events amongst other structures by e.g. inverted causal dependence ("I was surprised *because* there was a reasonable amount of money on my bank account *although* I haven't been paid for weeks"), sign language speakers usually sign events in the order that they occurred (or sometimes in the order in which they found out about them).

Neuropsychological research of sign language

We have seen that sign languages are independent from and fully developed to the extend of spoken languages, we will compare cerebral processes in speaker's of both. Studies from aphasic patients have shown that damage to anterior portions of the left hemisphere (e.g. Broca's aphasia) result in a loss of fluency and the disability of the patients to correctly use syntactic markers, inflection of verbs and other minor features, although the words signed are chosen semantically correct. In turn, patients with damages to posterior portions could still properly inflect verbs and set up and retrieve nouns from a discourse locus, but their sequences of signs have no meaning (Poizner, Klima & Bellugi, 1987). These findings show that the same underlying processes are responsible for production of sign language and spoken language - or in other words that the brain regions dealing mainly with langue are in no way restricted to spoken language, but may well be able to process any type of language system, as long as it underlies some syntax and semantics (a finding that may serve as evidence to a Universal Grammar as postulated by (Chomsky, 1965)).

Studies using brain imaging techniques such as fMRI proved these results from studies on aphasic subjects by comparing activation patterns of speakers and signers: Typical areas in the left hemisphere are activated for both native Rnglish speakers given written stimuli and native signers given signs as stimuli. However signers also show strong activation of right hemisphere. This is partly due to the necessity to process visually perceived spatial information (such as making the perceived signals indifferent to the angle of perception or individual physical attributes of the signer). However some of those areas, like the angular gyrus, are only activated in native singers - not in hearing subjects that learned ASL after puberty. This suggests that the way of learning sign languages (and languages in general) changes with puberty: Late learner's brains are unable to recruit brain regions specialised for processing this language (Newman et al., 1998).

References & Further Reading

Books - English

- Brigitte Stemmer, Harry A. Whitaker. Handbook of Neurolinguistics. Academic Press (1998). ISBN 0126660557
- Marie T. Banich: Neuropsychology. The neural bases of mental function (1997).
- Ewa Dąbrowska: Language, Mind and Brain. Edinburgh University press Ltd.(2004)
- *a review:* Evelyn C. Ferstl, The functional neuroanatomy of text comprehension. What's the story so far?" from: Schmalhofer, F. & Perfetti, C. A. (Eds.), Higher Level Language Processes in the Brain:Inference and Comprehension Processes. Lawrence Erlbaum. (2004)

Books - German

- Müller,H.M.& Rickert,G. (Hrsg.): Neurokognition der Sprache. Stauffenberg Verlag (2003)
- Poizner, Klima & Bellugi: What the hands reveal about the brain. MIT Press (1987)
- N. Chomsky: Aspects of the Theory of Syntax. MIT Press (1965). ISBN 0262530074
- Neville & Bavelier: Variability in the effects of experience on the development of cerebral specializations: Insights from the study of deaf individuals. Washington, D.C.: US Government Printing Office (1998)
- Newman et al.: Effects of Age of Acquisition on Cortical Organization for American Sign Language: an fMRI Study. NeuroImage, 7(4), part 2 (1998)

Links - English

- Robert A. Mason and Marcel Adam Just: How the Brain Processes Causal Inferences in

Text
- Neal J. Pearlmutter and Aurora Alma Mendelsohn: Serial versus Parallel Sentence Comprehension
- Brain Processes of Relating a Statement to a Previously Read Text: Memory Resonance and Situational Constructions
- Clahsen, Harald: Lexical Entries and Rules of Language: A Multidisciplinary Study of German Inflection.
- Cherney, Leora (2001): Right Hemisphere Brain Damage
- Grodzinsky, Yosef (2000): The neurology of syntax: Language use without Broca's area.
- Müller, H.M. & Kutas, M. (1996). What's in a name? Electrophysiological differences between spoken nouns, proper names and one's own name.NeuroReport 8:221-225.
- Müller, H. M., King, J. W. & Kutas, M. (1997). Event-related potentials elicited by spoken relative clausesCognitive Brain Research 4:193-203.

Links - German

- University of Bielefeld:
  - Müller, H. M., Weiss, S. & Rickheit, G. (1997). Experimentelle Neurolinguistik: Der Zusammenhang von Sprache und GehirnIn: Bielefelder Linguistik (Hrsg.) Aisthesis-Verlag, pp. 125-128.
- Müller, H.M. & Kutas, M. (1997). Die Verarbeitung von Eigennamen und Gattungsbezeichnungen: Eine elektrophysiologische Studie. In: G. Rickheit (Hrsg.). Studien zur Klinischen Linguistik - Methoden, Modelle, Intervention. Opladen: Westdeutscher Verlag, pp. 147-169.
- Müller, H.M., King, J.W. & Kutas, M. (1998). Elektrophysiologische Analyse der Verarbeitung natürlichsprachlicher Sätze mit unterschiedlicher Belastung des Arbeitsgedächtnisses. Klinische Neurophysiologie 29: 321-330.

- Michael Schecker (1998): Neuronale "Kodierung" zentraler Sprachverarbeitungsprozesse --> Debates (only a criticism)

live version • discussion • edit lesson • comment • report an error

11 SITUATION MODELS AND INFERENCING

live version • discussion • edit lesson • comment • report an error

Introduction

An important function and property of the human cognitive system is the ability to extract important information out of textually and verbally described situations. This ability plays a vital role in understanding and remembering. But what happens to this information after it is extracted, how do we represent it and how do we use it for inferencing?

This chapter aims to introduce you to an answer given to these questions - the Situation Model - which claims: *Information of the state of affairs of some circumscribed world situation in the human mind are represented in a so called situation model* (van Dijk&Kintsch, 1983) *or mental model* (Johnson-Laird, 1983). Without these mental representations of situation we would have to store all the input (e.g. this text) and each time we want to use it's information, go over and over through the whole text.

By assuming situations to be encoded by perceptual symbols (Barsalou, 1999), the theory of Situation Models touches many aspects of Cognitive Philosophy, Linguistics and Artificial Intelligence. In the beginning of this chapter, we will mention why Situation Models are important and what we use them for.

Next we will focus on the theory itself by introducing the four primary types of information - the situation model components (spatial-temporal framework, entities, properties of entities and relational information), its Levels of Representation (situation model, episodic model and comprehensive model) and finally two other basic types of knowledge used in situation model construction and processing (general world knowledge and referent specific knowledge).

Situation models do not only form a central concept in theories of situated cognition that helps us in understanding how situational information is collected and how new information gets inferred, but they can also explain many other phenomena. According to van Dijk&Kintsch situation models are responsible for processes like domain-expertise, translation, learning from multiple sources or completely understanding situations just by reading about them. These situation models consist according to most researches in this area out of five dimensions: time, space, causation, intentionality and persons/objects (Zwaan&Radvansky, 1998). When new information concerning one of these dimensions is extracted the situation model is changed according to the new information. The bigger the change in the situation model is, the more time the reader needs for understanding the situation with the new information. If there are contradictions, f.eg. new informations which do not fit into the model, the reader fails to understand the text and probably reread parts of the text again to build up a better model where this new information fits in or can be connected with. It was shown in several experiments that its easier to understand texts which have only small changes in the five dimensions of text understanding. (see Daniel Morrow 1987 for space, Zwaan 1996 for space and time). It also has been found, that it is easier for readers to understand a text if the important information is more explicitly mentioned. For this reason several researchers wrote about the importance of foregrounding important information (see Zwaan&Radvansky 1998 for a detailed list). These findings and how they influenced our understanding of the Situation Model will be addressed in the third part of this chapter.

The other important issue about situation models is the multidimensionality. Here the important question is how are the different dimensions related and what is their weight for constructing the model. Some researchers claim that the weight of the dimensions shifts according to the situation which is described. Introducing such claims will be the final part of this chapter and aims to introduce you to current and future research goals.

Why do we need situation models?

A lot of tasks which are based on language processing can only be explained by the usage of situation models. The so called situation model or mental model consists of five different dimensions, which refer to different sources. To comprehend a text or just a simple sentence situation models are useful. Further more the comprehension and combination of several texts and sentences can be explained by that theory much better. In the following some examples, are listed why we really need situation models.

Integration of information across sentences

Integration of information across sentences is more than just understanding a set of sentences. For example:

"Gerhard Schroeder is in front of some journalists. Looking forward to new ideas is nothing special for the Ex-German chancellor. It is like in the good old days, in 1971 when the leader of the Jusos was behind the polls and talked about changes."

This example only makes sense to the reader if he is aware of *"Gerhard Schroeder"*, *"Ex-German chancellor"* and *"the leader of the Jusos in 1971"* is one and the same person. If we build up a situation model, in this example *"Gerhard Schroeder"* is our token. Every information which comes up will be linked to this token, based on grammatical and world knowledge. The definite article in the second sentence refers to the individual in the first sentence. This is based on grammatical knowledge. Every definite article indicates a connection to an individual in a previous sentence. If there would be an indefinite article we had to build a new token for a new individual. The third sentence is linked by domain knowledge to the token. It has to be known that "Gerhard Schroeder" was the leader of the Jusos in 1971. Otherwise the connection can only be guessed. We can see that an integrated situation model is needed to comprehend the connection between the three sentences.

Explanation of similarities in comprehension performances across modalities

The explanation of similarities in comprehension performances across modalities can only be done by the usage of situation models. If we read a newspaper article, watch a report on television or listen to a report on radio, we come up with a similar understanding of the same information, which is conveyed through different modalities. Thus we create a mental representation of the information or event. This mental representation does not depend on the modalities itself. Further more there is empirical evidence for this intuition. Baggett (1979) found out that students who saw a short film and students who heard a spoken version of the events in the short film finally produced a structurally similar recall protocol. There were differences in the protocols of the two groups but the differences were due to content aspects. Like the text version explicitly stated that a boy was on his way to school and in the movie this had to be inferred.

Domain expertise on comprehension

Situation models have a deep influence for effects of domain expertise on comprehension. In detail this means that person A, whose verbal skills are less than from person B, is able to outperform person B, if he has got more knowledge of the topic domain. To give evidence for this intuition there was a study by Schneider and Körkel (1989). They compared the recalls of "experts" and novices of a text about a soccer match. In the study were three different grades: 3rd, 5th and 7th. One important example in that experiment was that the 3rd grade soccer experts outperformed the 7th grade novices. The recall of units in the text was 54% by the 3rd grade experts and 42% by the 7th grade novices. The explanation is quite simple: The 3rd grade experts built up a situation model and can use knowledge from their long-term memory (Ericsson & Kintsch, 1995). The 7th grade novices have just the text by which they can come up with a situation model. Some more studies show evidence for the theory that domain expertise may counteract with verbal ability, i.e. Fincher-Kiefer, Post, Greene & Voss, 1988 or Yekovich, Walker, Ogle & Thompson in 1990.

Multiple source learning

People are able to learn about a domain from multiple documents. This phenomenon can be explained by a situation model, too. For example, we try to learn something about the "*Cold War*" we use different documents with information. The information in one document may be similar to other documents. Referents can be the same or special relationships in the "Cold War" just can be figured out by the usage of different documents. So what we are really doing by learning and reasoning is, that we integrate information on the base of different documents into a common situation model, which has got an organized order of the information we've learned.

We have seen that we need situation models in different tasks of language processing, but situation models are not needed in all tasks of language processing. For example proofreading. A proofreader checks every word by its correctness. This ability does not contain the ability to construct situation models. This task uses the resources of the long-term memory in which the correct writing of each word is stored.

This is done word by word. It is unnecessary to create situation models in this task for language processing.

Multidimensionality of Situation Models

Space

Very often, objects that are spatially close to us are more relevant than more distant objects. Therefore, one would expect the same for situation models. consistent with this idea, comprehenders are slower to recognize words denoting objects distant from a protagonist than those denoting objects close to the protagonist (Glenberg, Meyer & Lindem, 1987).

When comprehenders have extensive knowledge of the spatial layout of the setting of the story (e.g., a building), they update their representations according to the location and goals of the protagonist. They have the fastest mental access to the room that the protagonist is currently in or is heading to. For example, they can more readily say whether or not two objects are in the same room if the room mentioned is one of these rooms than if it is some other room in the building (e.g., Morrow, Greenspan, & Bower, 1987). This makes perfect sense intuitively because these are the rooms that would be relevant to us if we were in the situation.

People's interpretation of the meaning of a verb denoting movement of people or objects in space, such as *to approach*, depends on their situation models. For example, comprehenders interpret the meaning of *approach* differently in *The tractor is just approaching the fence* than in *The mouse is just approaching the fence*. Specifically, they interpret the distance between the figure and the landmark as being longer when the figure is large (tractor) compared with when it is small (mouse). The comprehenders' interpretation also depends on the size of the landmark and the speed of the figure (Morrow & Clark, 1988). Apparently, comprehenders behave as if they are actually standing in the situation, looking at the tractor or mouse approaching a fence.

Time

We assume by default that events are narrated in their chronological order, with nothing left out. Presumably this assumption exists because this is how we experience events in everyday life. Events occur to us in a continuous flow, sometimes in close succession, sometimes in parallel, and often partially overlapping. Language allows us to deviate from chronological order, however. For example, we can say, "Before the psychologist submitted the manuscript, the journal changed its policy." The psychologist submitting the manuscript is reported first, even though it was the last of the two events to occur. If people construct a situation model, this sentence should be more difficult to process than its chronological counterpart (the same sentence, but beginning with "After"). Recent neuroscientific evidence supports this prediction. Event-related brain potential (ERP) measurements indicate that "before" sentences elicit, within 300 ms, greater negativity than "after" sentences. This difference in potential is primarily located in the left anterior part of the brain and is indicative of greater cognitive effort (Münte, Schiltz, & Kutas, 1998). In real life, events follow each other seamlessly. However, narratives can have temporal discontinuities, when writers omit events not relevant to the plot. Such temporal gaps, typically signaled by phrases such as *a few days later*, are quite common in narratives. Nonetheless, they present a departure from everyday experience. Therefore, time shifts should lead to (minor) disruptions of the comprehension process. And they do. Reading times for sentences that introduce a time shift tend to be longer than those for sentences that do not (Zwaan, 1996).

All other things being equal, events that happened just recently are more accessible to us than events that happened a while ago. Thus, in a situation model, *enter* should be less accessible after *An hour ago, John entered the building* than after *A moment ago, John entered the building*. Recent probeword recognition experiments support this prediction (e.g., Zwaan, 1996).

Causation

As we interact with the environment, we have a strong tendency to interpret event sequences as causal sequences. It is important to note that, just as we infer the goals of a protagonist, we have to infer causality; we cannot perceive it directly. Singer and his colleagues (e.g., Singer, Halldorson, Lear,

& Andrusiak, 1992) have investigated how readers use their world knowledge to validate causal connections between narrated events. Subjects read sentence pairs, such as 1a and then 1b or 1a' and then 1b, and were subsequently presented with a question like 1c:

(1a) Mark poured the bucket of water on the bonfire.
(1a') Mark placed the bucket of water by the bonfire.
(1b) The bonfire went out.
(1c) Does water extinguish fire?

Subjects were faster in responding to 1c after the sequence 1a-1b than after 1a'-1b. According to Singer, the reason for this is that the knowledge that water extinguishes fire was activated to validate the events described in 1a-1b. However, because this knowledge cannot be used to validate 1a'-1b, it was not activated when subjects read that sentence pair.

Intentionality

We are often able to predict people's future actions by inferring their intentionality, i.e. their goals. For example, when we see a man walking over to a chair, we assume that he wants to sit, especially when he has been standing for a long time. Thus, we might generate the inference "He is going to sit." Keefe and McDaniel (1993) presented subjects with sentences like *After standing through the 3-hr debate, the tired speaker walked over to his chair (and sat down)* and then with probe words (e.g., sat, in this case). Subjects took about the same amount of time to name sat when the clause about the speaker sitting down was omitted and when it was included. Moreover, naming times were significantly faster in both of these conditions than in a control condition in which it was implied that the speaker remained standing.

Protagonists and Objects

Comprehenders are quick to make inferences about protagonists, presumably in an attempt to construct a more complete situation model. Consider, for example, what happens after subjects read the sentence *The electrician examined the light fitting*. If the following sentence is *She took out her screwdriver*, their reading speed is slowed down compared with when the second sentence is *He took out his screwdriver*. This happens because she provides a mismatch with the stereotypical gender of an electrician, which the subjects apparently infer while reading the first sentence (Carreiras, Garnham, Oakhill, & Cain, 1996).

Comprehenders also make inferences about the emotional states of characters. For example, if we read a story about Paul, who wants his brother Luke to be good in baseball, the concept of "pride" becomes activated in our mind when we read that Luke receives the Most Valuable Player Award (Gernsbacher, Goldsmith, & Robertson, 1992). Thus, just as in real life, we make inferences about people's emotions when we comprehend stories.

Processing Frameworks

Introduction

In the process of language and text comprehension new information has to be integrated into the current situation model. This is achieved by a processing framework. There are various theories and insights on this process. Most of them only model one or some aspects of Situation Models and language comprehension.

A list of theories, insights and developments in language comprehension frameworks:

- an interactive model of comprehension (Kintsch and van Dijk, 1978)
- early Computatinal Model (Miller, Kintsch, 1980)
- Constructing-integration Model (Kintsch, 1988)
- Structure-Building-Framework (Gernsbacher,1990)
- Capacity Constraint Reader Model (Just, Carpenter, 1992)
- Constructivist framework (Graesser, Singer, Trabasso, 1994)
- Event Indexing Model (Zwaan, Langston, Graesser, 1995)
- Landscape Model (van den Brock, Risden, Fletcher, & Thurlow, 1996)
- Capacity-constrained construction-integration Model (Goldman, Varma, Coté, 1996)
- The Immersed Experiencer Framework (Zwaan, 2003)

In this part of the chapter on Situation Models we will talk about several models, we will start with some of the early stuff and then go to the popular later ones. We will start with the work of Kintsch in the 70s and 80s and then go on to later research which bases on this.

An interactive Model of Comprehension

This model was already developed in the 80s, it is the basis for many later models like the CI-Model, or even the Immersed-Experiencer Framework. According to Kintsch and van Dijk (1978) text comprehension proceeds in cycles. In every cycle a few propositions are processed, this number is determined by the capacity of the Short-Term Memory, so 7 plus or minus 2. In every cycle the new propositions are connected to existing ones, they therefore form a connected and hierarchical set.

Early Computational Model

This computational model from Miller and Kintsch tried to model earlier theroies of comprehension, to make predictions according to these and compare them to behavioural studies and experiments. It consisted of several modules. One was a chunking program: It's task is to read in one word at the moment, identify if it is a proposition and decide whether to integrate it or not. This part of the model was not done computationally. The next part in the input order was the Microstructure Coherence Program (MCP). The MCP sorted the propositions and stored them in the Working Memory Coherence Graph. The task of the the Working Memory Coherence Graph was then to decide which propositions should be kept active during the next processing cycle. All propositions are stored in the Long Term Memory Coherence Graph, this decided which propositions should be transferred back in to the Working Memory or it can construct a whole new Working Memory Graph with a differen superordinate node. The problem with this Computational Model was that it show a really low performance. But still it led to further research which tried to overcome it's shortcomings.

Construction-Integration Model

Event-Indexing Model

The *Event-Indexing Model* was first proposed by Zwaan, Langston and Graesser (1995). It makes claims about how the incoming information in comprehension is processed and how it is represented in the long-term memory.

According to the *Event-Indexing Model* all incoming actions events are splitted into five indexes. The five indexes are the same as the five situational dimensions, though Zwaan&Radvasnky(1998) claim that there are possibly more dimensions. These might be found in future research. One basic point of this model is the processing time of integrating new events into the current model. It is more easier to integrate a new incoming event if it shares indexes with a previous event. The more contiguous the new event is, the easier it is integrated into the new Situation Model. This prediction made by Zwaan & Radvanksy (1998) is supported by some prior research (Zwaan, Magliano and Graesser, 1995). The other important point of the *Event-Indexing Model* is the representation in long-term memory. Zwaan & Radvasnky (1998) predict that this representation is a network of nodes, these nodes encode the events. The nodes are linked with each other through situational links according to the indexes they share. This connection does not only encode if two nodes share indexes but it also encodes the number of shared indexes through its strength. This second point already hints what the *Event-Indexing Model* lacks. There are several things which it does not include. For example it does not encode the temporal order of the events nor the direction of the causal relationships. The biggest disadvantage of the *Event-Indexing Model* is clearly that it treats the different dimensions as different entities though they probably interact with each other.

Radvansky & Zwaan (1998) updated the *Event-Indexing Model* with some features. This new model splits the processed information into three types. These three types are the situational framework, the situational relations and the situational content. The situational framework grounds the situation in space and time and it's construction is obligatory. If no information is given this framework is probably build up by standard values retrieved from prior world knowledge or some empty variable would be instantiated. he situational relations are based on the five situational dimensions. These are analysed through the *Event-Indexing Model*. This kind of situational information includes not the basic information, which is given in the situational framework, but the relationships between the different entities or nodes in the network. In contrast to the situational framework the situational relations are not obligatory. If their is no information given or their are no possible inferences between entities, then there is simply no relationship there. There is also an index which addresses importance to the different relations. This importance consists of the necessity of the information to understand the situation, the easiness to inference it when it would not be mentioned and how easy the information can later be remembered. Another distinction this theory makes is the one between functional and non-functional relations (Carlson-Radvansky & Radvansky, 1996; Garrod & Sanford, 1989). Functional relations describe the interaction between different entities whereas non-functional relations are the ones between non-interacting entities. The situational content consists of the entities in the situation like protagonists and objects and their properties. These are only integrated explicitly in the Situation Model, like situational relations, if they are necessary for the understanding of the situation. None the less the central and most important entities and their properties are obligatory again. It is proposed that, in order to keep the processing time low, non-essential information is only represented by something like a pointer so that this information can be retrieved if necessary.

The Immersed Experiencer Framework

The Immersed Experiencer Framework (IEF) is based on prior processing framework models (see above for a detailed list) but tries to include several other research findings too. For example it was found that during comprehension brain regions are activated, which are very close or even overlap with brain regions which are active during the perception or the action of the words meaning (Isenberg et al., 2000; Martin & Chao, 2001; Pulvermüller, 1999, 2002). During comprehension there is also a visual representation of shape and orientation of objects (Dahan & Tanenhaus, 2002; Stanfield & Zwaan, 2002; Zwaan, Stanfield, & Yaxley, 2002; Zwaan & Yaxley, in press a, b). Visual-spatial information primes sentence processing (Boroditsky, 2000). These visual representations can interfer with the comprehension (Fincher-Kiefer, 2001). Findings from (Glenberg, Meyer, & Lindem, 1987; Kaup & Zwaan, in press; Morrow, Greenspan, & Bower, 1987; Horton & Rapp, in press; Trabasso & Suh, 1993; Zwaan, Madden, & Whitten, 2000) suggest that information which is part of the situation and the text is more active in the reader's mind than information which is not included. The fourth research finding is that people move their eyes and hand during comprehension in a consistent way with the described the situation. (Glenberg & Kaschak, in press; Klatzky, Pellegrino, McCloskey, & Doherty, 1989; Spivey, Richardson, Tyler, & Young, 2000).

The main point of the Immersed Experiencer Framework is the idea that words active experiences with their referents. For example "an eagle in the sky" activates a visual experience of a eagle with stretched-out wings while "an eagle in the nest" activates a different visual experience. According to Zwaan (2003) the IEF should be seen as an engine to make predictions about language comprehension. These predictions are then suggested for further research.

According to the IEF the process of language comprehension consists of three components, these are activation, construal and integration. Each component works at a different level. Activation works at the world level, construal is responsible for the clause level while integration is active at the discourse level. Though the IEF shares many points with earlier models of language comprehension it differs in some main points. For example it suggests that language comprehension involves action and perceptual representations and not amodal propositions (Zwaan, 2003).

Levels of Representation in Language and Text Comprehension

A lot of theories try to explain the situation model or so called mental model in different representations. Several theories of the representation deal with the comprehension from the text into the situation model itself. How many levels are included or needed and how is the situation model constructed, is it done by once like:

Sentence → Situation Model

Or are there levels in between which have to be passed until the model is constructed? Here are three different representations shown which try to explain the construction of the situation model by a text.

Propositional Representation

The propositional Representation claims that a sentence will be structured in another way and then it is stored. Included information does not get lost. We will have a look at the simple sentence:

"George loves Sally" the propositional representation is [LOVES(GEORGE, SALLY)]

It is easy to see that the propositional representation is easy to create and the information is still available.

Three levels of representation

This theory says that there exist three levels of representation the surface form, text base and the situation model. In this example the sentence "The frog ate the bug." Is already the surface form. We naturally create semantically relations to understand the sentence (semantic tree in the figure). The next level is the "Text base". [EAT(FROG, BUG)] is the propositional representation and *Text base* is close to this kind of representation, except that it is rather spatial. Finally the situation model is constructed by the "Text base" representation. We can see that the situation model does not include any kind of text. It is a mental picture of information in the sentence itself.

Two levels of representation

This theory is like the "three levels of representations" theory. But the "Text base" level is left out. The theory itself claims that the situation model is created by the sentence itself and there is no "Text base" level needed.

Further situation model theories directing experiences exist. So not only text comprehension is done by situation models, learning through direct experience is handled by situation models, too.

KIWi-Model

One unified model the so called KIWi-Model tries to explain how text representation and direct experience interact with a situation model. Additionally the domain knowledge is integrated. The domain knowledge is used by forming a situation model in different tasks like simple sentence comprehension (chapter: Why do we need Situation Models). The KIWi-Model shows that a permanent interaction between "text representation → situation model" and between "sensory encoding → situation model" exists. These interactions supports the theory of a permanent updating of the mental model.

Inferencing

Inferencing is used to build up complex situation models with limited information. For example: in 1973 John Bransford and Marcia Johnson made a memory experiment in which they had two groups reading variatons of the same sentence.

The first group read the text "*John was trying to fix the bird house. He was **pounding** the nail when is father came out to watch him do the work*"

The second group read the text "*John was trying to fix the bird house. He was **looking for** the nail when is father came out to watch him do the work*"

After reading some test statements were presented to the participants. These statements contained the word *hammer* which did not occur in the original sentences, e.g.: "*John was using a hammer to fix the birdhouse. He was looking for the nail when his father came out to watch him*". Participants of the first group said they had seen 57% of the test statements while the participants from the second group had seen only 20% of the test statements.

As one can see, in the first group there is a tendency of believing to have seen the word *hammer*. The participants of this group made the inference, that John used a hammer to pound the nail. This memory influence test is good example to get an idea what is ment by making inferences and how they are used to complete situation models.

While reading a text inferencing creates information which is not explicitly stated in the text, hence it is a creative process. It is very important for text understanding in general, because texts cannot include all informations needed to understand the sense of a story. Texts usually leaves out what is known as *worldknowledge*. Knowledge about certain situations, persons or items, that most people share and which therefore doesn't need to be explicitly stated again. Each person should be able to infer this kind of information, as for example that we usually use hammers to pound nails. It would be impossible to write a text, if it has to include all information it deals with; if there was no such thing like inferencing or if it was not automatically done by our brain.

There is a number of different kinds of inferences:

Anaphoric Inference

This kind of Inferencing usually connects objects or persons from one to another sentence. Therefore it is responsible for connecting cross-sentence information. E.g. in "*John hit the nail. He was proud of his stroke*", we directly infer that "he" and "his" relate to "John". We make this kind of inferences quite easy normally. But there can be sentences where more persons and other words relating to them are mixed up and people have problems understanding the story at first. This is normally regarded as bad writing style.

Instrumental Inference

This type of Inference is about the tools and the methods used in the text, like the hammer in the example above. Or for example if you read about somebody flying to New York you would not infer that this person has built a dragon-flyer and jumped off a cliff but that he or she used a plane, since there is nothing else mentioned in the text and a plane is the most common form of flying to New York. If there is no specific information about tools, instruments and methods we get this information from our *General World Knowledge*

Causual Inference

Causal Inference is the conclusion that one event caused another in the text, like in "He hit his nail. So his finger ached". The first sentence gives the reason why it came to the situation described in the second text. It would be more difficult to draw a causal inference in an example like "He hit his nail. So his father ran away", although one could create an inference on this with some fantasy.

Causual inferences create causual connections between text elements. These connections are separated into *local connections* and *global connections*. Local connections are made within a range of 1 to 3 sentences. This depends on factors like the capacity of the working memory and the concentration due reading. Global connections are drawn between the information in one sentence together with the background information gathered so far about the whole text. Problems can occur with Causal Inferences when a story is *inconsistent*. For example vegans eating a steak would be inconsistent. An interesting fact about Causal Inferences (Goldstein, 2005) is that the kind of Inferences we draw here who are not as easy seen at first, are easier to remember. This may be due to the fact that they required a higher mental processing capacity while drawing the inference. So this "not-so-easy"-inference seems to be marked in a way that it is easier to remember it.

Predictice / Forward Inference

Predictive/Forward Inferences uses the *General World Knowledge* of the reader to build his prediction of the consequences of what is currently happening in the story into the Situation Model.

Integrating Inferences into Situation Models

The question how models enter inferential processes is highly controversial in the two desciplines of cognitive psychologie and artificial intelligence. A.I. gave a deep insight in psychological procedures and since the two disciplines crossed their ways and give two man bases of the cognitive science. The arguments in these are largely independent from eacht other but they have much in common, though.

Johnson-Laird (1983) makes a distinction between three types of reasoning-theories in which inferencing plays an important role. The first class geares to logical calculi and have been implemented in many formal system. The programmin language Prolog arises from this way of dealing with reasoning and in psychologie many theories postulate formal rules of inference, a "mental logic". These rules shall work in a purley syntactic way and so are "context free"; blind for the context of its content. A simple example clarifies the problem with this type of theorie:

If patients have cystitis, then they are given penicillin.
and the logical conclusion:
If patients have cystitis and are allergic to penicillin, then they are given penicillin

This is logically correct, but seems to fail our common sense of logic.

The second class of theories postulate content specific rules of inference. Their origin lies in programmming languages and production systems. They work with forms like "If x is a, then x is b". If one wants to show that x is b, showing that x is a is a subgoal of this argumentation. The idea of basing psychological theories of reasoning on content specific rules was discussed by Johnson-Laird and Wason and various sorts of such theories have been proposed. A related idea is that reasoning depends on the accumulation of specific examples within a connectionist framework, where the distinction between inference and recall is blurred.

The third class of theories base on mental models and do not use any rules of inferencing. The process of building mental models of things heard or read. The models are in an permanent change of updates. A model built, will be equipped with new features of the new information as long as there is no information, which generates a conflict with that model. If this is the case the model is generally re-built, so that the conflict generating information fits into the new model.

Important Topics of current research

Linguistic Cues versus World Knowledge

According to many researchers language is the set of processing instructions on how to build up the Situation Model of the represented situation (Gernsbacher, 1990; Givon, 1992; Kintsch, 1992; Zwaan & Radvansky, 1998). As mentioned readers use the lexical cues and informations to connect the different situational dimensions and integrate them into the model. Another important point here is prior world knowledge. World knowledge also influences how the different informations in a situation model are related. The relation between linguistic cues and world knowledge is therefore an important topic of current and future research in the area of Situation Models.

Multidimensionality

Another important aspect of current research in the area of Situation Models is the Multidimensionality of the Models. The main aspect is here how the different dimensions relate to each other, how they influence and interact. The question here is also if they interact at all and which interact. Most studies in the field were only about one or a few of the situational dimensions.

References

Ashwin Ram Kenneth Moorman (1999) Understanding Language Understanding - chapter 5

Baggett, P. (1979). Structurally equivalent stories in movie and text and the effect of the medium on recall. Journal of Verbal Learning and Verbal Behavior, 18, 333-356.

Bertram F. Malle Louis J. Moses Dare A. Baldwin (2001) Intentions and Intentionality - chapter 9

Boroditsky, L. (2000). Metaphoric Structuring: Understanding time through spatial metaphors.

Cognition, 75, 1-28.

Carlson-Radvansky, L. A., & Radvansky, G. A. (1996). The influence of functional relations on spatial term selection. Psychological Science, 7, 56-60.

Carreiras, M., Garnham, A., Oakhill, J., & Cain, K. (1996). The use of stereotypical gender information in constructing a mental model: Evidence from English and Spanish. Quarterly Journal of Experimental Psychology, 49A, 639-663.

Dahan, D., & Tanenhaus, M.K. (2002). Activation of conceptual representations during spoken word recognition. Abstracts of the Psychonomic Society, 7, 14.

Dupoux, Emmanuel,(???) Language, Brain, and Cognitive Development - chapter5

Ericsson, K. A., & Kintsch, W. (1995). Long-term working memory. Psychological Review, 102, 211-245.

Farah, M. J., & McClelland, J. L. (1991). A computational model of semantic memory impairment: modality specificity and emergent category specificity. Journal of Experimental Psychology: General, 210, 339-357.

Fincher-Kiefer (2001). Perceptual components of situation models. Memory & Cognition, 29 , 336-343.

Fincher-Kiefer, R., Post, T. A., Greene, T. R., & Voss, J. F. (1988). On the role of prior knowledge and task demands in the processing of text. Journal of Memory and Language, 27, 416-428.

Garrod, S. C., & Sanford, A. J. (1989). Discourse models as interfaces between language and the spatial world. Journal of Semantics, 6, 147-160.

Gernsbacher, M.A. (1990), Language comprehension as structure building. Hillsdale, NJ: Erlbaum.

Glenberg, A. M., & Kaschak, M. P. (2002). Grounding language in action. Psychonomic Bulletin & Review, 9, 558-565.

Glenberg, A. M., Meyer, M., & Lindem, K. (1987) Mental models contribute to foregrounding during text comprehension. Journal of Memory and Language 26:69-83.

Givon, T. (1992), The grammar of referential coherence as mental processing instructions, Linguistics, 30, 5-55.

Goldman, S.R., Varma, S., & Coté, N. (1996). Extending capacityconstrained construction integration: Towards "smarter" and flexible models of text comprehension. Models of understanding text (pp. 73-113).

Goldstein, E.Bruce, Cognitive Psychology, Connecting Mind, Research, and Everyday Experience (2005) - ISBN: 0-534-57732-6.

Graesser, A. C., Singer, M., & Trabasso, T (1994), Constructing inferences during narrative text comprehension. Psychological Review, 101, 371-395.

Holland, John H. , Keith J. Holyoak, Richard E. Nisbett, Paul R. Thagard (1986) Induction

Horton, W.S., Rapp, D.N. (in press). Occlusion and the Accessibility of Information in Narrative Comprehension. Psychonomic Bulletin & Review.

Isenberg, N., Silbersweig, D., Engelien, A., Emmerich, K., Malavade, K., Beati, B., Leon, A.C., & Stern, E. (1999). Linguistic threat activates the human amygdala. Proceedings of the National Academy of Sciences, 96, 10456-10459.

Johnson-Laird, P. N. (1983). Mental models: Towards a cognitive science of language, inference, and consciousness. Cambridge, MA: Harvard University Press.

John R. Koza, David E. Goldberg, David B. Fogel, Rick L. Riolo (1996) Genetic Programming

Just, M. A., & Carpenter, P. A. (1992). A capacity hypothesis of comprehension: Individual differences ih working memory. Psychological Review, 99, 122-149.

Kaup, B., & Zwaan, R.A. (in press). Effects of negation and situational presence on the accessibility of text information. Journal of Experimental Psychology: Learning, Memory, and Cognition.

Keefe, D. E., & McDaniel, M. A. (1993). The time course and durability of predictive inferences. Journal of Memory and Language, 32, 446-463.

Kintsch, W. (1988), The role of knowledge in discourse comprehension: A construction-integration model, Psychological Review, 95, 163-182.

Kintsch, W., & van Dijk, T. A. (1978), Toward a model of text comprehension and production, Psychological Review, 85, 363-394.

Kintsch, W. (1992), How readers construct situation models for stories: The role of syntactic cues and causal inferences. In A. E Healy, S. M. Kosslyn, & R. M. Shiffrin (Eds.), From learning processes to cognitive processes. Essays in honor of William K. Estes (Vol. 2, pp. 261 - 278).

Klatzky, R.L., Pellegrino, J.W., McCloskey, B.P., & Doherty, S. (1989). Can you squeeze a tomato? The role of motor representations in semantic sensibility judgments. Journal of Memory and Language, 28, 56-77.

Martin, A., & Chao, L. L. (2001). Semantic memory and the brain: structure and processes. Current Opinion in Neurobiology, 11, 194-201.

McRae, K., Sa, V. R., de, & Seidenberg, M. S. (1997). On the nature and scope of featural representations of word meaning. Journal of Experimental Psychology: General, 126, 99-130.

Mehler, Jacques, & Franck, Susana. (1995) Cognition on Cognition - chapter 9

Miceli, G., Fouch, E., Capasso, R., Shelton, J.R., Tomaiuolo, F., & Caramazza, A. (2001). The dissociation of color from form and function knowledge. Nature Neuroscience, 4, 662-667.

Morrow, D., Greenspan, S., & Bower, G. (1987). Accessibility and situation models in narrative comprehension. Journal of Memory and Language, 26, 165-187.

Pulvermüller, F. (1999). Words in the brain's language. Behavioral and Brain Sciences, 22, 253-270.

Pulvermüller, F. (2002). A brain perspective on language mechanisms: from discrete neuronal ensembles to serial order. Progress in Neurobiology, 67, 85–111.

Radvansky, G. A., & Zwaan, R.A. (1998). Situation models.

Schmalhofer, F., MacDaniel, D. Keefe (2002). A Unified Model for Predictive and Bridging Inferences

Schneider, W., & Körkel, J. (1989). The knowledge base and text recall: Evidence from a short-term longitudinal study. Contemporary Educational Psychology, 14, 382-393.

Singer, M., Halldorson, M., Lear, J. C., & Andrusiak, E (1992). Validation of causal bridging inferences. Journal of Memory and Language, 31, 507-524.

Spivey, M.J., Richardson, D.C., Tyler, M.J., Young, E.E. (2000). Eye movements during comprehension of spoken scene descriptions. Proceedings of the Twenty-second Annual Meeting of the Cognitive Science Society (pp. 487-492).

Stanfield, R.A. & Zwaan, R.A. (2001). The effect of implied orientation derived from verbal context on picture recognition. Psychological Science, 12, 153-156.

Talmy, Leonard,(2000) Toward a Cognitive Semantics - Vol. 1 - chapter1

van den Broek, P., Risden, K., Fletcher, C. R., & Thurlow, R. (1996). A "landscape" view of reading: Fluctuating patterns of activation and the construction of a memory representation. In B. K. Britton & A. C. Graesser (Eds.), Models of understanding text (pp. 165-187).

Van Dijk, T. A., and W. Kintsch. (1983).Strategies of discourse comprehension.

Yekovich, F.R., Walker, C. H., Ogle, L. T., & Thompson, M. A. (1990). The influence of domain knowledge on inferencing in low-aptitude individuals. In A. C. Graesser & G. H. Bower (Eds.), The psychology of learning and motivation (Vol. 25, pp. 175-196). New York: Academic Press.

Zwaan, R.A. (1996). Processing narrative time shifts. Journal of Experimental Psychology: Learning, Memory and Cognition, 22, 1196-1207

Zwaan, R.A. (2003), The Immersed Experiencer: Toward an embodied theory of language comprehension.B.H. Ross (Ed.) The Psychology of Learning and Motivation, Vol. 44. New York: Academic Press.

Zwaan, R. A., Ericsson, K. A., Lally, C., & Hill, L. (1998). Situation-model construction during translation. Manuscript in preparation, Florida State University.

Zwaan, R. A., Langston, M. C., & Graesser, A. C. (1995). The construction of situation models in narrative comprehension: An event-indexing model. Psychological Science, 6, 292-297.

Zwaan, R. A., Magliano, J. P., & Graesser, A. C. (1995). Dimensions of situation model construction in narrative comprehension. Journal of Experimental Psychology." Learning, Memory, and Cognition, 21, 386-397.

Zwaan, R. A., Radvansky (1998), Situation Models in Language Comprehension and Memory. in Psychological Bulletin, Vol.123,No2 p.162-185.

Zwaan, R.A., Stanfield, R.A., Yaxley, R.H. (2002). Do language comprehenders routinely represent the shapes of objects? Psychological Science, 13, 168-171.

Zwaan, R.A., & Yaxley, R.H. (a). Spatial iconicity affects semantic-relatedness judgments. Psychonomic Bulletin & Review.

Zwaan, R.A., & Yaxley, R.H. (b). Hemispheric differences in semantic-relatedness judgments. Cognition.

Links

Cognitive Psychology Osnabrück
Summer School course on Situation Models and Embodied Language Processes
Dr. Rolf A. Zwaan's Homepage with many Papers
International Hanse-Conference on Higher level language processes in the brain: Inference and Comprehension Processes 2003
University of Notre Dame Situation Model Research Group
                    live version • discussion • edit lesson • comment • report an error

live version • discussion • edit lesson • comment • report an error

Knowledge Representation and Hemispheric Distribution/Specialisation

Introduction

The Latin word for "to know" is "cognoscere" and after Princeton's WordNet a possible synonym for "knowledge" is "cognition". This close etymological affinity between "knowledge" and "cognition" is an indicator for the importance of "knowledge" for cognitive psychology and cognitive science. Most human cognitive abilities rely on or interact with what we call knowledge. How do people navigate through the world? How do they solve problems, how do they comprehend their surroundings, on which basis do people make decisions and draw inferences? For all these questions, knowledge and mental representations of the world without doubt are part of the answer.

But what is knowledge? According to Merriam-Webster-OnLine-Dictionary knowledge is "the range of one's information and understanding" and "the circumstance or condition of apprehending truth or fact through reasoning". Thus, knowledge is a structured collection of information, that can be acquired through learning, perception or reasoning.

In this chapter we deal with what structures humans build to represent their knowledge about the world in their brain. First, we will introduce the idea of concepts and categories as a model for storing and sorting information to you , and then talk about semantic networks, which are similar to neural networks and also try to explain the way humans store and handle information. Apart from the human aspect, we are also going to talk about knowledge representation in artificial systems, which can be helpful tools to store and access knowledge and draw quick inferences.

After having looked at how knowledge is stored and made available in the human brain and artificial systems, we will talk about a quite different topic, namely hemispheric specialisation. This topic also connects to many other chapters of this book. Where, for example, is memory located, and which parts of the brain are relevant for emotions and motivation? Although these are interesting questions, in this chapter we focus on the general differences between right and left hemisphere. We consider the question whether they differ in what or in how they process and give an overview about experiments with which knowledge was gained in this field.

Historical and Philosophical Aspects

Is explaining the activity within our two hemispheres enough to explain our conscious selves? Is our true self really that spatially limited to this soft stuff in our skull? It seems obvious that this cannot be the case and that the brain rather is in constant interaction with our body and thereby with the environment we live in. Perceiving our environment is a human ability that is usually done unconsciously. Somatic marker are an good example for unconscious perception and the influence it has on our behavior. This knowledge is qualitative as well as quantitative. Hence, our decisions in each circumstance is based on more information than we are aware of.

There have been arguments going on for a long period of time how to value the information of sensory data in comparison to our 'mind'. Is just everything we are pure receiving and modeling of physical information and talking about a mind just a waste of time? Or is instead the body just a hindrance in gaining knowledge, as already Socrates claimed, because it does not "afford men any truth"?

Theories on Knowledge Representation in the Brain

Concepts and Categories

Concepts

For many cognitive functions concepts are important. Concepts are mental representations and are used for the use and understanding of language, for reasoning and memory. One function of concepts is the categorization which has been studied most intensively.In the following we will deal with this particular function of a concept.

Categories in our Life

Imagine to wake up every single morning and start wondering about all the things you have never seen before. Think about how you would feel if an unknown car parked in front of your house. You have seen thousands of cars but since you have never seen this specific car in this particular position, you would not be able to provide yourself with any explanation. But since we are able to find an explanation, the questions we need to ask ourselves are: How are we able to abstract from prior knowledge and why do we not start all over again if we are confronted with a slightly new situation? The answer is easy: We *categorize* knowledge. Categorization is the process of abstracting and assigning objects to categories. Categories are so called "pointers of knowledge". You can imagine a category as a box, inside which similar objects are grouped and which is labeled with common properties and other general information about the category. Our brain does not only memorize specific examples of members of a category, but also stores general information that all members have in common and which therefore defines the category. Coming back to the car-example, this means that our brain does not only store how your car, your neighbors and your friends car look like, but it also provides us with the general information that most cars have four wheels, need to be fueled and so on.

Because categorization allows us to quickly get a general picture of a scene by allowing us to recognize new objects as members of a category, it saves us much time and energy that we otherwise would have to spend in investigating new objects. It helps us to focus on the important details in our environment, and enables us to quickly draw the correct inferences. To make this obvious, imagine yourself standing at the side of a road, wanting to traverse it. A car approaches from the left. Now, the only thing you need to know about this car is the general information provided by the category, that it will run you over if you don't wait until it has passed. You don't need to care about the car's color, number of doors and so on. If you were not able to immediately assign the car to the category "car", and infer the necessity to step back, you would get hit because you'd still be busy with examining the details of that specific and unknown car. Therefore categorization has proved itself as being very helpful for surviving during evolution and allows us to quickly and efficiently navigate through our environment.

Definitional Approach

Take a look at the following picture, you will see three different kinds of cars. They differ in shape, color and other features save that they are all cars.

What makes us so convinced about the identity of these objects? Maybe we can try to find a definition which describes all the cars. All cars have four wheels? Really? There are some which have only three. All cars drive with petrol. That's not true for all cars either. Apparently we will fail to come up with a definition. The reason for this failure is that we have to generalize to make a definition. But because not all members of one category share identical features definitions are problematic especially concerning natural or human-made objects.

Wittgenstein (1953) was one of the people who dealt with this problem of the definitional approach. Wittgenstein claimed to have found a solution. He developed the idea of *family resemblance*. That means that members of a category resemble each other in several ways. For example cars differ in shape, color and many other properties but every car resembles somehow other cars.

Prototype Approach

The prototype approach was proposed by Rosch in 1973. A prototype is an average case of all members in a particular category, but it is not an actual, really existent member of the category. Even extreme various features of members within one category can be explained by this approach. Different degrees of prototypicality represent differences among category-members. Members which resemble the prototype in a very strongly are *high-prototypical*. Low-prototypicality is the opposite namely members which differ in a lot of ways from the prototype. There seem to be connections to the idea of family resemblance and indeed some experiments showed that high prototypicality and high family resemblance are strongly connected.

The *typicality effect* describes the fact that high-prototypical members are faster recognized as a member of a category. For example participants had to decide whether statements like "A penguin is a bird", "A sparrow is bird" are true. Their decisions were much faster concerning prototypical members as for the "sparrow" than for atypical members as "penguin". Participants also tend to prefer prototypical members of a category when asked to list objects of a category. Concerning the birds-example, they rather list "sparrow" than "penguin", which is a quite intuitive result. In addition prototypical objects are strongly affected by priming.

Exemplar Approach

The *typicality effect* can also be explained by the third approach which is concerned with exemplars. Similar to a prototype, an *exemplar* is very typical of the category. The difference between exemplars and prototypes is that exemplars are actually existent members of a category that a person has encountered in the past. It is proposed that objects which are similar to the majority of exemplars are classified faster. A sparrow would be classified very fast because it looks similar to many other birds. Therefore an atypical bird like a penguin would not be classified as fast because it doesn't share it appearance with many other exemplars of birds.

Prototype vs. Exemplar Approach

For both prototype and exemplar approach there are experiments whose results support either one approach. Some people claim that the exemplar approach has less problems with variable categories and with atypical cases within categories. The reason for that could be that "real" category-members are used and all information of the individual exemplars, which can be useful when encountering other members later, are stored. Another point where the approaches can be compared is how well they work for different sized categories. The exemplar approach seems to work better for smaller categories and prototypes do better for larger categories.

In the end one quote gives a good sense of how useless and even impossible it is to decide which approach is the "right" one: "We know generally what cats are (the prototype), but we know specifically our own cat the best (an exemplar)." (Minda & Smith, 2001)

Hierarchical Organization of Categories

Now that we know about the different approaches of how we go about forming categories and negotiating between their members, let us look at the structure of a category and the relationship between categories.

The basic idea is that larger categories can be split up into more specific and smaller categories. Rosch stated that by this process three levels of categorization are created:

It is interesting that the decrease of information from basic to superordinate is really high but that the increase of information from basic down to subordinate is rather low. Scientists wanted to find out if among these levels one is preferred over the others. They asked participants to name presented objects as quickly as possible. The result was that the subjects tended to use the basic-level name, which includes the optimal amount of stored information. So a picture of a retriever would mainly be named "dog" rather then "animal" or "retriever". It is important to note that the levels are different for each person depending on factors such as expertise and culture.

Affecting Factors on Categorization

One factor which influences our categorization is knowledge itself. Experts pay more attention to specific features of objects in their area than non-experts would do. For example after presenting some pictures of birds experts of birds tend to say the subordinate name (blackbird, sparrow) while non-experts just say "bird". The basic level in the area of interest of an expert is therefore lower than the basic level of a layperson. Therefore knowledge and experience of people affect categorization.

Another factor is culture. If something is of great importance in a culture people of that culture are like experts and have more knowledge about this topic than another people in whose culture this area does not play such an important role. A person coming from a Western culture is more likely to have more knowledge about computers than a person coming from an African tribe.

Representation of Categories in the Brain

There is evidence that some areas in the brain are selective for different categories. But it is not very probably that there is a corresponding brain area for each category. One prove for a selectivity of brain areas is the results of neurophysiological research. There seems to be a kind of double dissociation for living and non-living things. It has been proven by fMRI studies that non-living and living things are indeed represented in different brain areas. It is important to denote that nevertheless there is much overlap between the activation of different brain areas by categories. Moreover when going one step closer into the physical area there is a connection to mental categories, too. There seem to exist neurons which respond better to objects of a particular category, namely so called "category-specific neurons". These neurons fire not only as a response to one object but to many objects within one category. This leads to the idea that probably many neurons fire if a person recognizes a particular object and that maybe these combined patterns of the firing neurons represent the object.

Semantic Networks

The "Semantic Network approach" proposes that concepts of the mind are arranged into networks, in other words, in a functional storage-system for the `meanings' of words. Of course, the concept of a semantic net is very flexible. In a graphical illustration of such a semantic net, concepts of our mental dictionary are represented by nodes, which in this way represent a piece of knowledge about our world.

The properties of a concept could be placed, or "stored", next to a node representing that concept. Links between the nodes indicate the relationship between the objects. But the links can not only show, that there is a relationship. They can indicate the kind of relation by their length, for example.

Every concept in the net is in a dynamical correlation with other concepts, which maybe have protoypically similar characteristics or functions.

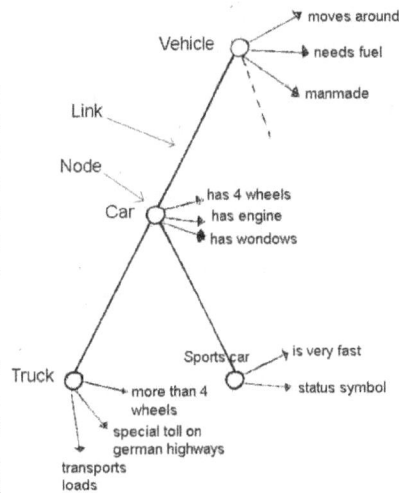

Semantic Network according to Collins and Quillian with nodes, links, concept names and properties. (GFDL - L bartels)

Collins and Quillian's Model

One of the first ones, who thought about such structure models of human memory that could be run on a computer, was Ross Quillian (1967). Together with Allan Collins, he developed the Semantic Network with related categories and with a hierarchical organization.

In the picture on the right hand side, Collins and Quillians network with added properties at each node is shown. As already mentioned, the skeleton-nodes are interconnected by links. At the nodes, concept names are added. Like in paragraph "Hierarchical Organisation of Categories", general concepts are on the top and more particular ones at the bottom. By looking at the concept "car", one gets the information, that a car has 4 wheels, has an engine, has windows, and furthermore moves around, needs fuel, is manmade. The properties of the higher concepts in line are inherited to the lower ones. This is called Cognitive Economy.

Cognitive Economy

In order not to produce redundancies, Collins and Quillian thought of this information inheritance principle. Information, that is shared by several concepts, is stored in the highest parent node, containing the information. So all son-nodes, that are below the information bearer , also can access the information about the properties.

But there are exceptions. Sometimes a special car has not four wheels, but three. This specific property is stored in the son-node.

Correlation between Distance of Concepts and Information Retrieval

The logic structure of the network is convincing. Since it can show, that the time of retrieving a concept and the distances in the network correlate. The correlation is proven by the sentence-verification technique. In experiments probands had to answer statements about concepts with "yes" or "no". It took actually longer to say "yes", if the concept bearing nodes were further apart.

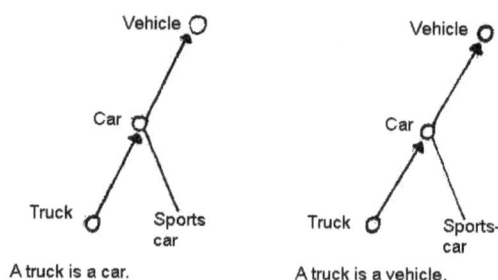

A truck is a car. A truck is a vehicle.

Correlation of distance of concepts and retrieval time for information (GFDL - Lbartels

Spreading Activation

The phenomenon, that adjacent concepts are activated is called Spreading activation. These concepts are far more easily accessed by memory, they are "primed".

As seen in the picture at the right, the starting point of that search activation is truck, going to car, as the participant thinks from truck to car. Spreading activation, coming from car, primes all surrounding concepts, namely sports car, van and vehicle.

This was studied and backed by David Meyer and Roger Schaneveldt (1971) with a lexical-decision task. Probands had to decide, if word pairs were words or non-words. They were faster at finding real word pairs, if the concepts of the two words were close-by in the intended network .

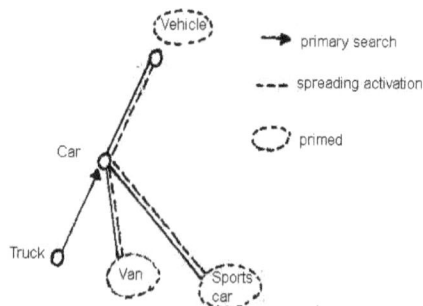

→ primary search

--- spreading activation

( ) primed

Spreading activation (GFDL - Lbartels

Criticism

While having the ability to explain many questions, the model has flaws.

The **Typicality Effect** is one of them. It is known that "reaction times for more typical members of a category are faster than for less typical members". (MITECS) This contradicts with the assumptions of Collins and Quillian's Model, that the distance in the net is responsible for reaction time.

Also **Cognitive Economy** is questioned. Since by means of experiments, it was found out, that some properties are stored at the specific node.

Furthermore, there are examples of faster concept retrieval, although the distances in the network are longer.

All this led to another version of the Semantic Network approach.

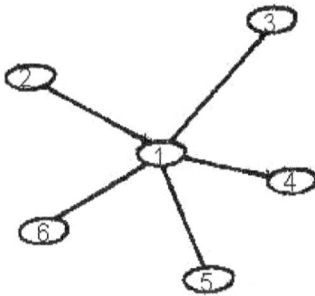

Link length of person 1.   Link length of person 2.

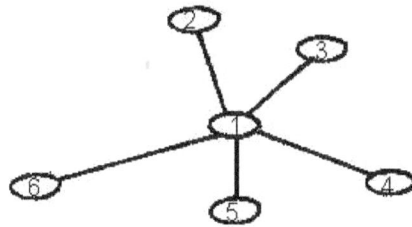

Interpersonal different link length and layout of concepts (GFDL - Lbartels

Collins and Loftus Model - A Developed C&Q-Model

Collins and Loftus (1975) tried to abandon these problems by using shorter or longer links depending on the relatedness and interconnections between formerly not directly linked concepts. Also the former hierarchic structure was substituted by a more individual structure of a person. Only to name a few of the extensions. Like shown in the picture on the right, the new model represents interpersonal differences, such as acquired during a humans lifespan. They manifest themselves in the layout and the various lengths of the links of the same concepts.

But after all these enhancements, the model is so omnipotent, that some researches scarced it for being too flexible. In their opinion, the model is no longer a scientific theory, because it is not disprovable.

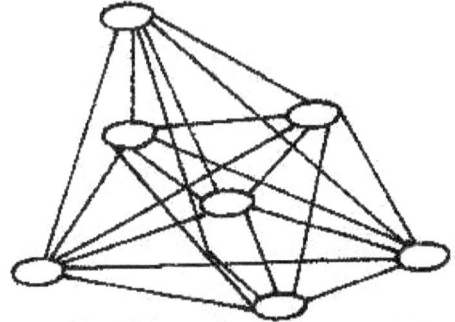

Semantic Network as proposed by Collins and Loftus,without speciflc hierarchy

Collins and Loftus Model (GFDL - Lbartels

Connectionist Approach

As written above, every concept in a semantic net is in a dynamical correlation with other concepts, which maybe have protoypically similar characteristics or functions. In the brain neural networks are organised similarly.

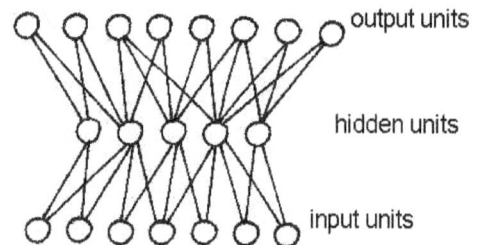

Parallel distributed processing (PDP) network

A parallel distributed processing (PDP) network (GFDL - Lbartels

Furthermore, it is useful to include the features of "spreading activation" and "parallel distributed activity" in a concept of such a semantic net, to explain the complexity of the very sophisticated environment.

The connectionists did this by modeling their networks after neural networks in the nervous system. Instead of nodes, the units of the networks are divided into subgroups like Input-, Output- and Hidden nodes, as shown on the picture on the left hand side.

Representation of Concepts in Networks

Excitatory and inhibitory connections between units just like in synapses in the brain allow 'input' to be analyzed and evaluated. For computing the outcome of such systems, it is useful to attach a certain 'weight' to the input of the connectionists system, that mimics the strength of a stimulus of the human nervous system.

Different inputs are represented in different output patterns. As shown in the picture on the right hand side, "truck" has the output pattern +7,+5,+1,+3. A sports car has another pattern, for example

+4,+9,+1,+8. So it is not possible to monitor only one output unit to get the whole information needed to specify the kind of car, or object.

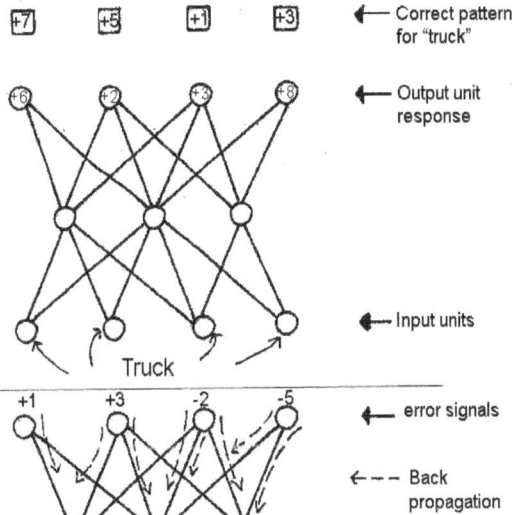

Basic Principles of Connectionism

It has to be emphasised, that connectionist networks are no models of how the nervous system works. It is a hypothetical approach to represent categories in network patterns. Another name for the connectionist approach is Parallel Distributed Processing approach, for short PDP, since processing takes place in parallel lines and the output is distributed across many units.

Operation of Connectionist Networks

The picture on the right shows a learning process in a PDP. Learning is necessary, since the patterns, for example for "truck", are not build-in.

First the stimulus, that stands for truck is presented to the input units. Then the links pass on the signal to the hidden units, that distribute the signal to the output units via further links.

In the first trial, the output units shows a wrong pattern, an error signal, that does not represent "truck". But after many repetitions, the pattern is correct. This is achieved by back propagation. The error signals are send back to the hidden units and the signals are reprocessed. During these repetive trials, the "weights" of the signal are gradually calibrated on behalf of the error signals in order to get a right output pattern at last.

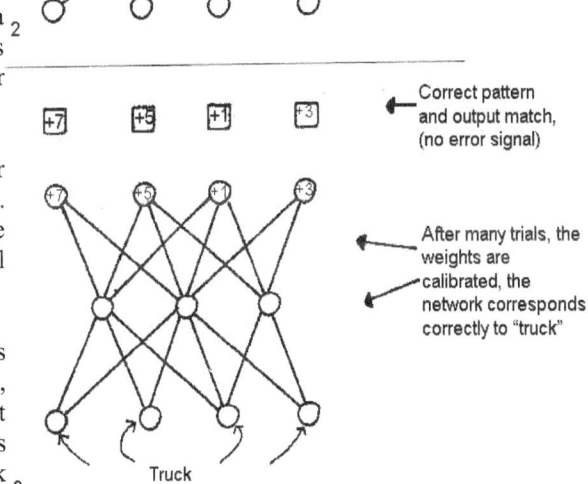

Processing steps of learning in a PDP (GFDL - Lbartels

After having achieved a correct pattern for "truck", the system is ready to learn a new concept. This new concept will then have a new and different output pattern in comparison to "truck". Yet, by learning the new concept, the old can be "forgotten" and if forgotten, needs to be relearned.

Evaluating Connectionism

The PDP approach is important for KR studies. It is far from perfect, but on the move to get there.

Some supporting arguments are the following: The process of learning enables the system to make generalizations, because similar concepts create similar patterns. After knowing one car, the system can recognize similar patterns as other cars, or may even predict how other cars look like. Furthermore, the system is protected against total wreckage. A damage to single units will not cause the system's total breakdown, but will delete only some patterns, which use those units. This is called **graceful degradation** and is often found at patients with brain lessions. These two arguments lead to the third. The PDP is organised similarly to the human brain. And some effective computer programmes have been developed on this basis, that were able to predict the consequences of human brain damage.

On the other hand, problems of the connectionist approach are: Formerly learned concepts can be superposed by new concept. In addition PDP can not explain more complex processes than learning concepts. Neither, can it explain the phenomenon of rapid learning. It is assumed, that rapid learning takes place in the hippocampus, and that conceptual and gradual learning is located in the cortex.

In conclusion, the PDP approach can explain some, but not everything. So, a combination of different approaches is most goal oriented.

Mental Representation

There are different theories on how living beings, especially humans encode information to knowledge. We may think of diverse mental representations of the same object. When reading the written word "car", we call this a **discrete symbol**. It matches with all imaginable cars and is therefore not bound to a special vehicle. It is an abstract, or amodal, representation. Else wise if seeing a picture of a car. It might be a red sport wagon. Now we speak of a **non-discrete symbol**, an imaginable picture that appears in front of our inner eye and that fits only to some similar cars.

Propositional Approach

The Propositional Approach is one possible way to model mental representation in the human brain. It works with discrete symbols which are strongly connected among each other. The usage of discrete symbols necessitates clear definitions of each symbol, as well as information about the syntactic rules and the context dependencies in which the symbols may be used. The symbol "car" is only comprehensible for people how do understand English and have seen a car before and therefore know what a "car" is about. The Propositional Approach in an explicit way to explain mental representation.

Propositions

Definitions of propositions differ in the different fields of research and are still in discussion. One possibility is the following:

> "*Traditionally in philosophy a distinction is made between sentences and the ideas underlying those sentences, called propositions. A single proposition may be expressed by an almost unlimited number of*

sentences. Propositions are not atomic, however; they may be broken down into atomic concepts called "Concepts". http://www.cs.vu.nl/~mmc/tbr/content_pages/repository/nel/glossary.html

Mental Propositions

In addition Mental Propositions deal with the storage, retrieval and interconnection of information as knowledge in the human brain.

There is a big discussion, if the brain really works with propositions or if the brain processes its information to and from knowledge in another way or perhaps in more ways.

Imagery Approach

One possible alternative to the Propositional Approach, is the Imagery Approach. Since here the representation of knowledge is understood as the storage of images as we see them, it is also called analogical or perceptual approach. In contrast to the Propositional Approach it works with non-discrete symbols and is modality specific. It is an implicit approach to mental representation. The picture of the sport wagon includes implicitly seats of any kind. If additionally mentioned that they are off-white, the image changes to a more specific one. How two non-discrete symbols are combined is not as predetermined as it is for discrete symbols. The picture of the off-white seats may exist without the red car around, as well as the red car did before without the off-white seats.

The Imagery and the Propositional Approaches are also discussed in chapter 8.

Knowledge Representation (KR) in Computational Models of Cognition

Almost all these theories evolved in symbiosis with the developing computer sciences. Computer processing was seen as a model of human brain processing.

Computer Science wants to understand the human brain by developing artificial models of its functioning and on the other hand uses the human brain as an inspiration for computational systems.

Knowledge Representation (KR), one of the crucial parts of Artificial Intelligence (AI), deals with **information encoding, storing and usage** for "computational models of cognition" (MITECS). KR has many connections to other fields concerning (human) information processing like logic, linguistics, reasoning, and the philosophical aspects of these fields, to name only a few. There are two main interest of KR: First, the **kind of information**, that is encoded. This is called knowledge engineering. Second, the **formalisms of information representations**. That means, how information is stored. Most KR applications are particularly developed for a specific use, for example a digital map for robot navigation or a graph like account of events for visualizing stories. Yet, the overall aim is to find an artificial way to draw conclusions with preferably short derivations. Humans can draw conclusions very well. But AI applications, like robots or programs are still very bad at that issue. Drawing conclusions is one of the most difficult tasks for artificial intelligence. Furthermore, there is a need for a uniform kind of knowledge representation, since there are many different ways of incompatible representations. For further information, read the passage about intertranslation between KR formalisms. In order to achieve these goals, it is necessary to create a "conceptual framework" for a common terminology.

Knowledge Engineering

Knowledge engineering deals with finding the right type of **conceptual vocabulary**. That means that each special knowledge type is expressed best by its own specific conceptual vocabulary. Different kinds of knowledge are, for example: Rules of games, attributes of objects and their relations to each other, temporal relations, chronologies, world knowledge...

Ontology

Related conceptual vocabularies, that are able to describe objects and their relationships are called **ontologies**. These conceptual vocabularies are highly formal and able to express meaning in a specific fields of knowledge. They are used for queries and assertions to knowledge bases and make knowledge sharing possible. In order to represent different kinds of knowledge, that means several ontologies, in one framework, Jerry Hobbs (1985) proposed the principle of **ontological promiscuity**. This means, to mix several ontologies together to cover a range of different knowledge types, as many as possible.

A query to such a system could be for example: "Take a cube from a table".

First, since we live in a temporal world, the action must be a progressive processing, that can be broken down in successive steps/states. Temporal information is often represented as functions on states of the world. E.g.: *to_grow(child,adult)*. After applying the function *to_grow* to *child*, the *child* becomes an *adult*.

Second, we make general statements about and rules for our system/world. Axioms on the rules of the environment are stated, like gravitational forces.

Third, we try out the chain of tasks, that have to be done to take a cube from a table. 1) Reach out for the cube with the hand, 2) grab it, 3) raise the hand with the cube, etc. Logical Reasoning is the perfect tool for this task, because the system can also recognize if the task is possible.

Frame Problem

But there is a problem with the procedure described above. It is called **Frame Problem**. The system in the example deals with changing states or in other words: the steps of actions that take place, change the environment. That is, the cube changes its place. Yet, the system does not make any propositions about the table so far. We need to make sure, that after picking up the cube from the table, the table does not change its state. It should not disappear or break down. This could happen, since the table is no longer needed. The systems tells that the cube is in the hand and omits any information about the table. In order to work out the Frame Problem there have to be stated some special axioms or similar things. The Frame Problem has not been solved completely. There are different approaches to a resolution. Some add object spatial and temporal boundaries to the system/world (Hayes 1985). Others try more direct modeling. They do transformations on state descriptions. For example: Before the transformation the cube is on the table, after transformation , the table still exists, but independent from the cube.

Knowledge Representation Formalisms

All KR formalisms need a strict syntax, semantics and inferring procedures in order to be clear and computable. Furthermore most formalisms have the following attributes to be able to express information more detailed: the Semantic Network Approach, concept hierarchies (Vehicle -> car -> truck) and property inheritance (A truck has four wheels, like a car). There are attributes that provide the possibility to add new information to the system without creating any inconsistencies, and the possibility to create a "closed-world" assumption. For example if the information that we have gravitation on earth is omitted, the closed-world assumption must be false for our earth/world.

Different Types of Formal Languages

There are symbolic, functional, logical, and object oriented notations, which formulate KR systems. These different kinds of encoding are inspired by Imagery, Semantic Networks, First-order logic, Second-order logic, Bayesian probabilistic inference, fuzzy reasoning, and others like nonmonotonic reasoning, that can displace old with more detailed information.

Expressive Power of Formalisms vs. Deductive Complexity

A problem for KR formalisms is the mutually exclusiveness of expressive power and deductive reasoning in one formalism. If a formalism has a big expressive power, it is able to describe a wide range of (different) information, but is not able to do brilliant inferring from (given) data. Propositional logic is restricted to Horn clauses. A Horn clause is a disjunction of literals with at most one positive literal. It has a very good decision procedure(inferring), but can not express generalizations. An example is given in the logical programming language Prolog. If a formalism has a big deductive complexity, it is able to do brilliant inferring, i.e. make conclusions, but has a poor range of what it can describe. An example is second-order logic. So, the formalism has to be tailored to the application of the KR system. This is reached by compromises between expressiveness and deductive complexity. In order to get a greater deductive power, expressiveness is sacrificed and vice versa.

Application of KR – Databases

KR can be and is used as extension of Database Technology. It is mostly not used as a computational model of cognition, but as a pool of information. In these cases general rules and models are not needed. With growing storage media, one is capable to create simple knowledge bases stating all specific facts. The information is stored in the form of sentential knowledge, that is knowledge saved in form of sentences comparable to propositions, or program code.

Intertranslation between KR Formalisms

With the growth of the field of knowledge bases, there have been developed many different standards. They all have different syntactic restrictions. To allow intertranslation, there have been created different "interchange" formalisms. For example the Knowledge Interchange Format, First-Order Set Theory plus LISP(Genesereth et al. 1992) or a Graph Notation (Peirce).

Gap between Human and Artificial KR

There is still a long way for researchers till they will be able to formalize all human kinds of knowledge. Intuitive, temporal and spatial knowledge defy themselves from control and can not be formalized today. Also the understanding of physical coherences and story comprehension is not framed properly. Whereas the complex strategies of chess playing are already formalized. The chess computer Deep Blue beat the world chess champion Kasparow in 1997.

KR in AI

As seen above KR is a key to process given unsystematic information of the world to get intelligibly knowledge. With this kind of knowledge, artificial intelligence research is willing to develop systems, that are able to act and react properly to the world; And some day, are able to act intelligent, perhaps.

Hemispheric Distribution

After having dealt with how knowledge is stored in the brain we now turn to the question of whether the brain is specialized and if it is which functions can be located where. These questions can be subsumed under the topic "hemispheric specialisation" or "lateralization of processing" which looks at the differences in processing between the two hemispheres of the human brain. Differences between the hemispheres can be traced back to as long as 3.5 million years ago. Evidence for this are fossils of australopithecines (which is an extinct ancestor of homo sapiens). Because differences have been present for so long and survived the selective pressure they must be useful in some way for our cognitive processes.

Differences in Anatomy and Chemistry

Although at first glance the two hemispheres look identically they differ in fact quite a lot in various ways.

Concerning the anatomy, some areas are larger and the tissue contains more dendritic spines in one hemisphere than in the other. An example of this is what used to be called "Broca's area" in the left hemisphere. This area which is –among other things- important for speech production shows greater branching in the left hemisphere than in the respective right hemisphere area. Because of the left hemisphere's importance for language, with which we will deal later, one can conclude that anatomical differences have consequences for lateralization in function.

Neurochemistry is another domain the hemispheres differ in: The left hemisphere is dominated by the neurotransmitter dopamine, whereas the right hemisphere shows higher concentrations of norepinephrine. Theories suggest that modules specialized on cognitive processes are distributed over the brain according to the neurotransmitter needed. Thus, a cognitive function relying on dopamine would be located in the left hemisphere.

Historic Approaches

Hemispheric specialisation has been of interest since the days of Paul Broca and Karl Wernicke, who discovered the importance of the left hemisphere for speech in the 1860s. Broca examined a number of patients who could not produce speech but whose understanding of language was not severed, whereas Wernicke examined patients who suffered the opposite symptoms (i.e. who could produce speech but did not understand anything). Both Broca and Wernicke found that their patients' brains had damage to distinct areas of the left hemisphere.

Because in these days language was seen as the cognitive process superior to all other processes, the left hemisphere was believed to be superior to the right which was expressed in the "cerebral dominance theory" developed by J.H. Jackson. The right hemisphere was seen as a "spare tire [...] having few functions of its own" (Banich, S.94). This view was not challenged until the 1930s. In this decade and the following, research dramatically changed this picture. Of special importance for showing the role of the right hemisphere was Sperry, who conducted several experiments in 1974 for which he won the Nobel Prize in Medicine and Physiology in 1981.

Experiments with Split-Brain-Patients

Sperry's experiments were held with people who suffered a condition called "split brain syndrom" because they underwent a *commissurotomy*. In a commissurotomy the *corpus callosum* which is the major cortical connection between the two hemispheres is cut so that communication between the hemispheres becomes severed in these patients. Before dealing with the role of the corpus callosum, we will talk about Sperry's pioneering experiments with which he wanted to find out whether the left hemisphere really played such an important role in speech processing as was suggested by Broca and Wernicke.

Sperry used different experimental designs in his studies, but the basic assumption behind all experiments of this type was that perceptual information received at one side of the body is processed in the contralateral hemisphere of the brain.

In one of the experiments the subjects had to recognize objects by touching it with merely one hand, while being blindfolded. He then asked the patients to name the object they felt and found that people could not name it when touching it with the left hand (which is linked to the right hemisphere). The question that arose was whether this inability was due to a possible function of the right hemisphere as "spare tire" or due to something else. Sperry now changed the design of his experiment so that patients now had to show that they recognized the objects by *using* it the right way. For example, if they recognized a pencil they would use it to write. With this changed design, no difference in performance between both hands were found.

Another experiment conducted by Sperry involved chimeric pictures. A chimeric picture is a picture that is made up of two things that are each cut in half and then put together as one.

Experiments with Patients with other Brain-Lesions

Other experiments that were conducted with the aim to find out about hemispheric specialisation was done with individuals who were about to receive surgery in which parts of one of their hemispheres was going to be removed due to epileptic seizures. Before the surgery was begun, it was important to find out which hemisphere was responsible for speech in this individual. This was done with the *Wada-technique*. Here, barbiturate was injected into one of the arteries supplying the brain with blood. Shortly after the injection, the contralateral side of the body is paralysed. If the person was now still able to speak, the doped hemisphere of the brain is not responsible for speech production in this individual. With the results of this technique it could be estimated that 95% of all adult right-handers use their left hemisphere for speech.

Drawbacks

Research with people who suffer brain lesions or even a commissurotomy has some major draw backs: The reason why they had to undergo such surgery is usually epileptic seizures. Because of this, it is possible that their brains are not typical or have received damage to other areas during the surgery. Also, these studies have been performed with very limited numbers of subjects, so the statistical reliability might not be high.

Experiments with Neurologically Intact Individuals

In addition to experiments with brain-severed patients, studies with neurologically intact individuals have been conducted to measure perceptual asymmetries. These are usually performed with one of three methods: Namely the "divided visual field technique", "dichaptic presentation" and "dichotic presentation". Each of them again has as basic assumption the fact that perceptual information received at one side of the body is processed in the contralateral hemisphere.

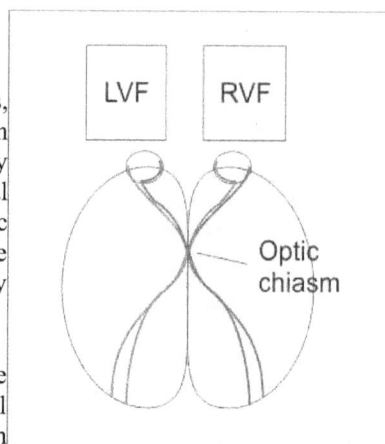

Highly simplified picture of the visual pathway.

The *divided visual field technique* is based on the fact that the visual field can be divided into the right (RVF) and left visual field (LVF). Each visual field is processed independently from the other in the contralateral hemisphere. The divided visual field technique includes two different experimental designs: The experimenter can present one picture in just one of the visual fields and then let the subject respond to this stimulus. The other possibility involves showing two different pictures in each visual field. A problem that can occur using the visual field technique is that the stimulus must be presented for less than 200 ms because this is how long the eyes can look at one point without shifting of the visual field.

In the *dichaptic presentation technique* the subject is presented two objects at the same time in each hand. (c.f. Sperry's experiments)

The dichotic presentation technique enables researchers to study the processing of auditory information. Here, different information is presented simultaneously to each ear. Experiments with these techniques found that a sensory stimulus is processed 20 to 100 ms faster when it is initially directed to the specialized hemisphere for that task and the response is 10% more accurate.

Explanations for this include three hypotheses, namely the *direct access theory*, the *callosal relay model* and the *activating-orienting model*. The direct access theory assumes that information is processed in that hemisphere to which it is initially directed. This may result in less accurate responses, if the initial hemisphere is the unspecialised hemisphere. The Callosal relay model states that information if initially directed to the wrong hemisphere is transferred to the specialized hemisphere over the corpus callosum. This transfer is time-consuming and is the reason for loss of information during transfer. The activating-orienting model assumes that a given input activates the specialized hemisphere. This activation then places additional attention on the contralateral side of the activated hemisphere, "making perceptual information on that side even more salient". (Banich)

Results

All experiments had some basic findings in common: The left hemisphere is superior at verbal tasks such as the processing of speech, speech production and recognition of letters whereas the right hemisphere excels at non-verbal tasks such as face recognition or tasks that involve spatial skills such as line orientation, or distinguishing different pitches of sound. This is evidence against the cerebral dominance theory which appointed the right hemisphere to be a spare tire! In fact both hemispheres are distinct and outclass at different tasks, and neither one can be omitted without this having high impact on cognitive performance.

Although the hemispheres are so distinct and are experts at their assigned functions, they also have limited abilities in performing the tasks for which the other hemisphere is specialized.

Do the Hemispheres Differ in What or How They Process?

There are two sets of approaches to the whole question of hemispheric specialisation. One set of theories goes about the topic by asking the question "What tasks is each hemisphere specialized for?". Theories that belong to this set, assign the different levels of ability to process sensory information to the different levels of abilities for higher cognitive skills. One theory that belongs to this set is the "spatial frequency hypothesis". This hypothesis states that the left hemisphere is important for fine detail analysis and high spatial frequency in visual images whereas the right hemisphere is important for low spatial frequency. We have pursued this approach above.

Local and global processing

Experiment on local and global processing with patients with left- or right-hemisphere damage

The other approach does not focus on what type of information is processed by each hemisphere but rather on *how* each hemisphere processes information. This set of theories assumes that the left hemisphere processes information in an analytic, detail- and function-focused way and that it places more importance on temporal relations between information, whereas the right hemisphere is believed to go about the processing of information in a holistic way, focusing on spatial relations and on appearance rather than on function.

The picture above shows an exemplary response to different target stimuli in an experiment on global and local processing with patients who suffer right- or left-hemisphere damage. Patients with damage to the right hemisphere often suffer a lack of attention to the global form, but recognize details with no problem. For patients with left-hemisphere-damage this is true the other way around. This experiment supports the assumption that the hemispheres differ in the way they process information.

Communication Between the Hemispheres via the Corpus Callosum

After we have looked at the different functions of each hemisphere and how researchers went about finding this out, we will now look at the role of the corpus callosum. With its 250 million nerve fibres the corpus callosum is like an Autobahn for neural data connecting the two hemispheres. There are in fact smaller connections between the hemispheres but these are little paths in comparison to the corpus callosum. All detailed higher order information must pass through the corpus callosum when being transferred from one hemisphere to the other. The transfer time which can be measured with ERP takes between 5 to 20 ms.

So why is this transfer needed at all if the hemispheres are so distinct concerning functioning, anatomy, chemistry and the transfer results in degrading of quality of information and takes time? The reason is that the hemispheres, although so different, do interact. This interaction has important advantages because as studies by Banich and Belger have shown it may "enhance the overall processing capacity under high demand conditions" (Banich). (Under low demand conditions the transfer does not make as much sense because the cost of transferring the information to the other hemisphere are higher than the advantages of parallel processing.)

The two hemispheres can interact over the corpus callosum in different ways. This is measured by first computing performance of each hemisphere individually and then measuring the overall performance of the whole brain.

In some tasks one hemisphere may dominate the other in the overall performance, so the overall performance is as good or bad as the performance of one of the single hemispheres. What's surprising is that the dominating hemisphere may very well be the one that is less specialized, so here is another example of a situation where parallel processing is less effective than processing in just one half of the brain.

Another way of how the hemispheres interact is that overall processing is an average of performance of the two individual hemispheres.

The third, most surprising way the hemispheres can interact is that when performing a task together the hemispheres behave totally different than when performing the same task individually. This can be compared to social behavior of people: Individuals behave different in groups than they would when being by themselves.

Individual Factors may Influence Lateralization

After having looked at hemispheric specialization from a general point of view, we now want to focus on differences between individuals concerning hemispheric specialization. Aspects that may have an impact on lateralization might be age, gender or handed-ness.

Age

Let's first look at whether the age of an individual decides in how far each hemisphere is used at specific tasks. Researchers have suggested that lateralization develops with age until puberty. Thus infants should not have functionally-lateralized brains. Here are four pieces of evidence that speak against this hypothesis:

Infants already show the same brain anatomy as adults. This means the brain of a new born is already lateralized. Following the hypothesis that anatomy is linked to function this means that lateralization is not developed at a later period in life.

Differences in perceptual asymmetries that means superior performance at processing verbal vs. non-verbal material in the different hemispheres cannot be observed in children aged 5 to 13, i.e. children aged 5 process the material the same way 13 year olds do.

Experiments with 1-week-old infants showed that they responded with increased interest to verbal material when this was presented to the right ear than when presented to the left ear and increased interest to non-verbal material when presented to the left ear. The infants' interest was hereby measured by the frequency of soother sucking.

Although children who underwent hemispherectomy (the surgical removal of one hemisphere) do develop the cognitive skills of the missing hemisphere (in contrast to adults or adolescents who cannot compensate for missing brain parts), they do not develop these skills to the same extent as a child with hemispherectomy of the other hemisphere. For example: A child whose right hemisphere has been removed will develop spatial skills but not to the extent that a child whose left hemisphere has been removed, and thus still possesses the right hemisphere.

Handedness

Another factor that might influence brain lateralization is handedness. There is statistical evidence that left-handers have a different brain organization than right-handers. 10% of the population is left-handed. Whereas 95% of the right-handed people process verbal material in a superior manner in the left-hemisphere, there is no such a high figure for verbal superiority of one hemisphere in left-handers: 70% of the left-handers process verbal material in the left-hemisphere, 15% process verbal material in the right hemisphere (so the functions of the hemispheres are simply switched around), and the remaining 15% are not lateralized, meaning that they process language in both hemispheres. Thus as a group, left-handers seem to be less lateralized. However a single left-handed-individual can be just as lateralized as the average right-hander.

Gender

Gender is another aspect that is believed to have impact on the hemispheric specialization. In animal studies, it was found that hormones create brain differences between the genders that are related to reproductional functions. In humans it is hard to determine to which extent it is really hormones that cause differences and to which extent it is culture and schooling that are responsible.

One brain area for which a difference between the genders was observed is the corpus callosum.

Although one study found that the c.c. is larger in women than in men these results could not be replicated. Instead it was found that the posterior part of the c.c. is more bulbous in women than in men. This might however be related to the fact that the average woman has a smaller brain than the average man and thus the bulbousness of the posterior section of the c.c. might be related to brain size and not to gender.

In experiments that measure performance in various tasks between the genders the cultural aspect is of great importance because men and women might use different problem solving strategies due to schooling.

Summary

Although the two hemispheres look like each other's mirror images at first glance, this impression is misleading. Looking closer, the hemispheres not only differ in their conformation and chemistry, but most importantly in their function. Although both hemispheres can perform all basic cognitive tasks, there exists a specialization for specific cognitive demands. In most people, the left hemisphere is an expert at verbal tasks, whereas the right hemisphere has superior abilities in non-verbal tasks. Despite the functional distinctness the hemispheres communicate with each other via the corpus callosum.

This fact has been utilized by Sperry's experiments with split-brain-patients. These are outstanding among other experiments measuring perceptual asymmetries because they were the first experiments to refute the hemispheric dominance theory and received recognition through the Nobel Prize for Medicine and Physiology.

Individual factors such as age, gender or handed-ness have no or very little impact on hemispheric functioning.

References

Editors: Robert A. Wilson and Frank C. Keil.(Eds.) (online version july 2006). The MIT Encyclopedia of the Cognitive Sciences (MITECS), Bradford Books

Knowledge Representation

Goldstein, E. Bruce.(2005). Cognitive Psychology - Connecting, Mind Research, and Everyday Experience. Thomson, Wadsworth. Ch 8 Knowledge, 265-308.

Sowa, John F.(2000). Knowledge Representation - Logical, Philosophical, and Computational Foundations. Brooks/Cole.

Slides concerning Knowledge from: http://www.cogpsy.uos.de/ , Knowledge: Propositions and images. Knowledge: Concepts and categories.

Hemispheric Specialisation/Distribution

Banich, Marie T.(1997).Neuropsycology - The Neural Bases of Mental Function. Hougthon Mifflin Company. Ch 3 Hemispheric Specialisation, 90-123.

Hutsler, J. J., Gillespie, M. E., and Gazzaniga (2002). The evolution of hemispheric specialization. In Bizzi, E., Caliassano, P. and Volterra V. (Eds.) Frontiers of Life, Volume III: The Intelligent Systems Academic Press: New York.

Birbaumer, Schmidt(1996). Biologische Psychologie. Springer Verlag Berlin-Heidelberg. 3.Auflage. Ch 24 Plastizität, Lernen, Gedächtnis. Ch 27 Kognitive Prozesse (Denken).

Kandel, Eric R.; Schwartz, James H.; Jessel, Thomas M.(2000). Principles of Neural Science. Mc Graw Hill. 4.th edition. Part IX, Ch 62 Learning and Memory.

Ivanov, Vjaceslav V.(1983). Gerade und Ungerade - Die Assymmetrie des Gehirns und der Zeichensysteme. S.Hirzel Verlag Stuttgart.

David W.Green ; et al.(1996). Cognitive Science - An Introduction. Blackwell Publishers Ltd. Ch 10 Learning and Memory(David Shanks).

Links

Knowledge Representation

From Stanford Encyclopedia of Philosophy: knowledge analysis, knowledge by acquaintance and knowledge by description

Lecture on Knowledge and Reasoning, University of Erlangen Germany

Links to Knowledge-Base and Ontology Projects Worldwide

Links on Ontologies and Related Subjects

Knowledge Representation: Logical, Philosophical, and Computational Foundations, by Sowa, John F.

Hemispheric Specialisation

Evolution of Hemispheric Specialisation, by Hutsler, Gillespie, Gazzaniga

Cerebral specialisation and interhemispheric communication, by Gazzaniga,in Oxford Journals

live version • discussion • edit lesson • comment • report an error

13 Decision Making and Reasoning

live version • discussion • edit lesson • comment • report an error

Introduction

No matter which public topic you discuss or which personal aspect you worry about – one thing you definitely need are reasons for your opinion and argumentation. People need justifications to satisfy themselves as well as they need backed up arguments in order to express themselves in society.

But how do such reasons develop? What are conclusions based on? This complex topic is very important for any person, independent of the age, the gender or the life situation, especially because it always inhales consequences and can influence life enormously.

The following chapter gives an overview about the different methods and types of reasoning considering its psychological background. Additionally it deals with the topic Executive Functions.They connect to the complex of decision making and reasoning, as they encompass 'higher-order' mental abilities such as attention, planning, organization, abstract reasoning and self-monitoring.

The problem of reasoning can be split into two important types of reasoning: Deductive reasoning (drawing conclusions based on premises) and Inductive reasoning (drawing conclusions based on evidence). Additionally there are the fields of *Reasoning and the Brain* as well as Decision making.

Deductive reasoning refers to the process of concluding that something must be true since it is a special case of a general principle that is already known to be true. Hence, one can deduce from the whole process how its single states could or should work. It implies two ways of thinking, on the one hand to think in categories – the so called *thinking categorically field* - and on the other hand to think conditional – *thinking conditionally*.

The field of inductive reasoning covers the topic on how people do reason from evidence. Inductive reasoning is the process of reasoning that a general principle is true because the special cases you do know about are true, so you conclude from the parts onto how the whole process or state must be like.

A more complex part of this article tries to show how the brain is involved in reasoning processes. Furthermore it is important to know where exactly inside the brain these cognitive skills take place and how different brain regions work together during the process of reasoning. The prefrontal cortex is known to play one of the essential roles in reasoning.

Coming now to the topic of executive functions, we will at first discuss the breakdown of them and goal-directed behavior which deals with problems such as deficits in initiation, cessation and control of action, impairments in abstract and conceptual thinking, lack of cognitive flexibility and deficits in the response to novelty and deficits in goal directed behaviors.

Second, theories of frontal lobe function in executive control are presented. These include the role of working memory, the role of controlled versus automatic processes, the use of scripts and the role of a goal list.

Deductive Reasoning

Thinking Categorically

The basic principle of deductive reasoning is that a conclusion follows from two premises. An example of such a syllogism is:

All flowers are plants.
No plants are artificial.
Therefore no flowers are artificial.

The statements of the premises begin typically with "all", "none" or "some" (as in the example) and the conclusion starts with "therefore". These kinds of syllogisms fulfil the task of describing a relationship between two categories. Two different approaches serve the study of syllogisms which are the **normative approach** and the **descriptive approach**.

The Normative Approach

The normative approach is based on logic and deals with the problem of categorizing conclusions as either valid or invalid. Two basic principles and a method called **Euler circles** have been developed to help judging about the validity. The first principle was created by Aristotle and says "If the two premises are true, the conclusion of a valid syllogism must be true" (Goldstein, 2005, page 431). The second principle explains why the following syllogism is (surprisingly) valid:

All flowers are animals.
All animals can jump.
Therefore all flowers can jump.

Even though it is quite obvious that the first premise is not true and further that the conclusion is not true, the whole syllogism is still valid. The second principle inhales that "The validity of a syllogism is determined only by its form, not its content."

Due to this precondition it is possible to display a syllogism formally with symbols or letters and explain its relationship graphically with the help of diagrams. As shown in the picture, there are various ways to demonstrate a premise graphically. Starting with a circle to represent the first premise and adding one or more circles for the second one, the crucial move is to compare the constructed diagram with the conclusion. It should be clearly laid out whether the diagrams are contradictory or not. Agreeing with one another, the syllogism is valid.

The Descriptive Approach

The descriptive approach is concerned with estimating people's ability of judging validity and explaining judging errors. This psychological approach uses two methods in order to determine people's performance. For the method of **evaluation** (which is the preferred one) people are given two premises, a conclusion and the task to judge whether the syllogism is true or not. The method of **production** supplies the participants with two premises and asks them to develop a logically valid conclusion (if possible).

With the **method of evaluation** researchers found typical reasons misjudgements about syllogisms. Premises starting with "All", "Some" or "No" imply a special atmosphere and influence a person in his decision. One mistake often occurring is judging a syllogism incorrectly as valid, in which the two premises as well as the conclusion starts with "All". The influence of the provided atmosphere leads to the right decision at most times, but is definitely not reliable and guides the person to a rash decision. This phenomenon is summarized by the **atmosphere effect**. In addition to the form of a syllogism, the content is likely to influence a person's decision as well and cause the person to neglect his logical thinking. Given a conclusion as " Some bananas are pink", hardly any participants would judge the syllogism as valid, even though it might be valid according to its premises (e.g. Some bananas are fruits. All fruits are purple.) The **belief bias** states that people tend to judge syllogisms with believable conclusions as valid, while they tend to judge syllogisms with not believable conclusions as invalid.

Mental Models of Deductive Reasoning

From the data already given it is still not possible to consider what mental processes might be occurring as people are trying to determine if a syllogism is valid. After finding out that Euler circles can be used to determine the validity of a syllogism Phillip Johnson – Laird (1999) wondered whether people would use such circles naturally when not haven been taught to them. At the same time he found out that they do not work for some more complex syllogisms and that a problem can be solved by applying logical rules, but most people most people solve them by imagining the situation. This is the base idea of people using mental models – a specific situation that is represented in a person's mind that can be used to help determine the validity of syllogisms – to solve deductive reasoning problems. The basic principle behind such a mental model theory is: A conclusion is valid only if it cannot be refuted by any mode of the premises. This theory is attractive because it makes predictions that can be tested and because it can be applied without training in the rules of logic. But there are still problems that face researchers when trying to determine how people reason about syllogisms. These problems include the fact that a variety of different strategies are used by people in reasoning and that some people are better in solving syllogisms than others.

Effects of Culture on Deductive Reasoning

Now it is known that people can be influenced by the content of syllogisms rather then by focusing on logic when judging their validity. Psychologists have wondered whether people are influenced by their cultures when judging. Therefore they have done cross – cultural experiments in which reasoning problems were presented to people in different cultures. They found out that people from different cultures judge differently to these questions. For example, a man from a traditional tribe in Liberia would give a wrong answer to such a reasoning problem when the question is considered purely in terms of formal logic, but for justifying his answer he would use logic. This shows that the man uses evidence from his own experience (empirical evidence) but is ignoring evidence presented in the syllogism (theoretical evidence). When asking people to explain their answers it becomes clear that they often base their response on empirical evidence. Another fact that becomes by these experiments is the difference between educated and uneducated participants. Uneducated people are often affected by the believability of the conclusion, while educated people base their judgments on logic. These results might occur because of the difference in raising up their children. It also shows that European Americans for example are less susceptible to the belief bias then Eastern Asians. Such experiments strengthen the idea that people in different cultures may use different strategies for reasoning.

Thinking Conditionally

Another type of syllogisms is called 'conditional syllogism'. Just like the categorical one, it also has two premises and a conclusion. In difference the first premise has the form 'If ... then'. Syllogisms like this one are common in everyday life. Consider the following example:

1. assumption: If it is raining, Frank gets wet.
2. assumption: Frank gets wet.
3. conclusion: therefore it is raining.

Forms of conditionla syllogisms

Now it can be differenciated between four forms of conditional syllogisms, which all do have abstract terms p and q indicated in parenthesis. These notations p and q are typically used for conditional syllogisms where p is the antecedent (the 'If' term in 'If p then q') and q is the consequent (the 'then' term in 'If p then q'). The first form of conditional syllogisms which will be explained is called modus ponens (which means 'method of affirmation' in Latin, because the antecedent p is affirmed in the second premise/ assumption). This rule of inference says: 'If p then q, and also given p' (affirming the antecedent). To make it more clearly the example given before is used, but this time the antecedent is affirmed in the second premise:

If it is raining, Frank gets wet.
It is raining.
Therefore Frank gets wet.

The conclusion of this example is valid.

Another rule of inference which is the second form of conditional syllogisms is called modus tollens (which means 'method of denying' in Latin, because the consequent is negated in the second premise).It says: 'If p then q, and q is false.' Again the same example is used but it is differs a bit because of negating the consequent in the second premise:

If it is raining, Frank gets wet.
Frank does not get wet.
Therefore it is not raining.

This conclusion is also valid.

Now the following two forms are invalid. It will be soon considered why. Denying the antecedent is the third form which procedes the negation of p in the second premise:

If it is raining, Frank gets wet.
It is not raining.

Therefore Frank does not get wet.

Many people argue the above conclusion is valid, but it is not. The reason for invalidity is that it does not have to be raining for Frank to get wet (e.g he might have jumped into a swimming pool). Last but not least the forth form is called affirming the consequent. It is called so, because q is affirmed in the second premise, which is described more clearly by the following example:

If it is raining, Frank gets wet.
Frank gets wet.
Therefore it is raining.

This conclusion is also invalid for the same reason as before. The fact that Frank gets wet can follow from another antecedent (again he might have been swimming). The results of many experiments have shown that most people (close to 100 percent) correctly judge that modus ponens is valid, but perform lower on modus tollens and the other two forms. Another important point for people's performance in conditional reasoning tasks is the way the task is stated. This means people's performance is dependent on whether the task is stated abstractly or concretely. The knowledge possessed by the person who is evaluating the syllogism is also important for the performance.

Why people make errors in conditional reasoning: The Wason Four- Card- problem

People are often better at judging the validity of syllogisms when real – world items are substituted for abstract symbols. But it is also known that real – world items can sometimes lead to errors as when people are influenced by the belief bias. There are many experiments which provide the evidence for the effect of using real – world items in a conditional reasoning problem. The Wason Four – Card – problem is one of these experiments. Four cards are shown to the participants. There is a letter on one side of each card and a number on the other side. The participants task was to indicate the minimum number of cards they would need to turn over to test the following rule: If there is a vowel on one side then there is an even number on the other side. In one of the most used versions of this experiment the cards have the following four symbols visible: 'E' 'K' '4' '7' 55 percent of participants selected the 'E' card which is correct, because turning this card over tests the rule. However still another card needed to be turned over to fully test the rule. 64 percent indicated the '4' card to be turned over after 'E'. This answer indeed is not the best one, because if there is a vowel on the other side of the card it is consistent with the rule, but if there is a consonant on the other side, then turning the '4' wouldn't tell anything about the rule since having a consonant on one side and a vowel on the other side does not violate the rule. In Wasons's experiment only 4 percent of participants answered correctly that the '7'`card also needs to be turned over. This is important because turning this card over would disconfirm the rule by revealing a vowel. Now for solving such a card problem one should be aware of the falsification principle which says for testing a rule it is necessary to look for situations that falsify the rule.

Stating the Four – Card task in real – world terms: the role of 'Regulations'

The main reason researchers are interested in the Wason Four – Card problem is that they want to figure out why participants make so many errors. For answering this, they determined how participants perform when the problem is restarted in real – world terms. One of the experiments for determining this was the beer/drinking-age problem used by Richard Griggs and James Cox (1982). This experiment is identical to the Wason Four – Card problem except that instead of numbers and letters on the cards everyday terms (beer, soda and ages) were used. Griggs and Cox found out that 73 percent of participants provided the correct response for the following rule: 'If a person is drinking beer then he or she must be over 19 years old.' As mentioned before few of the participants answered the abstract Four - Card task correctly. Now, why is it easier to solve such a problem when using real – world terms? Apparently being able to relate the beer task to regulations about drinking makes it easier to pick the right card to turn over. Another experiment was done, the instructions following: 'Pretend you are a postal worker sorting letters. A letter which is sealed must have a '5d' stemp on it according to the postal regulations. Which of the four envelopments (one is shown from the sealed side, the other one is shown unsealed, the third one is shown with a '5d' stemp and the last one is shown with a '4d' stemp) would you have to turn over to determine whether the rule is being obeyed?' The experiment was done with English and American participants. The fact that English participants performed better (a higher percentage of them chose the sealed envelope and the one with a 4d-stamp on it to be turned over) than American was very striking. The reason for this result appeared to be that the American participants were not familiar with postal regulations like this one but the English were.

Pragmatic Reasoning Schemas in the Wason Task: The role of 'Permission'

Patricia Chena and Keith Holyoak (1985) proposed the concept of pragmatic reasoning schemas. A pragmatic reasoning schema is a way of thinking about case and effect in the world that is learned as part of experiencing everyday life. One of these schemas that people learn is called the permission schema which states that if a person satisfies condition A, then he/ she get to carry out action B. As an example the permission schema for the beer'/ drinking – age problem ('If you are 19 years old, then you are allowed to drink beer.') has already been learned by most of the participants, so they were able to apply that schema to the card task.

This makes it easier to people to understand the difference between the abstract version or the 'drinking beer' or 'postal regulation' version of the card task. Apparently activating the permission schema helps people to focus on attention on the right card, which is often ignored by them in the abstract task.

An evolutionary approach to the Four – Card – problem: The role of 'Cheating'

The Wason Four – Card – problem did not only prove the evidence for the effect on using it in a conditional reasoning problem, but it also had led cognitive psychologists to another controversy in which there were different explanations offered for the result of various experiments. As already mentioned the permission schema is one of them. Now there is a proposed alternative to this idea which states that the performance on the Wason task is governed by a built – in cognitive program for detecting cheating.

Some psychologists (among them are Leda Cosmides and John Tobby (1992)) do have an evolutionary perspective on cognition in which they argue that human beings can trace many properties of their minds to the evolutionary principle of natural selection. Now according to this natural selection adaptive characteristics (characteristics that help a person or an animal to survive to pass their genes to the next generation) will become a basic characteristic of humans.

Applying to this idea it follows that a highly adaptive feature of the mind would become a basic characteristic of the mind. According to the evolutionary approach, one such characteristic is related to the idea of social exchange theory. This theory states that an important aspect of human behavior is the ability for two persons to cooperate in a way that is beneficial to both of them. As long as each person is receiving a benefit for whatever he/ she gives up, everything works well in social exchange. But if someone cheats, some problem arises. Therefore it is important that people are able to detect cheating behavior to avoid it. Because this is an important tool for them to have better chances to survive, 'detecting cheating' has become a part of the brain's cognitive makeup.

Now with this evolutionary approach the Wason Four – Card – problem can be understood in terms of cheating. Cosmides and Tobby devised a number of experiments to determine whether 'detecting cheating' is helping by decisions or not. They created unfamiliar situations in Four – Card scenarios which include cheating. It was obvious that the participants' performance was high, though even task was unfamiliar to them. They also ran some other experiments which did not include cheating to prove that participants perform better in experiments which include it.

However other researchers have created scenarios with unfamiliar situations, but which did not include cheating. It was astonishing that stating problems in this way caused an increase in performance. An example of these experiments was one devised by Ken Maktelow and David Over (1990) in which they tested people using a rule that says 'If you clean up spillt blood, you must wear gloves'. Now there are a lot more examples for controversial research in the field of cognitive reasoning and for each of the mechanisms presented for and against it.

What will be left is the important finding that the context within which conditional reasoning occurs makes a big difference. All this controversy can be inferred from the behavioral evidence. This shows how complex the mind is and that it can have a number of different ways of approaching such a task like the Wason task, depending on the situation.

Inductive Reasoning

In the previous chapters we discussed deductive reasoning, reaching conclusions based on logical rules applied to a set of premises.

However, many problems cannot be represented in a way that would make it possible to use these rules to get a conclusion. In this chapter we will talk about a way to be able to decide in terms of these problems as well: inductive reasoning.

Inductive reasoning means making simple observations of a certain kind and apply these observations via generalization to a different problem to make a decision.

One famous example for this kind of reasoning is the following:

All crows I have ever seen are black.
Therefore, every crow in the world is black.

This is an example for the so called 'strong inductive reasoning'. It is easy to see that inductive reasoning leads to a quick conclusion that is likely but not certain, since it is impossible to check the color of every crow in the world. An example for 'weak inductive reasoning' would be a statement like this:

I always cook noodles in a frying pan.

Therefore, noodles are cooked in a frying pan.

(For this kind of reasoning the same conditions hold than stated before for strong inductive reasoning.)

This is the difference between inductive and deductive reasoning. While deduction brings conclusions that are inevitably based on certain rules (arguments are called 'sound' or 'valid), induction is concerned rather with the probability of an event or a statement based on previously gathered evidence (the correct terminology here is 'cogent').

Induction vs deduction

Induction is the form of reasoning that is used more often and much more easily. Most of the time we use it without even realizing that we do some kind of reasoning at the moment. Whether it is the sunrise every morning and the sunset in the evening, the change of seasons, the TV program, the fact that a chair does not collapse when we sit on it or the lightbulb that flashes after we have pushed a button, all of these are examples for inductive reasoning. We think that certain events will occur or that our actions have certain kinds of effects because this is the way it always is and has been and therefore we have good reason to believe that it is going to happen in just the same way. It would take way too much time and effort to think about all these things every time anew.

Deduction and induction are also regarded as being the complement of one another and inductively reached conclusions are usually deductively invalid. But it would be a mistake to say that these two are totally independent from each other. It is often the case that one needs inductive reasoning first to get to deductive reasoning. A good example for this is the whole field of science. To be able to compile a formula in physics for example, one needs a theory at first that can be tested. This is nothing but inductive reasoning:

I realize that everything I see, including myself, is somehow fixed to the surface of the earth. I have been to different places on this planet and noticed the same. Although I have not seen every single corner in the world, I assume that this principle holds for every piece of matter with a certain mass.

This is a prime example for inductive reasoning because it shows that it can be regarded as making an assumption that is thought quite probable to be the case but not foolproof.

How reliable are conclusions reached through induction?

What it also shows is an important aspect for evaluating conclusions reached through induction: The size of the sample, also called the 'law of large numbers'.

If I have been to many countries and saw the same circumstances everywhere, it is much more likely that these circumstances can be found on the whole planet than if I have seen nothing but my own town. It might be the case that in the next town people are walking on the ceiling. I cannot say anything about that because I have never been out of town to check on it.

Other factors that contribute to the so-called 'strength' of the argument is the representativeness of the observations and the quality of the evidence.

To ask only members of a reigning political party about the current government of their country is certainly not very representative because it only takes into account the opinion of people that are very likely to approve it.

And it is no better idea to ask other people the same question when it is in the middle of the night and they have spent the last five hours in a pub. It would be quite doubtful that their answers were of the quality we want for doing proper reasoning.

Processes and constraints of inductive reasoning

But how does inductive reasoning happen in more special cases than strong inductive reasoning? And what kinds of psychological pitfalls are there to it? To get a little bit deeper into this subject, we will introduce some processes and consraints related to inductive reasoning:

The availability heuristic

Things that are more easily remembered are judged to be more prevalent. Examples are two experiments that have been made. One of them asked people to say which one of two different causes of death occurs more often (Lichtenstein et al., 1978). Because of the availability heuristic people judged more 'spectacular' causes like homicide or pregnancy to cause more deaths than others, like asthma. In another similar experiment participants had to say whether there were more words in a list starting with an 'r' or more words having 'r' as the third letter (Tversky & Kahneman, 1973). Most people picked the former although there were actually three times as many words having 'r' in third position.

The representativeness heuristic

Judgements are often made based on how much an event resembles another event. If I hear loud scratching noises in the back of my car while parking, I know that I bumped into another car. If I hear the same kind of noise from the front of the car, I will be much more likely to think about an accident than if I heard a soft sound like when I drive my car into a heap of freshly fallen snow in winter. Even if the noise comes from another direction, it is much more similar to the first scenario than the snow scenario.

Illusory correlations

People tend to judge according to stereotypes. This is what is known by the term 'prejudice'. It means that a much oversimplified generalization about a group or a class of people is made. Usually this focuses on the negative and has absolutely no proof in reality. This property of inductive reasoning can be very dangerous. Examples for this are racist believes about Afro-Americans or Jews during the time of the Third Reich.

The conjunction rule

The conjunction of two events is never more likely to be the case than the single events alone. An example for this is the case of the femininist bank teller (Tversky & Kahneman, 1983). If we are introduced to a woman of whom we know that she is very interested in women's rights and has participated in many political activities in college and we are to decide whether it is more likely that she is a bank teller or a feminist bank teller, we are drawn to conclude the latter based on our knowledge about her. But it is in fact much more likely that somebody is just a bank teller than it is that someone is a feminist in addition to being a bank teller.

Confirmation bias

This phenomenon describes the fact that people tend to decide in terms of what they themselves believe to be true or good. If we go back to the example of the members of the political party, let us imagine that they are strictly against abortion. If they are presented with a bill that prohibits abortion but features in addition to that a list of some arguments pro and contra abortion, they would judge the prohibition as being a good thing although the list might contain twice as many arguments for abortion than against it.

The hindsight bias

Estimations are reconsidered after getting more infromation. If you ask someone about the percentage of water on the planet's surface and after a while you give him the answer and ask what it was that he had estimated before, he is quite likely to give another number that is closer to the actual percentage.

The probability heuristic

This is simply the term for the fact that the subjective probabilities one would give for an event might differ to a smaller or larger extent from the actual probabilities of the event. Reasons for this can be all of the above.

The gambler's fallacy

And a little tidbit at the end of the list: Against most intuitions the rolling of a dice is totally independent from earlier outcomes, of course. Throwing a six has exactly the same probability after the throwing of five, one and four than it has after three sixes have been thrown already. This is also an example for the representativeness heuristic.

So, why inductive reasoning at all?

All of these introduced phenomenons are responsible for leading our reasoning by induction. And as we can easily see, quite often they lead us on the wrong track. But they are important nevertheless because they act as shortcuts for our reasoning. We have said that inductive reasoning is used in everyday situations much more often than deductive reasoning because it is faster and easier. The attributes featured in the above list are the reason for that.

And this shows exactly what inductive reasoning is and why it is so useful:

It is a way of making decisions that might not ground on real facts, but on what best suits the purposes of the individual in a particular situation and it is a very quick way of making these decisions. And this is much more important because most of the time decisions are supposed to serve the purposes of a person and are made within parts of seconds without us even noticing that we just made a decision.

Decision Making: Choosing Among Alternatives

About the Process

The psychological process of decision making constantly goes along with situations in daily life. Determining preferences among different alternatives can have minor consequences (e.g. deciding between chocolate and vanilla ice cream), but it can also have relevant influence on important circumstances of life in the future (e.g. job decisions, influencing also family life, hobbies, self-esteem, salary, ...). The mentioned examples are both characterized by **personal** decisions, whereas **professional** decisions, dealing for example with economic or political issues, are just as important.

According to the different levels of consequences, each process of making a decision requires appropriate effort and various aspects to be considered. Such a process can be roughly structured into three steps, beginning with the **information-gathering stage**, proceeding through **likelihood estimation and deliberation** and being completed by the **final act of choosing**.

There are three different approaches to the analysis of decision making. The **normative** approach assumes a rational decision-maker with well-defined preferences. While the rational choice theory is based on a priori considerations, the **descriptive** approach is based on empirical observation and on experimental studies of choice behavior. The **prescriptive** enterprise develops methods in order to improve decision making.

The Utility Approach

According to Manktelow and Reber´s definition, "**utility** refers to outcomes that are desirable because they are in the person's best interest" (as cited in Goldstein, 2005, p. 468). An early economic approach characterizes optimal decision making by the maximum expected utility (in terms of monetary value). This approach can be helpful in gambling theories, but simultaneously inhales several disadvantages. People do not necessarily focus on the monetary payoff, since they find value in things other than money, such as fun, free time, family, health, ... Therefore not choosing the maximal monetary value does not automatically describe an irrational decision process.

Misleading Effects

Situation Models

By imagining the most intuitive consequences of different decisions, people often create **situation models** (Kahneman & Tversky, 1982; Dunning & Parpal, 1989) which might be misleading, since they rely on subjective speculations. An example could be deciding where to move by considering typical prejudices of the countries (e.g. always good pizza, nice weather and a relaxed life-style in Italy in contrast to some kind of boring food and steady rain in Great Britain). The predicted events are not equal to the events occurring indeed.

Focusing Illusion

Another misleading effect is the so-called **focusing illusion**. By considering only the most obvious aspects in order to make a certain decision (e.g. the weather) people often neglect various really important outcomes (e.g. circumstances at work). This effect occurs more often if people judge about others than in case of judging about their own life conditions.

Framing Effect

A problem can be described in different ways and therefore evoke different decision strategies. If a problem is specified in terms of gains, people tend to use a risk-aversion strategy, while a problem description in terms of losses leads to apply a risk-taking strategy. An example of the same problem and predictably different choices is the following: A group of people asked to imagine themselves $300 richer than they are, is confronted with the choice of a sure gain of $100 or an equal chance to gain $200 or nothing. Most people avoid the risk and take the sure gain, which means they take the risk-aversion strategy. Alternatively asked to assume themselves to be $500 richer than in reality, given the options of a sure loss of $100 or an equal chance to lose $200 or nothing, the majority opts for the risk of losing $200 by taking the risk seeking or risk-taking strategy. This phenomenon is known as **framing effect**. (text)

Justification in Decision Making

Decision making often includes the need to assign a reason for the decision and therefore justify it. This factor is illustrated by an experiment by Tversky and Eldar Shafir (1992). A very attractive vacation package has been offered to a group of students who have just passed an exam and to another group of students who have just failed the exam and have the chance to rewrite it after the holidays coming up. All students have the options to buy the ticket straight away, to stay at home, or to pay $5 to keep open the option and to buy it later. At this point, there is no difference between the two groups, since the number of students who passed the exam and deciding to book the flight (with the justification of a treat), is the same as the number of students who failed and booking the flight (justified by a consolation with time to reoccupate).

A third group of students who were informed to receive their results in two more days was confronted with the same problem. The majority decided to pay $5 and keep the option open until they would get their results. Even though the actual exam result does not influence the decision, it is required in order to provide a rationale.

Executive Functions

The talk about decision making leads us deeper into the brain and gives us the chance to look at this and similar psychological abilities on a more neurological level: the executive functions.

As in part already introduced in the overview section of this chapter, executive functions include (among others) having a master plan or a general conception about reaching some specific goal, assimilating new information, modifying plans and being responsive to change, keeping track of multiple tasks simultaneously and understanding relations among them, prioritizing both decisions and actions and, in a more abstract way, social skills and political savvy. For short you could say that your executive functions altogether act as the executive manager of your behavior. As you can see, the above list of abilities is already quite long though still incomplete. This shows that providing an exact definition is very difficult. They are not completely separated from one another but have multifaceted and shared characteristics. Furthermore, each function cannot be linked to a specific brain region either, but has to be connected with overlapping regions.

For the most part, though not in every case, these regions are located in the frontal or more precisely, the prefrontal lobe. If these regions are damaged, this can lead to profound deficits in a patient's executive functions, called executive dysfunction, whereas this does not mean that his or her overall intelligence is affected, as can be shown through IQ-tests. But depending on the extent of the damage, it can be nonetheless impossible for this person to ever lead a 'normal' life without constant help and support from the outside.

In the following we would like to explain why this is so by describing the most common executive dysfunctions.

Deficits in initiation, cessation and control of action

We start by describing the effects of the loss of the ability to start something, to initiate an action. A person with executive dysfunction is likely to have trouble beginning to work on a task without strong help from the outside, while people with left frontal lobe damage often show impaired spontaneous speech and people with right frontal lobe damage rather show poor nonverbal fluency. Of course, one reason is the fact that this person will not have any intention, desire or concern on his or her own of solving the task since this is yet another characteristic of executive dysfunction. But it is also due to a psychological effect often connected with the loss of properly executive functioning: psychological inertia.

Like in physics, inertia in this case means that an action is very hard to initiate, but once started, it is again very hard to shift or stop. This phenomenon is characterized by engagement in repetitive behavior, is called perseveration and can best be observed in a famous experiment, the Wisconsin Card Sorting Test or short, WCST.

A participant is presented with cards that show certain objects. These cards are defined by shape, color and number of the objects on the cards. These cards now have to be sorted according to a rule based on one of these three criteria. The participant does not know which rule is the right one but has to reach the conclusion after positive or negative feedback of the experimenter. Then at some point, after the participant has found the correct rule to sort the cards, the experimenter changes the rule and the correct sorting will lead to negative feedback. The participant has to realize the change and adapt to it by sorting the cards according to the new rule.

Patients with executive dysfunction have problems identifying the rule in the first place. It takes them noticeably longer because they have trouble using already given information to make a conclusion (will be explained later). But once they got to sorting correctly and the rule changes, they keep sorting the cards according to the old rule although many of them notice the negative feedback. They are just not able to switch to another sorting-priciple, or at least they need many tries to learn the new one. They perseverate.

Another problem caused by executive dysfunction can be observed in patients suffering from the so called environmental dependency syndrome. Their actions are impelled or obligated by their physical or social environment. This manifests itself in many different ways and depends to a large extent on the individual's personal history. Examples are patients who begin to type when they see a computer key board, who start washing the dishes upon seeing a dirty kitchen or who hang up pictures on the walls when finding hammer, nails and pictures on the floor. This makes these people appear as if they were acting impulsively or as if they have lost their 'free will'. It shows a lack of control for their actions. This is due to the fact that an impairment in their executive functions causes a disconnection between thought an action, these patients know that their actions are wrong but like in the WCST, they cannot control what they are doing. Even if they are told by which attribute to sort the cards, they will still keep sorting them sticking to the old rule due to major difficulties in the translation of these directions into action.

What is needed to avoid problems like these are the abilities to start, stop or change an action but very likely also the ability to use information to direct behavior.

Impairments in abstract and conceptual thinking

To solve many tasks it is important that one is able to use given information. Often this means that material has to be processed in an abstract rather than in a concrete manner. Patients with executive dysfunction have abstraction difficulties. This is proven by another card sorting experiment (Delis et al., 1992).

This time, the cards show names of animals and black or white triangles placed above or below the word. Again, the cards can be sorted with attention to different attributes of the animals (living on land or in water, domestic or dangerous, large or small) or the triangles (black or white, above or below word). Unlike in the WCST, people with frontal lobe damage fail to solve the task because they cannot even conceptualize the properties of the animals or the triangles, thus are not able to deduce a sorting-rule for the cards (in contrast, there are some individuals with only perseverative tendencies, they find a sorting-criterion but then are unable to switch it).

As we have seen in other examples before, these problems in abstract conceptualization remain after the participants have been given abstract or even concrete cues. Therefore, it is sometimes believed that their problem might be caused by, once again, the difficulty in translating thought to action. Furthermore, once they found a rule to sort, they are unable to describe their sorting-criterion.

In general, all these problems are not connected to perseverative tendencies but rather to major difficulties for patients with frontal lobe damage to conceptualize information in an abstract manner. Plus, that information cannot be used to guide behavior. A reason for these problems might be a general difficulty in strategy formation (will be discussed later).

Deficits in cognitive estimation

Cognitive estimation is the ability to use known information to make reasonable judgements or deductions about the world. Now the inability for cognitive estimation is the third type of deficits often observed in individuals with executive dysfunction. It is already known that people with executive dysfunction have a relatively unaffected knowledge base. This means they cannot retain knowledge about information or at least they are unable to make inferences based on it. There are various effects which are shown on such individuals. Now for example patients with frontal lobe damage have difficulty estimating the length of the spine of an average woman. Making such realistic estimation requires inference based on other knowledge which is in this case, knowing that the height of the average woman is about 5ft 6 in (168cm) and considering that the spine runs about one third to one half the length of the body and so on.

Patients with such a dysfunction do not only have difficulties in their estimates of cognitive information but also in their estimates of their own capacities (such as their ability to direct activity in goal – oriented manner or in controlling their emotions).

Prigatuno, Altman and O'Brien (1990) reported that when patients with anterior lesions associated with diffuse axonal injury to other brain areas are asked how capable they are of performing tasks such as scheduling their daily activities or preventing their emotions from affecting daily activities, they grossly overestimate their abilities. From several experiments Smith and Miler (1988) found out that individuals with frontal lobe damages have no difficulties in determining whether an item was in a specific inspection series they find it difficult to estimate how frequently an item did occur. This may not only reflect difficulties in cognitive estimation but also in memory task that place a premium on remembering temporal information.

Later the fact that individuals with such dysfunction and frontal lobe damage are impaired on a variety of sequencing tasks will be explained more in detail. Thus both difficulties (in cognitive estimation and in temporal sequencing) may contribute to a reduced ability to estimate frequency of occurrence.

Despite these impairments in some domains the abilities of estimation are preserved in patients with frontal lobe damage. Such patients also do have problems in estimating how well they can prevent their emotions for affecting their daily activities. They are also as component as patients with temporal lobe damage or neurologically intact patients at judging how many dues they will need to solve a puzzle. For solving a puzzle patients with frontal lobe damage try to guess the answer. Therefore the ability for estimating is not entirely lost but is compromised in a number of areas.

Lack of Cognitive Flexibility and Deficits in the Response to Novelty

People with executive dysfunction are unable to look at situations from more than one point and to produce a variety of behavior and therefore unable to be cognitively flexible. Now this cognitive inflexibility can be called distinct from and related to cognitive estimation. But when dealing with new situations this flexibility is very important. It is also required when a person has to react newly to an old stimulus. Because damage to the prefrontal areas in the brain leads to difficulties in dealing with novel situations some theorists suggest that this area plays an important role.

Deficits in goal directed behavior

The last part that is affected by the breakdown of executive functions we want to discuss are the problems in goal-directed behavior. This topic is closely related to the area of problem solving since this is nothing else than organizing behavior towards a goal.

To make this more plastic, for the course of this topic we want to introduce an example that requires an individual to behave goal-directed. Let us imagine that a person, call him John, has just got up in the morning and wants to get dressed, in this case John's goal is being dressed. For neurologically intact people this task is not at all hard to master, they might not even realize that it is any task because it is so trivial. But if you look closely, there are a lot of things that have to be taken into account while working towards being fully dressed and any other task – trivial or not – in general.

What characterizes goal directed behavior?

Now, in the case of John, which are these?

Goal must be kept in mind

During the whole process it is improtant to always remember what it actually was that John wanted to do. If he starts getting dressed and forgets that he wanted to get dressed quickly because he might have overslept and is late in time, and starts making his breakfast, he definitely will not reach his goal of getting fully dressed.

Dividing into subtasks and sequencing

Most tasks have to de divided into subtasks, in John's case: getting clothes, such as underwear, a shirt, trousers, socks and a tie, and putting them on one after the other in a sensible order. This means that John has to sequence the subtasks. He has to think about the fact that he cannot put on any clothes that are still inside of the wardrobe and that he cannot put on the underwear after he has put on his trousers.

Completed portions must be kept in mind

John has to remember which of the subtasks he has performed already, meaning that he need not do them again. He only needs to get one piece (or pair) of clothes of each kind out of the wardrobe and after he has put on his tie he must know that he does not have to look for another one and put this on as well.

Flexibility and adaptability

Imagine that John has a shirt that is his favourite one and he plans on wearing it today. He looks into the wardrobe and does not find it. Now he has to realize that the shirt is not inside the wardrobe and has to develop alternative ways to complete the task of getting dressed. Maybe his wife has put the shirt into the laundry because it was dirty? In this case, John has to adapt to this situation and has to pick another shirt that was not in his plan originally.

Evaluation of actions

Along the way of reaching his ultimate goal John constantly has to evaluate his performance in terms of 'How am I doing considering that I have the goal of being dressed?'. If he is looking for socks or is working on the knot of his tie (after he has put on all the other clothes), he should know that he is doing perfectly fine in completing the subtasks required to reach his goal. But if he is distracted by his new tuxedo inside the wardrobe and starts getting dressed in it just to see how it looks on him, he has to realize that he is not working towards his goal of being properly dressed for a day at the office. He also will not reach his goal if he has the opinion that he is done getting dressed when he is only wearing his underpants and socks.

As we have seen, goal directed bahaviour is by far not as easy as it looks on first sight. Most people still will not have any trouble though, but think about what we have said about executive functions already.

Executive dysfunction and goal directed behavior

The breakdown of executive functions impairs goal directed behavior to a large extend. In which way cannot be stated in general, it depends on the specific brain regions that are damaged. So it is quite possible that an individual with a particular lesion has problems with two or three of the five points described above and performs within average regions when the other abilities are tested, however, if only one link is missing from the chain, the whole plan might get very hard or even impossible to master. Furthermore, the particular hemisphere affected plays a role as well. Patients with lesions in the left hemisphere have difficulties with one aspect of a task and patients with lesions ind the right hemisphere have difficulties with other aspects of the same tasks.

Problems in sequencing

For example, in an experiment (Milner, 1982) people were shown a sequence of cards with pictures. The experiment included two different tasks: recognition trials and recency trials. In the former the patients were shown two different pictures, one of them has appeared in the sequence before, and the participants had to decide which one it was. In the latter they were shown two different pictures, both of them have appeared before, they had to name the picture that was shown more recently than the other one. The results of this experiment showed that people with lesions in temporal regions have more trouble with the recognition trial and patients with frontal lesions have difficulties with the recency trial since anterior regions are important for sequencing. This is due to the fact that the recognition trial demanded a properly functioning recognition memory, the recency trial a properly functioning memory for item order. These two are dissociable and located in different areas of the brain.

Another interesting result was the fact that lesions in the frontal lobes of left and right hemisphere impaired different abilities. While a lesion in the right hemisphere caused trouble in making recency judgements, a lesion in the left hemisphere impaired the patient's performance only when the presented material was verbal or in a variation of the experiment that required self-ordered sequencing. Because of that we know that the ability to sequence behavior is not only located in the frontal lobe but in the left hemisphere particularly when it comes to motor action.

The frontal lobe is not only important for sequencing but also for working memory because the patient has to keep track of the items presented to them to make recency judgements. This idea is supported by the fact that lesions in the lateral regions of the frontal lobe are much more likely to impair this ability than damage to other areas of the frontal cortex.

But this is not the only thing there is to sequencing. For reaching a goal in the best possible way it is important that a person is able to figure out which sequence of actions, which strategy, best suits the purpose, in addition to just being able to develop a correct sequence. This is proven by an experiment called 'Tower of London' (Shallice, 1982) which is similar to the famous 'Tower of Hanoi' task with the difference that this task required three balls to be put onto three poles of different length so that one pole could hold three balls, the second one two and the third one only one ball, in a way that a changeable goal position is attained out of a fixed initial position in as few moves as possible. Especially patients with damage to the left frontal lobe proved to work inefficiently and ineffectively on this task, they needed many moves and engaged in actions that did not lead toward the goal. But in the end, although there are differences in how executive functions are affected depending on the particular hemisphere where the frontal lobe lesion is located, abilities connected with sequencing are mostly provided by overlapping structures in both frontal lobes.

Problems in shifting and modifying strategies

The intact neuronal tissue in the frontal lobe is also crucial for another exectuvie function connected with goal directed behavior that we described above: flexibility and adaptability. This means that a person with frontal lobe damage will have difficulties in shifting in set - meaning creating a new plan after it has been found out that the original one cannot be carried out for some reason - and in modifying the initial strategy according to this new set. In what particular way this can be observed in patients can again not be stated in general but depends on the nature of the shift that has to be made.

An experiment (Owen, 1991) that presented patients with pictures that required different kinds of conceptual shifts, discrimination between two black shapes, between two black shapes while ignoring intermingled white shapes ('intradimensional') and between the two white shapes ('extradimensional'), showed that patients with lesions in the frontal lobe have difficulties only with the extradimensional shift. This shows that these people cannot apply general rules to situations that are different from the origninal situations when these rules were learned. Besides, they are unable to create alternatives to their original plans because they stay fixed on their original way of dealing with a situation and cannot disengage from it. This is also part of the usual perseveration problems found in patients with executive dysfunction.

Another problem of patients with frontal lobe damage is that they do not use as many appropriate hypotheses for creating a strategy as people with damage to other brain regions do or they suddenly abandon it when they have found an appropriate hypothesis. Also, it seems not very surprising that they have big trouble switching beteen hypotheses indicated by Owen's experiment. Even when it is clear that one hypothesis cannot be the right one, patients will stick to it nevertheless and are unable to abandon it (called 'tunnel vision').

These earlier described problems of 'redirecting' of one's strategies stand in contrast to the atcual 'act of switching' between tasks. This is yet another problem for patients with frontal lobe damage. Since the control system that leads task switching as such is independent from the parts that actually perform these tasks, the task switching is particularly impaired in patients with lesions to the dorsolateral prefrontal cortex while at the same time they have no trouble with performing the single tasks alone. This of course, causes a lot of problems in goal directed behavior because as it was said before, most tasks consist of smaller subtasks that have to be completed.

Problems with the interpretation of available information

Quite often, if we want to reach a goal, we get hints on how to do it best. This means we have to be able to interpret the available information in terms of what the appropriate strategy would be. For many patients of executive dysfunction this is not an easy thing to do either. They have trouble to use this information and thus, engage in inefficient actions and it takes them much longer to solve a task than it would if they took into account the extra information and developed an effective strategy.

Problems with self-criticism and -monitoring

The last problem for people with frontal lobe damage we want to present here is the last point in the above list of properties important for proper goal directed behavior. It is the ability to evaluate one's actions, an ability that is missing in most patients. These people are therefore very likely to 'wander off task' and engage in behavior that does not help them to attain their goal. In addition to that, they are also not able to determine whether their task is already completed at all. Reasons for this are thought to be a lack of motivation or lack of concern about one's performance (frontal lobe damage is usually accompanied by changes in emotional processing) but these are probably not the only explanations there are for these problems.

Another important brain region in this context – the medial portion of the frontal lobe – is responsible for detecting behavioral errors made while working towards a goal. This has been shown by ERP experiments where there was an error-related negativity 100ms after an error has been made. If this area is damaged, this mechanism cannot work properly anymore and the patient loses the ability to detect errors and thus monitor his own behavior.

However, in the end we must add that although executive dysfunction causes an enormous number of problems in behaving correctly towards a goal, most patients when assigned with a task are indeed anxious to solve it but are just unable to do so which can manifest in all the various ways discussed in the passages above.

Theories of Frontal Lobe Function in Executive Control

In order to explain that patients with frontal lobe damage have difficulties in performing executive functions, four major approaches have developed. Each of them leads to an improved understanding of the role of frontal regions in executive functions, but none of these theories covers all the deficits occurred.

Role of Working Memory

The most anatomically specific approach assumes the dorsolateral prefrontal area of the frontal lobe to be critical for working memory. The working memory which has to be clearly distinguished from the long term memory keeps information on-line for use in performing a task.

Not being generated for accounting for the broad array of dysfunctions it focuses on the three following deficits. Sequencing information and directing behavior toward a goal, understanding of temporal relations between items and events, and some aspects of environmental dependency and perseveration.

Research on monkeys has been helpful to develop this approach (the delayed-respone paradigm, Goldman-Rakic, 1987, serves as a classical example.

In 2000 the working memory was defined by Baddeley as "a limited capacity system for temporary storage and manipulation of information for complex tasks such as comprehension, learning, and reasoning" (Goldstein) consisting of three components. The central executive coordinating the activity of the phonological loop (which holds verbal and auditory information) and the visuospatial sketch pad (which holds visual and spatial information) and pulling information from long-term memory is the most important part.

Role of Controlled Versus Automatic Processes

There are two theories based on the underlying assumption that "the frontal lobes are especially important for controlling behavior in nonroutine situations and for overriding typical stimulusresponse associations, but contribute little to automatic and effortless behavior." (Banich, p. 397).

Stuss and Benson (1986) consider control over behavior to occur in a hierarchical manner. They distinguish between three different levels, of which each is associated with a particular brain region. In the first level sensory information is processed automatically by posterior regions, in the next level (associated with the executive functions of the frontal lobe) conscious control is needed to direct behavior toward a goal and at the highest level controlled self-reflection takes place in the prefrontal cortex.

This model is appropriate for explaining deficits in goal-oriented behavior, in dealing with novelty, the lack of cognitive flexibility and the environmental dependency syndrome. Furthermore it can explain the inability to consciously control action and to self-criticize.

The second model developed by Shalice (1982) proposes a system consisting of two parts to influence the choice of behavior. The first part, a cognitive system called contention scheduling, is in charge of more automatic processing. Various links and processing schemes cause a single stimulus to result in an automatic string of actions. Once an action is initiated, it remains active until inhibited.

The second cognitive system is the supervisory attentional system which directs attention and guids action through decision processes and is only active "when no processing schemes are available, when the task is technically difficult, when problem solving is required and when certain response tendencies must be overcome" (Banich).

This theory supports the observations of few deficits in routine situations, but relevant problems in dealing with novel tasks (e.g. the Tower of London task, Shallice), since no schemes in contention scheduling exist for dealing with it. Impulsive action is another characteristic of patients with frontal lobe damages which can be explained by this theory. Even if asked not to do certain things, such patients stick to their routines and cannot control their automatic behavior.

Use of Scripts

The approach based on scripts, which are sets of events, actions and ideas that are linked to form a unit of knowledge was developed by Schank (1982) amongst others.

Containing information about the setting in which an event occurs, the set of events needed to achieve the goal and the end event terminating the action, such managerial knowledge units (MKUs) are stored in the prefrontal cortex. They are organized in a hierarchical manner being abstract at the top and getting more specific at the bottom.

Damage of the scripts leads to not being able to behave goal-directed, finding it easier to cope with usual situations (due to the difficulty of retrieving a MKU of a novel event) and deficits in the initiation and cessation of action (because of MKUs specifying the beginning and ending of an action.)

Role of a goal list

The perspective of artificial intelligence and machine learning introduced an approach which assumes that each person has a goal list, which contains the tasks requirements or goals. This list is fundamental to guiding behavior and since a frontal lobe damage disrupts the ability to form a goal list, the theory helps to explain difficulties in abstract thinking, perceptual analysis, verbal output and staying on task. It can also account for the strong environmental influence on patients with frontal lobe damages, due to the lack of internal goals and the difficulty of organizing actions toward a goal.

References

- Goldstein, E. Bruce (2005). Cognitive Psychology - Connecting, Mind Research, and Everyday Experience. Thomson Wadsworth.
- Marie T. Banich (1997). Neuropsychology. The neural bases of Mental Function. Houghton Mifflin.
- Wilson, Robert A.& Keil, Frank C. (1999). The The MIT Encyclopedia of the Cognitive Sciences. Massachusetts: Bradford Book.
- Schmalhofer, Franz. Slides from the course: Cognitive Psychology and Neuropsychology, Summer Term 2006, University of Osnabrueck.

Links

Reasoning

Quizz to check whether you understood the difference of deduction and induction
Short text with graphics
Reasoning in geometry

Decision making

How to make good decisions
Making ethical decisions
Web-published journal by the Society for Judgement and Decision Making

Executive functions

Elaborate document (pdf) from the Technical University of Dresden (in German)
Text from the Max Planck Society, Munich (in English)
Short description and an extensive link list

Executive functions & ADHD
live version • discussion • edit lesson • comment • report an error

14 PRESENT AND FUTURE OF RESEARCH

live version • discussion • edit lesson • comment • report an error

"It's hard to make predictions - especially about the future." — Robert Storm Petersen

Introduction

Until now

Developing from the information processing approach, today's cognitive psychology differs from classical psychological approaches in the methods they use as well as in the interdisciplinary connections to other sciences. Apart from rejecting introspection as a valid method to analyze mental phenomenon, cognitive psychology introduces further, mainly computer-based, techniques that had not been in the range of methods used by classical psychology so far.

Introducing new methods

By using imaging-techniques like fMRI scans cognitive psychology is able to analyze the relation between the physiology of the brain and mental processes. In the future cognitive psychology will even more concentrate on computer-related methods. Hereby it profits from improvements in this area. E.g. fMRI scans nowadays still have many possible error sources, which should be solved in the future. Thereby the approach becomes more powerful and precise. In addition to that the computer approach can be combined with the classical behavior approach, where one inferes a participant's mental states from the behavior that is shown.

Possible development

Apart from using the methods developed by other sciences cognitive psychology also collaborates with topic-related sciences like artificial intelligence, neuroscience, linguistics and philosophy. The different perspectives on the topic made it possible to confirm one's results as well as gaining new accesses to the study of the mind. Modern studies of cognitive psychology more and more critize the classical information processing approach. Instead of that other theories acquire more importance. E.g. the classical approach is modified to a parallel information processing approach, which more resembles the method of working of the mind. Furthermore different theories based on the different sciences concerned with the study of the mind come up.

Methods

In order to give an appropriate overview over the significant developments in the field of cognitive psychology in general first of all a we will focus on its subfields and their current approaches, problems and possible trends. Hereby hints of possible future developments should be given. Finally the method of converging operators is introduced which combines the different areas of cognitive psychology and furthermore areas that are related to it.

Experimental Cognitive Psychology

Psychological experimentation studies mental functions and it is done with indirect methods meaning reasoning. These studies are performed to find the cause and the consequence relation and the factors influencing the behavior. The researcher observes visible action and makes conclusions based on these observations. Variables are changed one at a time and the effect of it is observed. The benefits of experimental researching are that it is possible to find the causal relations and that the manipulated factors can be altered in the way the researcher wants.

In being the classical approach within the field of Cognitive Psychology the experimental approach has been the basis for the development of the multiple modern approaches within contempeorary Cognitive Psychology. Its empirical methods have been developed and verified over long periods of time and the so gained results contributed to the enhancements in many areas of psychology.

Taking the established character of experimental cognitive psychology into consideration one might suggest that the modifications in the way of working in this field are rather inconsiderable. In contrast to that in recent years a discussion was initiated concerning the question whether the findings of experimental cognitive psychology remain valid in the "real world" since the environment created in an experiment suppresses influencing factors that may affect the results. The resulting conditions of the experiment are artificial and may unintentionally cause the ignoration of facts and coherences (cf. Eysenck & Keane, Cognitive Psychology, pp.514-515).

A possible demonstrative example for this is the research concerning attention. Since the attention of the participant is mainly governed by the experimenter's instructions, it's focus is basically determined. Therefore "relatively little is known of the factors that normally influence the focus of attention." (ibid, p.514)

Beside this it turns out to be problematic that in experimental psychology mental phenomenons are often examined in isolation. While trying to make the experimental setup as concise as possible in order to get clearly interpretable results, one decouples the aspect at issue from adjacent and interacting mental processes. This tends to the situation that the results only turn out to be valid in the idealized experimental setting but not in "real life" where multiple mental phenomena interact and multiple outside stimuli influence the behavior of a mental process. The validity gained by such studies could only be characterized as an internal validity (which means that the results are valid in the special circumstances created by the experimenter) but not as an external validity (which means that the results stay valid in changed and more realistic circumstances) (cf. ibid, p.514).

Based on such objections concerning the approach of experimental cognitive psychology several experiments have been developed that refer closer to "real life". According to that experiments related to "real-world" phenomena like absent-mindedness, everyday memory or reading gain in importance.

Nevertheless the disscussion remains whether such experiments really deliver new information about mental processes. Accordingly whether such everyday phenomenon studies really become established or not in future experimental psychology will heavily depend on the results nowadays experiments of this field will deliver.

Another issue concerning experimental setups in cognitive psychology is the way individual differences are handled. In general the results from an experiments are generated by an analysis of variance. Thereby different results which are due to individual differences are averaged out and accordingly are not taken into consideration. Such a procedure seems highly questionable especially against the background of an investigation of Bowers in 1973 which showed that over 30% of the variance in such studies are due to individual differences or their interaction with the current situation (cf. ibid, p.515). Based on such facts one challenge for future experimental cognitive psychology is the analysis of individual differences and the finding of a way to include the knowledge about such differences in general studies.

Cognitive Neuropsychology

Cognitive Neuropsychology maps the connection between brain functions and the cognitive behavior. Patients with brain damages have been the most important source of research in neuropsychology. Neuropsychology also examines dissociation ("forgetting"), double dissociation and associations (connection between two things formed by cognition). Neuropsychology uses technological reseach methods to create images of the brain functioning. There are many differences in techniques to scan the brain. The most common ones are EEG (Electroencephalography), MRI and fMRI (functional Magnetic Resonance Imaging) and PET (Positron Emission Tomography).

Cognitive Neuropsychology became very popular because it delivers good evidence. Theories developed for normal individuals can be verified by patients with brain damages. Apart from that new theories could have been established because of the results of neuropsychological experiments.

Nevertheless certain limitations to the approach as it is today have to be taken into consideration. First of all the fact that people having the same mental disability often do not have the same lesion needs to be pointed out (cf. ibid, pp.516-517). In such cases the researchers have to be careful with their interpretation. In general it could only be concluded that all the areas that the patients have injured could play a role in the mental phenomenon. But not which part really is decisive. Based on that future experiments in this area tend to make experiments with a rather small number of people with pretty similar lesion respectively compare the results from groups with similar syndroms and different lesions.

In addition to that the situation often turns out to be vice versa. Some patients do have pretty similar lesions but show rather different behaviour (cf. ibid, p.517). One probable reason therfor is that the patients differ in their age and lifestyle (cf. Banich, Neuropsychology, p.55). With better technologies in the future one will be better able to distinguish the cases in which really the various personalities make the difference and in which cases the lesions only on the first look seem to be equal. In addition to that the indiviual brain structures which may cause the different reactions to the lesions will become a focus of research.

Another problem for Cognitive Neuropsychology is that their patients are rare. The patients which are interesting for such research have lesions of an accident or suffered during war. It would be highly philosophical the suggest whether the amount of possible patients increases or decreases in future. But in addition there are differences in the manner of the lesion. Often multiple brain regions are damaged which makes it very hard to determine which of the is responsible for the examined phenomenon. The dependency on chance whether there are patients available for the studies will remain in future. Thereby predictions concerning this aspect of the research are not very reliable.

Apart from that it is not possible to localise some mental processes in the brain. Creative thought or organisational planning could not have been unitised (cf. Eysenck & Keane, Cognitive Psychology, p.517). A possible outcome of the research is that those activities rely on parallel processing. This would support the idea of the modification of the information processing theory that will be discussed later on. But if it shows up that a lot of mental processes depend on such parallel processing it would turn out to be a big drawback for Cognitive Psychology since its core is the modularization of the brain and the according phenomena.

In this context the risk of overestimation and underestimation has to be mentioned. The latter occurs because Cognitive Psychology often only identifies the most important brain region for the mental task. Other regions that are related thereto could be ignored. This could turn out to be fundamental if really parallel processing is crucial to many mental activities. Overestimation occurs when fibers that only pass the damaged brain region are lesioned, too. The researcher concludes that the respective brain region play an important role in the phenomenon he analyses even though only the deliverance of the information passed that region (cf. ibid). Modern technologies and experiments here have to be developed in order to provide valid and precise results.

Cognitive Science

Cognitive science is multidisciplinary science. It comprises areas of cognitive psychology, linguistics, neuroscience, artificial intelligence, cognitive anthropology, computer science and philosophy. Cognitive sciences concentrates to study the intelligent behavior of humans, which includes perception, learning, memory, thought and language. Research in cognitive sciences are based on naturalistic research methods such as cognitive neuropsychology, introspection, psychological experimentation, mathematical modeling and philosophical argumentation.

In the beginning of the cognitive sciences the most common method was introspection. It meant that the test subject evaluated his/her own cognitive thinking. In these experiments the researchers were using experienced subjects because they had to analyze and report their own cognitive thinking. Problems can occur when the results are interpreted and the subject has different reports from the same action. In the research should be clearly separated the matters that can be studied by introspection and the ones that are not to be studied with this method.

Computational modeling in cognitive science means that the mind is seen as a machine. This modeling seeks to express theoretical ideas through computational modeling that generate behavior similar to humans. Mathematical modeling is based on flow charts. The quality of the modeling is very important to ensure the equivalence of the input and results.

Nowadays the researchers in cognitive sciences use often theorizing and computational modeling.

"This does not exclude their primary method of experimentation with human participants. In cognitive sciences it is also important to bring the theories and the experimenting together. Because it comprises so many fields of science it is important to bring together the most appropriate methods from all these fields. The psychological experiments should be interpreted through a theory that expresses mental representations and procedures. The most productive and revealing way to perform research in cognitive sciences is to combine different approaches and methods together. This ensures overall picture from the research area and it comprises the viewpoints of all the different fields." (Thagard, Cognitive Science)

Nevertheless Cognitive Science has not yet managed to succeed in bringing the different areas together. Nowadays it is criticized for not establishing a science on its own. Rather few scientist really address themselves as cognitive scientist. Furthermore the basic metaphor of the brain functioning like a computer is challenged as well as the distinctions between their models and nature (cf. Eysenck & Keane, Cognitive Psychology, pp. 519-520).

Here a lot of work has to be done in future. Cognitive Science has to work on better models that explain natural processes and that are reliably able to make predictions. Furthermore these models have to combine multiple mental phenomenon. In addition to that a general "methodology for relating a computational model's behaviour to human behaviour" has to be worked out. Hereby the strength of such models can be increased. Apart from that Cognitive Science needs to establish an identity with prominent researchers that avow themself to Cognitive Science. And finally its biggest goal the creation of a general unifying theory of human cognition (see Theory Part) has to be reach (cf. ibid, p. 520). If Cognitive Science fails on too much of these challenges the danger arises that it becomes labeled as a deadend. Therefor the highest rate to development can be expected in the field of Cognitive Science.

Cognitive Neuroscience

Another approach to get a better understanding of human cognition is from cognitive neuroscience. Cognitive neuroscience lies at the interface between traditional cognitive psychology and the brain sciences. Cognitive neuroscience is a science with approach chatacterized by attempts to derive cognitive level theories from a variety types of information, such as computational properties of neural circuits, patterns of behavioral damage as a result of brain injury, measures of brain activity during the performance of cognitive tasks (cf. www.psy.cmu.edu). Cognitive neuroscience helps to get the understanding of how the human brain supports thought, perception, affection, action, social process and other aspects of cognition and behaviour, including how such processes develop and change in the brain and through time (cf. www.nsf.gov).

Cognitive neuroscience has emerged in the last decade as an intensely active and influential discipline, forged from interactions among the cognitive sciences, neurology, neuroimaging, physiology, neuroscience, psychiatry, and other fields. Of particular importance for this discipline have been new methods for non-invasive functional neuroimaging of humans performing psychological tasks (cf. www.nsf.gov). The findings from cognitive neuroscience are directed toward enabling basic scientific understanding of a broad range of issues involving brain, cognition and behavior. One example non-invasive functional neuroimaging, this includes: positron emission tomography (PET), functional magnetic resonance imaging (fMRI), magnetoencephalography (MEG), optical imaging (near infrared spectroscopy or NIRS), anatomical MRI, and diffusion tensor imaging (DTI) (cf. www.nsf.gov).

Cognitive neuroscience becomes a very important approach to understand human cognition, since findings from cognitive neuroscience can elucidate functional brain organization, such as the operations performed by a particular brain area and the system of distributed, discrete neural areas supporting a spesific cognitve representation. These findings can reveal the effect on brain organization of individual differences (including even genetic variation) (cf. www.psy.cmu.edu, www.nsf.gov).

Another importance of cognitive neuroscience is that cognitive neuroscience provides some ways that allow us to "obtain detailed information about the brain structures involved in different kind of cognitive processing" (Eysenck & Keane, Cognitive Psychology, p. 521). Techniques such as MRI and

CAT scans have proved of particular value when used on patients to discover which brain areas are damaged. Before non-invansive methods of cognitive neuroscience were developed, examination to know the location of "brain damage could only be established by postmortem examination" (ibid). Knowing which brain areas related to which cognitive process would surely lead to obtain a clearer view of brain region, hence, in the end would help in better understanding for human cognition process.

Another strength of cognitive neuroscience is that it serves as a tool to demonstrate the reality of theoretical distinctions. For example, it has been argued by many theorists that implicit memory can be diveded into perceptual and conceptual implicit memory; support for that view has come from PET studies, which show that perceptual and conceptual priming tasks affected different areas of the brain (cf. ibid, pp. 521-522).

However, cognitive neuroscience is not that perfect as a science to be able to stand alone and answer all questions dealing with human cognition. Cognitive neuroscience has some limitations, dealing with data collecting and data validity. In most neuroimaging studies, data are collected from several individuals and then averaged. Some concern has arose about such averaging because of the existence of significant individual differences. The problem was answered by Raichle (1998), who stated that the differ in individual brain should be appreciated, however general organizing principles emerge that transcend these differences (cf. ibid, p. 522).

Converging operations

The four approaches of experimental cognitive psychology, cognitive neuropsychology, cognitive science and cognitive neuroscience differ in their strengths and weaknesses. Because of this reason, it is clear that no science can stand alone in answering the questions dealing with human cognition, also for future researches. We should use and combine the knowledge, and use the method of converging operations "in order to maximize our understanding of human cognition" (ibid, p. 523). The method of converging operations involves making use of a variety approaches to consider any given issue from different perspectives (cf. ibid).

An example for such a procedure is Davachi's memory experiment(2003). First the participants one of the words *place* and *read*, then they saw an adjective which they had to mentally pronounce backwards if the previous word was *read* or they had to imagine a scene that could be described by that adjective if the previous word was *place*. After learning a list of words in the described manner the participants got a list with the learned words and the same number of new words the next day. Their task now was to decide whether a presented word was new or one of them learned the day before. The experiment showed that the words learned by the *place* method were remembered better.

So far the experiment seems to be a normal behavioral experiment characteristically for the experimental approach. But while learning the words Davachi used an fMRI on the participants in order to determine the activated brain regions. It became obvious that the perirhinal cortex only was activated during the *place* task but not during the *read* task. According to that it could be concluded that memory is better when the perirhinal cortex is activated during learning (cf. Goldstein, Cognitive Psychology, pp. 16-19). In this case the physiological approach in this experiment explained the results gained by the behavioral.

When the method of converging operations is applied, there are two possible outcomes: first, the findings obtained are broadly comparable. The second is that the "findings differ significantly"

(Eysenck & Keane, Cognitive Psychology, p. 523). When the findings from two approaches are similar, this increases the confidence in the validity of the findings and in the usefulness of both approaches. When the findings are different, this indicates the need of further research to clarify what happens. Thus, the method of converging operations helps to prevent researchers from drawing incorrect conclusions on the basis of limited findings from a single approach (cf. ibid, p. 523).

Theory

The field Cognitive Psychology derived from an analogy between the mind and a computer. The idea that the mind works on the brain just as a programm does work on a computer nowadays is know as the information-processing theory. Thereby existed an identical theoretical basis for all subfields of Cognitive Psychology. Nevertheless in practical application when explaining concrete phenomenon researcher tended to establish models that only focused on their subfield. Some examples handled in this book are Baddeley's model of working memory or Pylyshyn's and Kosslyn's different theories about imagery. Hereby a fragmentation of Cognitive Psychology emerged. In 1972 Allen Newell criticised this tendency in his paper "You can't play 20 questions with nature and win". He stated:

"Suppose that in the next thirty years we continued as we are now going. Another hundred phenomena, give or take a few dozen, will have been discovered and explored. [...] It seems to me that clarity is never achieved. Matters simply become muddier and muddier as we go down through time. Thus, far from providing the rungs of a ladder by which psychology gradually climbs to clarity, this form of conceptual structure leads rather to an ever increasing pile of issues, which we weary of or become diverted from, but never really settle." (Anderson, The Atomic Components of Thought, pp. 1-2)

Over thirty years later several attempts to create a unified theory which should avert Newell's prediction were presented. But a widely accepted unified theory that includes at least most of the mental phenomena still could not have been established. So the main focus of theoretical development in Cognitive Psychology still lays on the constitution of such an overarching and unifing model. Possible ways of reaching this goal will be discussed in the following.

Unifying Theories

Newell's own solution to the dilemma he described was based on a production system. Such a system consist of a set of conditions and actions. Based on the given data an action is performed if the corresponding condition is fulfilled. Hereby the data structure is changed and new conditions are generated. The system stops either when no conditions are fulfilled or when an action includes a stop operation. The theory Newell developed from his approach is called Soar theory of human cognition (cf. ibid, pp. 2-3). Apart from that several other theories based on production systems exist. Here primarily Anderson's ACT-R theory has to be mentioned since it has been partially validated against behavioral timing data and fMRI brain localizations and timing data.

ACT-R is a cognitive architecture. It is constructed based on actual assumptions of the functioning of human cognition. It can be used to fulfill different tasks related with human cognition like language comprehension or the Towers of Hanoi. Apart from that researchers are able to modify the programm in order to add their own assumptions. Here ACT-R functions quite similar to a programming language. Thereby it is possible to compare the results gained by the model with results from human participants and to verify respectively to correct the model (cf. act-r.psy.cmu.edu and http://www.carleton.ca/ics/ccmlab/actr/).

In addition to that EPIC from Meyer and Kieras and 3CAPS from Just and Carpenter are production system theories with potential (cf. Anderson, The Atomic Components of Thought, p. 3). But the fact that several candidates for such an overarching theory have to be referred to makes it obvious that none of the systems really managed to be accepted from most of the researchers in Cognitive Psychology. So far the goal to create a unifying theory has not been reached. Some possible theories exist but the future development has to show if one of them really manages to become globally established.

Parallel Processing

Another possibility how to reach a reunification of the field is to create a new theory. In this case the analogy with the computer which was already the basis for the whole cognitive psychological approach seems to be the attempt with the best chances. It has to be taken into considertation that the information processing theory already developed over time. The traditional theory e.g. was only able to explain bottom-up processes (like used in Atkinson's and Shiffrin's memory theory) based on its sequential structure. But it failed to give an appropriate explanation for top-down processing which occurs e.g. when one has certain expectations based on the circumstances and context (cf. Eysenck & Keane, Cognitive Psychology, p. 2).

This limitation could have been overcome by keeping track with the developments in computer science and thereby with a modification of the analogy. As more and more parallel processing computer were build one changed the theory from sequential working to parallel processing. Thereby one was able to explain both bottom-up and top-down processes. Furthermore the highly parallel activation of the brain was integrated in the theory.

These developments in the theoretical view of the functioning of the brain may also give a hint to future changes. As computer science moves on the analogy may have to be modified again. Based on that new theories could be developed which maybe reach the goal to become an overarching theory that includes all human cognitive abilities and that is globally accepted.

Levels of Analysis

The realization that there are important links between brain activity and cognitive functions is the key assumption for present and future research. Complete psychological accounts of cognitive functioning require considerations of the computational level, algorithmic level (implementation of the computational theory, representation of the input and the algorithm of the transformation) and the brain levels, about how the representation and the algorithm be realized physically (cf. ibid, pp. 523-524).

Here a possible reason for the differences in the theories shows up. Some of these might occur because the descriptions used in the different theories refer to different levels of analysis. In order to avoid misunderstandings an overarching theory therefor has to include all of these levels.

Conclusion

Today's work in the field of Cognitive Psychology gives several hints how future work in this area may look like. In practical applications improvements will probably mainly be driven by the limitations one faces today. Here in particular the newer subfields of Cognitive Psychology will develop quick. How such changes look like heavily depends on the character of future developments in technology. Especially improvements in Cognitive Neuropsychology and Cognitive Neuroscience depend on the advancements of the imaging techniques.

In addition to that the theoretical framework of the field will be influenced by such developments. The parallel processing theory may still be modified according to new insights in computer science. Thereby or eventually by the acceptance of one of the already existing overarching theories the theoretical basis for the current research could be reunified.

But if it takes another 30 years to fulfill Newell's dream of such a theory or if it will happen rather quick is still open. As a rather young science Cognitive Psychology still is subject to elementary changes. All its practical and theoretical domains are steadily modified. Whether the trends mentioned in this chapter are just deadends or will cause a revolution of the field could only be predicted which definitely is hard.

References

- E. Br. Goldstein, Cognitive Psychology, Wadsworth, 2004
- M. W. Eysenck, M. T. Keane, Cognitive Psychology - A Student's Handbook, Psychology Press Ltd, 2000
- Thagard, Paul, Cognitive Science in Edward N. Zalta (ed.), The Stanford Encyclopedia of Philosophy, 2004
- Banich, Marie T., Neuropsycology - The Neural Bases of Mental Function, Hougthon Mifflin Company, 1997
- Anderson, John R., Lebiere, Christian, The Atomic Components of Thought, Lawrence Erlbaum Associates, 1998

Links

- http://www.psy.cmu.edu/home/research/index.html
- http://www.nsf.gov/pubs/2006/nsf06557/nsf06557.html
- http://act-r.psy.cmu.edu

live version • discussion • edit lesson • comment • report an error

15 HISTORY & DOCUMENT NOTES

Wikibook History

This book was created on 2006-04-08 and was developed on the Wikibooks project by the contributors listed in the next section. The latest version may be found at http://en.wikibooks.org/wiki/Cognitive_Psychology_and_Cognitive_Neuroscience.

PDF Information & History

This PDF was created on 2007-04-26 based on the 2007-04-25 version of the Cognitive Psychology and Cognitive Neuroscience Wikibook. A transparent copy of this document is available at http://en.wikibooks.org/wiki/Cognitive Psychology and Cognitive Neuroscience. An OpenDocument Text version of this PDF document and the template from which it was created is available upon request at Wikibooks:User talk:Hagindaz. A printer-friendly version of this document may be available at Wikibooks:Image:Cognitive Psychology and Cognitive Neuroscience printable version.pdf.

16 AUTHORS & IMAGE CREDITS

Authors

Achim, AkumAPRIME, Annschro, Apape, Arothert, ArrowStomper, Asarwary, Aschoeke, Az1568, Bluebirch, CyrilB, Darklama, Ddeunert, Ekrueger, Ervinn, Evan.Wilson, Eyu100, FlyingGerman, Hagindaz, Herbys bot, Herbythyme, Hknepper, Hnasir, Hu, Ifranzme, Iroewer, Itiaden, Jbuergle, Jcunliff, Jgerhard, Jguk, Jkeyser, Kellen, Kkase, Kvoncarl, LanguageGame, Lbartels, Loettl, Lyagoub, MFJoe, Maebert, Marplogm, Mheimann, MichaelFrey, Mkoguchi, Mstocks, Npraceju, Pbenner, Pehrenbr, Poogyist, Robert Huber, Rymwoo, Sahab, Smieskes, Soschnei, Sspoede, Swaterka, Tannersf, Tbittlin, Themsted, Thkruege, Thorben, Timoschm, Tkrieger, Urbane, Vmoenter, Xania, Ykisi

Image Credits

Authors for GFDL-licensed images are listed in image captions. All other images are in the public domain.

17 GNU FREE DOCUMENTATION LICENSE

Version 1.2, November 2002

```
Copyright (C) 2000,2001,2002  Free Software Foundation, Inc.
51 Franklin St, Fifth Floor, Boston, MA  02110-1301  USA
Everyone is permitted to copy and distribute verbatim copies
of this license document, but changing it is not allowed.
```

0. PREAMBLE

The purpose of this License is to make a manual, textbook, or other functional and useful document "free" in the sense of freedom: to assure everyone the effective freedom to copy and redistribute it, with or without modifying it, either commercially or noncommercially. Secondarily, this License preserves for the author and publisher a way to get credit for their work, while not being considered responsible for modifications made by others.

This License is a kind of "copyleft", which means that derivative works of the document must themselves be free in the same sense. It complements the GNU General Public License, which is a copyleft license designed for free software.

We have designed this License in order to use it for manuals for free software, because free software needs free documentation: a free program should come with manuals providing the same freedoms that the software does. But this License is not limited to software manuals; it can be used for any textual work, regardless of subject matter or whether it is published as a printed book. We recommend this License principally for works whose purpose is instruction or reference.

1. APPLICABILITY AND DEFINITIONS

This License applies to any manual or other work, in any medium, that contains a notice placed by the copyright holder saying it can be distributed under the terms of this License. Such a notice grants a world-wide, royalty-free license, unlimited in duration, to use that work under the conditions stated herein. The "Document", below, refers to any such manual or work. Any member of the public is a licensee, and is addressed as "you". You accept the license if you copy, modify or distribute the work in a way requiring permission under copyright law.

A "Modified Version" of the Document means any work containing the Document or a portion of it, either copied verbatim, or with modifications and/or translated into another language.

A "Secondary Section" is a named appendix or a front-matter section of the Document that deals exclusively with the relationship of the publishers or authors of the Document to the Document's overall subject (or to related matters) and contains nothing that could fall directly within that overall subject. (Thus, if the Document is in part a textbook of mathematics, a Secondary Section may not explain any mathematics.) The relationship could be a matter of historical connection with the subject or with related matters, or of legal, commercial, philosophical, ethical or political position regarding them.

The "Invariant Sections" are certain Secondary Sections whose titles are designated, as being those of Invariant Sections, in the notice that says that the Document is released under this License. If a section does not fit the above definition of Secondary then it is not allowed to be designated as Invariant. The Document may contain zero Invariant Sections. If the Document does not identify any Invariant Sections then there are none.

The "Cover Texts" are certain short passages of text that are listed, as Front-Cover Texts or Back-Cover Texts, in the notice that says that the Document is released under this License. A Front-Cover Text may be at most 5 words, and a Back-Cover Text may be at most 25 words.

A "Transparent" copy of the Document means a machine-readable copy, represented in a format whose specification is available to the general public, that is suitable for revising the document straightforwardly with generic text editors or (for images composed of pixels) generic paint programs or (for drawings) some widely available drawing editor, and that is suitable for input to text formatters or for automatic translation to a variety of formats suitable for input to text formatters. A copy made in an otherwise Transparent file format whose markup, or absence of markup, has been arranged to thwart or discourage subsequent modification by readers is not Transparent. An image format is not Transparent if used for any substantial amount of text. A copy that is not "Transparent" is called "Opaque".

Examples of suitable formats for Transparent copies include plain ASCII without markup, Texinfo input format, LaTeX input format, SGML or XML using a publicly available DTD, and standard-conforming simple HTML, PostScript or PDF designed for human modification. Examples of transparent image formats include PNG, XCF and JPG. Opaque formats include proprietary formats that can be read and edited only by proprietary word processors, SGML or XML for which the DTD and/or processing tools are not generally available, and the machine-generated HTML, PostScript or PDF produced by some word processors for output purposes only.

The "Title Page" means, for a printed book, the title page itself, plus such following pages as are needed to hold, legibly, the material this License requires to appear in the title page. For works in formats which do not have any title page as such, "Title Page" means the text near the most prominent appearance of the work's title, preceding the beginning of the body of the text.

A section "Entitled XYZ" means a named subunit of the Document whose title either is precisely XYZ or contains XYZ in parentheses following text that translates XYZ in another language. (Here XYZ stands for a specific section name mentioned below, such as "Acknowledgements", "Dedications", "Endorsements", or "History".) To "Preserve the Title" of such a section when you modify the Document means that it remains a section "Entitled XYZ" according to this definition.

The Document may include Warranty Disclaimers next to the notice which states that this License applies to the Document. These Warranty Disclaimers are considered to be included by reference in this License, but only as regards disclaiming warranties: any other implication that these Warranty Disclaimers may have is void and has no effect on the meaning of this License.

2. VERBATIM COPYING

You may copy and distribute the Document in any medium, either commercially or noncommercially, provided that this License, the copyright notices, and the license notice saying this

License applies to the Document are reproduced in all copies, and that you add no other conditions whatsoever to those of this License. You may not use technical measures to obstruct or control the reading or further copying of the copies you make or distribute. However, you may accept compensation in exchange for copies. If you distribute a large enough number of copies you must also follow the conditions in section 3.

You may also lend copies, under the same conditions stated above, and you may publicly display copies.

3. COPYING IN QUANTITY

If you publish printed copies (or copies in media that commonly have printed covers) of the Document, numbering more than 100, and the Document's license notice requires Cover Texts, you must enclose the copies in covers that carry, clearly and legibly, all these Cover Texts: Front-Cover Texts on the front cover, and Back-Cover Texts on the back cover. Both covers must also clearly and legibly identify you as the publisher of these copies. The front cover must present the full title with all words of the title equally prominent and visible. You may add other material on the covers in addition. Copying with changes limited to the covers, as long as they preserve the title of the Document and satisfy these conditions, can be treated as verbatim copying in other respects.

If the required texts for either cover are too voluminous to fit legibly, you should put the first ones listed (as many as fit reasonably) on the actual cover, and continue the rest onto adjacent pages.

If you publish or distribute Opaque copies of the Document numbering more than 100, you must either include a machine-readable Transparent copy along with each Opaque copy, or state in or with each Opaque copy a computer-network location from which the general network-using public has access to download using public-standard network protocols a complete Transparent copy of the Document, free of added material. If you use the latter option, you must take reasonably prudent steps, when you begin distribution of Opaque copies in quantity, to ensure that this Transparent copy will remain thus accessible at the stated location until at least one year after the last time you distribute an Opaque copy (directly or through your agents or retailers) of that edition to the public.

It is requested, but not required, that you contact the authors of the Document well before redistributing any large number of copies, to give them a chance to provide you with an updated version of the Document.

4. MODIFICATIONS

You may copy and distribute a Modified Version of the Document under the conditions of sections 2 and 3 above, provided that you release the Modified Version under precisely this License, with the Modified Version filling the role of the Document, thus licensing distribution and modification of the Modified Version to whoever possesses a copy of it. In addition, you must do these things in the Modified Version:

A. Use in the Title Page (and on the covers, if any) a title distinct from that of the Document, and from those of previous versions (which should, if there were any, be listed in the History section of the Document). You may use the same title as a previous version if the original publisher of that version gives permission.

B. List on the Title Page, as authors, one or more persons or entities responsible for authorship of the modifications in the Modified Version, together with at least five of the principal authors of the Document (all of its principal authors, if it has fewer than five), unless they release you from this requirement.

C. State on the Title page the name of the publisher of the Modified Version, as the publisher.

D. Preserve all the copyright notices of the Document.

E. Add an appropriate copyright notice for your modifications adjacent to the other copyright notices.

F. Include, immediately after the copyright notices, a license notice giving the public permission to use the Modified Version under the terms of this License, in the form shown in the Addendum below.

G. Preserve in that license notice the full lists of Invariant Sections and required Cover Texts given in the Document's license notice.

H. Include an unaltered copy of this License.

I. Preserve the section Entitled "History", Preserve its Title, and add to it an item stating at least the title, year, new authors, and publisher of the Modified Version as given on the Title Page. If there is no section Entitled "History" in the Document, create one stating the title, year, authors, and publisher of the Document as given on its Title Page, then add an item describing the Modified Version as stated in the previous sentence.

J. Preserve the network location, if any, given in the Document for public access to a Transparent copy of the Document, and likewise the network locations given in the Document for previous versions it was based on. These may be placed in the "History" section. You may omit a network location for a work that was published at least four years before the Document itself, or if the original publisher of the version it refers to gives permission.

K. For any section Entitled "Acknowledgements" or "Dedications", Preserve the Title of the section, and preserve in the section all the substance and tone of each of the contributor acknowledgements and/or dedications given therein.

L. Preserve all the Invariant Sections of the Document, unaltered in their text and in their titles. Section numbers or the equivalent are not considered part of the section titles.

M. Delete any section Entitled "Endorsements". Such a section may not be included in the Modified Version.

N. Do not retitle any existing section to be Entitled "Endorsements" or to conflict in title with any Invariant Section.

O. Preserve any Warranty Disclaimers.

If the Modified Version includes new front-matter sections or appendices that qualify as Secondary Sections and contain no material copied from the Document, you may at your option designate some or all of these sections as invariant. To do this, add their titles to the list of Invariant Sections in the Modified Version's license notice. These titles must be distinct from any other section titles.

You may add a section Entitled "Endorsements", provided it contains nothing but endorsements of your Modified Version by various parties--for example, statements of peer review or that the text has been approved by an organization as the authoritative definition of a standard.

You may add a passage of up to five words as a Front-Cover Text, and a passage of up to 25 words as a Back-Cover Text, to the end of the list of Cover Texts in the Modified Version. Only one passage of Front-Cover Text and one of Back-Cover Text may be added by (or through arrangements made by) any one entity. If the Document already includes a cover text for the same cover, previously added by you or by arrangement made by the same entity you are acting on behalf of, you may not add another; but you may replace the old one, on explicit permission from the previous publisher that added the old one.

The author(s) and publisher(s) of the Document do not by this License give permission to use their names for publicity for or to assert or imply endorsement of any Modified Version.

5. COMBINING DOCUMENTS

You may combine the Document with other documents released under this License, under the terms defined in section 4 above for modified versions, provided that you include in the combination all of the Invariant Sections of all of the original documents, unmodified, and list them all as Invariant Sections of your combined work in its license notice, and that you preserve all their Warranty Disclaimers.

The combined work need only contain one copy of this License, and multiple identical Invariant Sections may be replaced with a single copy. If there are multiple Invariant Sections with the same name but different contents, make the title of each such section unique by adding at the end of it, in parentheses, the name of the original author or publisher of that section if known, or else a unique number. Make the same adjustment to the section titles in the list of Invariant Sections in the license notice of the combined work.

In the combination, you must combine any sections Entitled "History" in the various original documents, forming one section Entitled "History"; likewise combine any sections Entitled "Acknowledgements", and any sections Entitled "Dedications". You must delete all sections Entitled "Endorsements."

6. COLLECTIONS OF DOCUMENTS

You may make a collection consisting of the Document and other documents released under this License, and replace the individual copies of this License in the various documents with a single copy that is included in the collection, provided that you follow the rules of this License for verbatim copying of each of the documents in all other respects.

You may extract a single document from such a collection, and distribute it individually under this License, provided you insert a copy of this License into the extracted document, and follow this License in all other respects regarding verbatim copying of that document.

7. AGGREGATION WITH INDEPENDENT WORKS

A compilation of the Document or its derivatives with other separate and independent documents or works, in or on a volume of a storage or distribution medium, is called an "aggregate" if the copyright resulting from the compilation is not used to limit the legal rights of the compilation's users beyond what the individual works permit. When the Document is included in an aggregate, this License does not apply to the other works in the aggregate which are not themselves derivative works of the Document.

If the Cover Text requirement of section 3 is applicable to these copies of the Document, then if the Document is less than one half of the entire aggregate, the Document's Cover Texts may be placed on covers that bracket the Document within the aggregate, or the electronic equivalent of covers if the Document is in electronic form. Otherwise they must appear on printed covers that bracket the whole aggregate.

8. TRANSLATION

Translation is considered a kind of modification, so you may distribute translations of the Document under the terms of section 4. Replacing Invariant Sections with translations requires special permission from their copyright holders, but you may include translations of some or all Invariant Sections in addition to the original versions of these Invariant Sections. You may include a translation of this License, and all the license notices in the Document, and any Warranty Disclaimers, provided that you also include the original English version of this License and the original versions of those notices and disclaimers. In case of a disagreement between the translation and the original version of this License or a notice or disclaimer, the original version will prevail.

If a section in the Document is Entitled "Acknowledgements", "Dedications", or "History", the requirement (section 4) to Preserve its Title (section 1) will typically require changing the actual title.

9. TERMINATION

You may not copy, modify, sublicense, or distribute the Document except as expressly provided for under this License. Any other attempt to copy, modify, sublicense or distribute the Document is void, and will automatically terminate your rights under this License. However, parties who have received copies, or rights, from you under this License will not have their licenses terminated so long as such parties remain in full compliance.

10. FUTURE REVISIONS OF THIS LICENSE

The Free Software Foundation may publish new, revised versions of the GNU Free Documentation License from time to time. Such new versions will be similar in spirit to the present version, but may differ in detail to address new problems or concerns. See http://www.gnu.org/copyleft/.

Each version of the License is given a distinguishing version number. If the Document specifies that a particular numbered version of this License "or any later version" applies to it, you have the option of following the terms and conditions either of that specified version or of any later version that has been published (not as a draft) by the Free Software Foundation. If the Document does not specify a version number of this License, you may choose any version ever published (not as a draft) by the Free Software Foundation.

External links

- GNU Free Documentation License (Wikipedia article on the license)
- Official GNU FDL webpage

www.ingramcontent.com/pod-product-compliance
Lightning Source LLC
Chambersburg PA
CBHW080612270326
41928CB00016B/3028